GARLAND LIBRARY
OF MEDIEVAL LITERATURE
VOL. 89 SERIES B

HILDEGARD
OF BINGEN

The Garland Library
of Medieval Literature

General Editors
James J. Wilhelm, Rutgers University
Lowry Nelson, Jr., Yale University

Literary Advisors
Ingeborg Glier, Yale University
Frede Jensen, University of Colorado
Sidney M. Johnson, Indiana University
William W. Kibler, University of Texas
Norris J. Lacy, Washington University
Fred C. Robinson, Yale University
Aldo Scaglione, New York University

Art Advisor
Elizabeth Parker McLachlan, Rutgers University

Music Advisor
Hendrik van der Werf, Eastman School of Music

HILDEGARD
OF BINGEN

*The Book of the
Rewards of Life
(Liber Vitae Meritorum)*

translated by

Bruce W. Hozeski

GARLAND PUBLISHING, Inc.
New York & London / 1994

Library of Congress Cataloging-in-Publication Data

Hildegard, Saint, 1098–1179.
    [Liber vitae meritorum. English]
    Hildegard of Bingen : the Book of the rewards of life
(Liber vitae meritorum) / [translated] by Bruce W.
Hozeski.
      p.   cm. — (Garland library of medieval litera-
ture ; vol 89B)
    Includes bibliographical references.
    ISBN 0–8153–0818–3 (alk. paper)
    1. Mysticism—Catholic Church—Early works to
1800. 2. Sin—Early works to 1800. 3. Virtues—Early
works to 1800. I. Hozeski, Bruce. II. Title. III. Title:
Book of the rewards of life. IV. Series: Garland library
of medieval literature ; v. 89.
BV5080.H5313   1994
248.2'2—dc20   93–30621
                                          CIP

Printed on acid-free, 250-year-life paper
Manufactured in the United States of America

Preface of the General Editors

The Garland Library of Medieval Literature was established to make available to the general reader modern translations of texts in editions that conform to the highest academic standards. All of the translations are originals, and were created especially for this series. The translations usually attempt to render the foreign works in a natural idiom that remains faithful to the originals, although in certain cases we have published more poetic versions.

The Library is divided into two sections: Series A, texts and translations; and Series B, translations alone. Those volumes containing texts have been prepared after consultation of the major previous editions and manuscripts. The aim in the edition has been to offer a reliable text with a minimum of editorial intervention. Significant variants accompany the original, and important problems are discussed in the Textual Notes. Volumes without texts contain translations based on the most scholarly texts available, which have been updated in terms of recent scholarship.

Most volumes contain Introductions with the following features: (1) a biography of the author or a discussion of the problem of authorship, with any pertinent historical or legendary information; (2) an objective discussion of the literary style of the original, emphasizing any individual features; (3) a consideration of sources for the work and its influence; and (4) a statement of the editorial policy for each edition and translation. There is also a Select Bibliography, which emphasizes recent criticism on the works. Critical writings are often accompanied by brief descriptions of their importance. Selective glossaries, indices, and footnotes are included where appropriate.

The Library covers a broad range of linguistic areas, including all of the major European languages. All of the important literary forms and genres are considered, sometimes in anthologies or selections.

The General Editors hope that these volumes will bring the general reader a closer awareness of a richly diversified area that has for too long been closed to everyone except those with precise academic training, an area that is well worth study and reflection.

James J. Wilhelm
Rutgers University

Lowry Nelson, Jr.
Yale University

CONTENTS

PREFACE

When I began working on the writings of Hildegard von Bingen in the late 1960's, I was the only one in this country doing so at the time, but I realized very quickly that there were lifetimes of research for hundreds of scholars in this and other English-speaking countries. Since most of her writings are very long and in complex Latin, readily available English translations were a necessary first step, although I believed then and still do that scholarly researchers need to work with the original Latin.

This volume is the second of my translations of Hildegard's three collections of her mystical visions, *Scivias* (1986) being the first. Like *Scivias, Liber Vitae Meritorum* was written in Latin under Hildegard's immediate and direct supervision. My approach has been to take Hildegard's original Latin and to render it into a Modern English version that captures as much of Hildegard's style of writing as is possible in our language, so different from hers, and yet to keep it reasonably readable. It would be inappropriate to translate in such a way that Hildegard would read like a twentieth-century novel. However, no translation can capture the beauty, complexity and subtlety of the original. Hildegard's positioning, for example, of a particular adjective and noun between two very long and complex subordinate clauses so that their meaning applies to both cannot be captured in Modern English without syntax that would be more suitable for puzzling than for reading.

My aim has been to make this important writer known to a wide variety of readers: the many English-speaking Hildegard scholars throughout the world, those interested in mysticism, those interested in the history of religion, those interested in religious reading, and those interested in major woman writers who have been previously neglected.

ACKNOWLEDGMENTS

The writer wishes to thank the following persons who are responsible in various ways for the completion of this translation:

Joannes Baptista Pitra for his Latin edition of Hildegard's *Liber Vitae Meritorum* in *Analecta Sanctae Hildegardis Opera Spicilegio Solesmensi Parata*. Analecta Sacra 8. 1882. Reprint. Farnborough, England, 1966.

Lowry Nelson, Jr., professor at Yale University; Arnold Williams and George Radimersky, professors emeriti at Michigan State University; C. Warren Vander Hill, provost, and Charles L. Houck and Linda K. Hanson, successive chairs of the Department of English, Ball State University; M. John Eiden, Ball State University; the many scholars researching the various mystics and those researching Hildegard von Bingen, particularly Pozzi Escot, professor at Wheaton College and the New England Conservatory of Music as well as the current president of the International Society of Hildegard von Bingen Studies.

Kathleen, my wife, by her continuous enthusiasm and encouragement during the length of this entire project and Alison, our daughter, whose youthful excitement and joy in learning new things are strong motivating forces in this scholarly pursuit.

INTRODUCTION

LIFE OF THE AUTHOR

Hildegard was born in Bockelheim, the diocese of Mainz, on the Nahe River in 1098. Her father Hildebert was a knight in the service of Meginhard, the count of Spanheim. As a child at the age of six, she began to have the visions that continued the rest of her life and that she later recorded. At the age of eight, she was entrusted to the care of Jutta, who was the sister of Count Meginhard of Spanheim. The two lived in a small cottage adjoining the church of the abbey founded by Saint Disibod at Disibodenberg. A sickly child, she nevertheless continued her education under Jutta, learning to read and sing Latin, as well as studying the typical subjects thought proper for medieval women. At the age of fifteen, she was clothed in the habit of a nun in Jutta's hermitage that by this time had attracted enough followers to become a community, following the Rule of Saint Benedict. When Jutta died in 1136, Hildegard at the age of thirty-eight became the abbess of the community.

As her visions continued, word of them spread to her confessor, the monk Godfrey, and to Godfrey's abbot, Conon. Conon brought them to the attention of the archbishop of Mainz who examined her visions with his theologians and ruled that they were divinely inspired and that she should begin recording her visions in writing. In the year 1141, Hildegard began writing her principal work, *Scivias*. In 1147, when Pope Eugenius III came to the region, the archbishop of Mainz brought Hildegard's visions to him. The pope appointed a commission to examine them, received a favorable report from the commission, discussed them with his advisers—including Saint Bernard of Clairvaux—and authorized her to write whatever the Holy Spirit inspired her to write. Her resulting fame caused Hildegard's community at Disibodenberg to grow so that it became necessary for her to transfer her convent to Rupertsberg, near Bingen. The monks of Saint Disibod, whose importance depended somewhat on the growing reputation of Hildegard, resented the move, but sometime between 1147 and 1150, Hildegard moved her community to a dilapidated church and unfinished buildings near Bingen. Hildegard saw to the building of a commodious convent that continued to attract increasing numbers. Here she lived, except during her extensive travels in Western Europe, did most of her writing, and continued as abbess until her death. She died on 17 September 1179 and was buried in her convent church where her relics remained until the convent was destroyed by the Swedes in 1632, when her relics were moved to Eibingen.

INFLUENCE AND REPUTATION

Hildegard von Bingen is the first major German mystic. She wrote profusely as a prophet, a poet, a dramatist, a musical composer, a physician, and a political moralist, communicating often with popes and princes, influential persons and common folk. Exerting a tremendous influence on the Western Europe of her time, she was an extraordinary woman who stood out from the corruption, misery and ruin—both temporal and spiritual—of the twelfth century.

In spite of all her writings and correspondence, Hildegard was not confined to her convent. She traveled considerably for her time and circumstances. She visited many places along the Nahe River, the Main, the Moselle, and the Rhine—the highway of Western Germany, traveling most likely by boat. The exact dates of her various travels are difficult to ascertain, but her various letters make many references to her travels. Sometimes she founded convents as she did at Eibingen, on the opposite side of the Rhine, near Rudesheim, and only a mile from her own convent. Sometimes she visited courts and palaces. In 1155, Frederick Barbarossa invited Hildegard to visit him at the old royal palace that he had restored at Ingelheim (traditionally held to be the birthplace of Charlemagne). Frederick Barbarossa was king at the time, but he was hoping to receive the Imperial Crown. In a letter to Hildegard that Frederick wrote several years after the visit, he comments that some of the prophecies she had made to him at Ingelheim had come true.

In a letter to the people of Cologne, Hildegard comments on her earlier visit to Treves or Cologne and also comments that she was exceedingly tired, having been traveling for the last two years and preaching to various masters, doctors, and other learned men. Sometime in her life she also visited Trier, Metz, Wurzburg, Ulm, Werden, Bamberg, and other places as distant as Belgium and Switzerland. Near the end of her life, she visited France. In the Act of Inquisition concerning Hildegard's life and miracles, it is stated that she made a pilgrimage to the shrine of St. Martin of Tours and then went on to Paris. It is also stated that she took three or four of her books with her on this journey. Finally, her correspondence indicates that she preached and prophesied during her various travels, exerting a tremendous influence that most certainly needs more detailed study by present-day scholars.

LITERARY ACHIEVEMENT

Being a woman of extraordinarily energetic and independent mind, Hildegard wrote voluminously. She recorded her visions in three books: *Scivias (May You Know, or Know the Ways)* written between 1141 and 1151, *Liber Vitae Meritorum (The Book of the Rewards of Life)* written between 1158 and 1163, and *Liber Divinorum Operum Simplicis Hominis (The Book of the Divine Works of a Simple Person)* written between 1163 and 1173. The illuminated manuscript of Hildegard's *Scivias*, the Riesenkodex, Hessische Landesbibliothek, Wiesbaden, cod. 2 (Rupertsberg, c. 1189-90), is in excellent preservation and is of the highest value to scholars of mysticism and history, as well as those studying medieval art. It was prepared near Bingen at about the time of Hildegard's death. The miniatures are extremely detailed and greatly help in visualizing the narrative of her complex visions. They were prepared either under Hildegard's immediate supervision or under her immediate tradition. *Scivias* itself is divided into three parts, the first part containing six visions, the second seven visions, and the third thirteen visions, along with her lengthy commentary on each vision. The visions of *Scivias* develop Hildegard's views on the universe, on the theory of macrocosm and microcosm, the structure of man, birth, death, and the nature of the soul. They also treat the relationship between God and humans in creation, the Redemption, and the Church. Besides, *Scivias* discusses the importance of the virtues through an explanation of the idea of "viriditas." "Viriditas" literally means greenness and symbolically it connotes growth or the principle of life. According to Hildegard and other thinkers of her time, life from God was transmitted into plants, animals, and precious gems. People, in turn, eat plants and animals and acquire gems, thereby obtaining "viriditas." People then give out "viriditas" by practicing the virtues, hence their importance in the chain of being. The last vision of *Scivias*, the thirteenth in the third part, contains her play *Ordo Virtutum*. Written between the years 1141 and 1151, the play is extremely noteworthy since it appears to be the earliest liturgical morality play yet to be discovered. Previously, scholars like E. K. Chambers, Karl Young, O. B. Hardison, Jr., and Arnold Williams had believed that no morality plays existed before the fourteenth century when they seem to have flourished.

The text of *Liber Vitae Meritorum* is preserved in three twelfth-century manuscripts that were probably written under Hildegard's supervision. The oldest of these is the Codex Afflighemiensis 9, at Kloster Dendermonde in Brabant (Rupertsberg, c. 1170). The second manuscript is the Codex Latinus Theologicus, Fol. 727, in the Preussischen Staatsbibliothek in Berlin (Rupertsberg, c. 1170). The third manuscript from the twelfth century belongs to the Kloster St. Eucharius in Trier and is known as Codex 68 in the Seminarbibliothek of Trier. Further versions of the text can be found in the thirteenth century, such as the Codex Latinus 1016 of the Osterreichischen Nationalbibliothek and the Codex Helmstadiensis 951, now in the Herzoglichen Bibliothek of Wolfenbuttel.

Liber Divinorum Operum Simplicis Hominis, the third collection of Hildegard's visions, is found in an important illuminated manuscript, the Codex 1942 of the Bibliothek Governativa at Lucca. This collection contains many of the same dogmatic and ascetic thoughts that are found in *Scivias*, but it is arranged differently, being divided into short sections, each beginning with a brief summary of the contents of that section. The fundamental idea of the whole book is the unity of creation. Hildegard herself does not use the terms macrocosm and microcosm, but she succeeds in synthesizing into one great whole her theological beliefs along with her knowledge of the elements of the universe and the structures within the human body. This work is often considered as the epitome of the science of her time.

Besides these three books recording her visions, Hildegard also wrote a long physical treatise entitled *Physica: Subtilitatum Diversarum Naturarum Creaturarum (Physical Things: Of the Simplicities of Various Natural Creatures)* and her book of medicine entitled *Causae et Curae (Causes and Cures)*. Although her theoretical knowledge of medicine as found in these works may seem crude today, she must have been successful because large numbers of sick and suffering persons were brought to her for cures. And indeed there is today a thriving clinic in Konstanz, Germany, where Hildegard's remedies are still practiced.

In addition, Hildegard wrote *Vita Sancti Disibodi (The Life of Saint Disibod)* and *Vita Sancti Ruperti (The Life of Saint Rupert.)* She wrote *Vita Sancti Disibodi* in 1170 at the request of Abbot Hillinger, who was then abbot at the monastery of Mount Saint Disibod. This work contains only a few facts and details about Saint Disibod, facts that Hildegard probably learned from the monks when she lived with Jutta near the monastery at Disibodenberg. The rest of the work contains long interpretations of Scripture and other moral teachings. Her *Vita Sancti Ruperti* is interesting in what it has to say about Saint Rupert, but most interesting for the long explanation of the Athanasian Creed that she wrote for the benefit of the nuns of her own convent.

Her *Solutiones Triginta Octo Quaestionum (Answers to Thirty-eight Questions)* comments on various theological and scriptural subjects. Her *Explanatio Symboli Sancti Athanasii (Explanation of the Symbol of Saint Athanasius)* is self-explanatory, as is her *Explanatio Regulae Sancti Benedicti (Explanation of the Rule of Saint Benedict)*, which she wrote at the request of the Benedictine monastery of Huy in Belgium.

For the nuns of her own convent, Hildegard wrote hymns and canticles—both words and music. She tells us in the beginning of her *Liber Vitae Meritorum* that between 1151 and 1158 she collected her songs into a cycle entitled *Symphonia Armonie Celestium Revelationum (The Symphony of the Harmony of Heavenly Revelations)*. Much work is being done by modern scholars on the music and text of her *Symphonia*. Approximately seventy sequences and hymns, antiphons and responsories are found in the cycle and were written for a wide range of liturgical celebrations, from important Church feasts to feasts of lesser known saints. The cycle is comparable to *Liber Hymnorum (The Book of Hymns)* composed by Notker between 860 and 870. For the nuns of her convent, Hildegard also wrote fifty allegorical homilies. And for her own diversion, she originated a language of her own, composed of 900 words and an alphabet of twenty-three letters.

Finally, Hildegard wrote letters to popes, cardinals, bishops, abbots, kings and emperors, monks and nuns, men and women of varied levels of society both in Germany and abroad. Her letters helped Hildegard become known throughout Europe, and a thorough study of her letters would reveal important political and ecclesiastical information concerning the history of her time. Migne prints one hundred and forty-five of her letters in *Patrologiae Cursus Completus, Series Latina.*

Saint Bernard, with whom Hildegard corresponded, was preaching his crusade at this time and he urged Hildegard to use her influence to stir up enthusiasm for what he preached. Over the years she did just that, corresponding with four popes (Eugenius III, Anastasius IV, Adrian IV, and Alexander III) and with two emperors (Conrad III and his son and successor Frederick Barbarossa). Such correspondence brought her into the mainstream of general European history. Her letters also include correspondence with the English King Henry II and his queen Eleanor who was the divorced wife of Louis VII. She urged Henry to beware of the flattery of his courtiers and she warned Queen Eleanor to beware of unrest and inconstancy. In a letter to the Greek emperor and his empress Irene, or Berta as she was also called, she wished them the blessings of a child. When Philip, Count of Flanders, wrote for Hildegard's advice before beginning his crusade, she responded, telling him to be just, but to suppress with an iron hand those who did not believe and who threatened to destroy the faith.

Hildegard was in constant correspondence with the archbishop of Mainz, in whose See Bingen lay. She also had extensive communication with various bishops and clergy in Cologne, Speyer, Hildesheim, Trevers, Bamberg, Prague, Nuremberg, and Utrecht; and with others in Germany, the Low Countries, and Central Europe. Twenty-five abbesses of various convents corresponded with her, but most of her letters to these are more personal, whereas the majority of her other letters are more mystical treatises, prophecies, sermons, and very strong exhortations concerning various corruptions. Hildegard's clear intelligence foresaw that the abuse in the political situation, the corrupt government of the episcopal electors and the princely abbots was exasperating to the Germans and that the volatile situation would eventually burst into flames in some event such as the eventual Reformation or the Thirty Years' War.

OUTLINE OF THE *LIBER VITAE MERITORUM*

While *Scivias* discusses, among many things, the importance of the virtues, *Liber Vitae Meritorum* is a study of the weakness, seemingly inherent in the human consciousness, that separates us from God, a study of moral flaws and of the true nature of sin. *Liber* is one of the most subtle, psychologically fascinating, and intense works ever written on the relationship of the various sins to their corresponding virtues. There are thirty-five antithetical pairs of sins set against virtues. Whereas *Scivias* might be considered a handbook of belief, *Liber Vitae Meritorum* might be considered a handbook of life.

Structure and Content

FOREWORD

Hildegard prefaces *Liber Vitae Meritorum* with a foreword in which she explains how God gave her the command to write down what she saw and heard. She says that nine years after her visions in *Scivias*, she saw another strong and wonderful vision that she labored over for five years. In 1158, when she was sixty-one years old while she was under pressure from the Apostolic See and while Frederick I (Barbarossa) was the reigning emperor, she heard a voice from heaven tell her that she had been taught, not bodily but spiritually, by true vision from the Holy Spirit and that she should speak and write what she saw and heard.

THE FIRST PART: CONCERNING THE MAN LOOKING TO THE EAST AND TO THE SOUTH

In the first of six parts, Hildegard records her vision of a man so tall that he reaches from the summit of the clouds down to the abyss. His head is in the highest ether. From his shoulders to his thighs he is under the clouds. From his thighs to his knees, he is in the earth's air. From his knees to his calves he is in the earth, and from his calves to the soles of his feet he is in the waters of the abyss, standing upon the abyss. He looks East and South. His face is very bright. He blows into a white cloud that is in front of him and this cloud in turn holds up three other clouds: a fiery one, a stormy one, and a light one. Various holy ones live in these clouds. The devil and various wicked ones live in the darkness surrounding these clouds and in a dark cloud coming from the North. The devil spews a horrible mist from his mouth that contains images of seven sins. The image of each sin is described and speaks before each receives a response from its corresponding virtue. The seven sins and antithetical virtues in the first part are worldly love / heavenly love, impudence / discipline, jesting / shyness, hard-heartedness / mercy, slothfulness / divine victory, anger / patience, and foolish joy / sighing for the Lord.

With this and each successive vision, Hildegard is, of course, explaining and interpreting her vision as she presents what is necessary to repent of the sin and to acquire the corresponding virtue.

THE SECOND PART: CONCERNING THE MAN LOOKING TO THE WEST AND TO THE NORTH

In the second vision, the man mentioned above turns West and looks both West and North. He has a wing on each shoulder as well as one on his back and one on his chest. The wings on each shoulder contain open books. The pages of the book on the left shoulder tell of Noah and of being reborn in water. The pages of the book on the right shoulder tell of the coming of the Word. The wing on his back is inscribed by the finger of God; the wing on his chest contains the writings of philosophers and other wise ones. There is a white cloud in front of this man that contains more souls of the just and eight further sins are found in the dark cloud and its surrounding darkness. The eight sins and antithetical virtues are gluttony of the belly / abstinence, bitterness / bountifulness, impiety / piety, falseness / truth, strife / peace, unhappiness / blessedness, immoderation / discretion, and destruction of souls / salvation of souls.

THE THIRD PART: CONCERNING THE MAN LOOKING TO THE NORTH AND TO THE EAST

In the third vision, the man mentioned above turns North and looks both North and East. The winds, the air and the greenness of the earth cover him from his thighs to his knees, like a garment. The powers of the elements work around the middle of his hip bones, but they complain to this man that they cannot finish their journey since their master pushes them aside and men subvert their ways. This man, who is God, answers the elements, telling them that he will purge them with his branches and that he will torment men again and again until they return to him. Seven more sins appear in the horrible mist coming from the devil's mouth. The sins and their antithetical virtues are pride / humility, envy / charity, empty glory / fear of the Lord, disobedience / obedience, unfaithfulness / faith, despair / hope, and luxury / chastity.

THE FOURTH PART: CONCERNING THE MAN LOOKING TO THE SOUTH AND TO THE WEST

In the fourth vision, the man mentioned turns South and looks both South and West. He stands in the earth from his knees to the calves of his legs. This earth is moist and green and is sprouting. In other words, his virtues flourish and are beautiful. In addition, the material of the earth is found in God's work, which is man, and it is also the material of the humanity of the Son of God. Eight other sins appear in the surrounding mist and darkness. The sins and their antithetical virtues are injustice / justice, numbness / strength, forgetfulness / holiness, changeableness / steadiness, care of earthly things / heavenly desire, obstinacy / sorrow of the heart, desire / contempt of the world, and discord / concord.

THE FIFTH PART: CONCERNING THE MAN LOOKING OVER THE WHOLE EARTH

In the fifth vision, the man mentioned looks over the whole earth. From his calves to the soles of his feet he is in the waters of the abyss, standing upon the abyss. The waters of the abyss are the strength of his virtues because they restore all things, purify them, support them, and make them strong, just as the soul makes the body strong. The abyss is the strength of his power since it supports all his institutions and his institutions rest upon it. This man speaks and tells people that he will punish them with his rod if they do not repent. Five other sins then appear. The sins and their antithetical virtues are scurrility / reverence, aimlessness / quiet stability, wrong doing / true care of God, avarice / pure contentment, and sorrow of time / joy of heaven.

THE SIXTH PART: CONCERNING THE MAN MOVING HIMSELF WITH THE FOUR ZONES OF THE EARTH

In the sixth vision, the man mentioned moves, as it were, in the four zones of the earth. And a unicorn appears on his left thigh, licking his knee. The man, who is God, moving in the four zones of the earth symbolizes his strength at the end of the world. The unicorn, who is the Son of God, appears on his left thigh since he is the one who resisted the devil with his holy humanity and who struck the devil down with his sword of chastity. The unicorn licks the man's knee since the Son of God receives the power of judgment from God the Father. The unicorn declares: "What has been done will be pulled down, and what has not been done will be built up. Indeed, man's sin will be examined and his good will be completed with just works. He will then enter into another life."

No further sins appear in this vision, but a comparison is made between the four elements and the virtues. As the elements in general are in people, so also the virtues are in the faithful. And each of the four specific elements is related to a particular function of the virtues. As fire inflames the body, so also the virtues inflame the soul; as a person blows out air, so also the virtues make the soul draw in heavenly things; as water moistens the body, so also the virtues water a person's soul; and as the earth quickens the flesh, so also the virtues make people bear good fruit.

The rest of Part Six explains what else happens at the end of the world and after the last judgment. The devil will no longer be able to produce evil and those in Gehenna will suffer torments forever without any hope. Heaven will be fulfilled. The rewards of those who had renounced their sins by repenting are described. The rewards of those who had obeyed God's commandments in the active life are described, as well as those who had obeyed them as members of the religious life. Further, the rewards of teachers, rulers, martyrs and virgins are also presented. This vision ends with discussions of the fact that the glory and splendor and joy of heaven are so great that humans cannot understand them while they are alive and the fact that once humans gaze upon God they will forget all about earthly things.

CONCLUSION

Considering that Hildegard is the first major German mystic; that the illuminated manuscript of *Scivias* recording her visions and their commentary are important to the art historians and those studying mysticism as well; that her *Ordo Virtutum* at the end of *Scivias* is the earliest morality play yet discovered; that her *Liber Vitae Meritorum* is a major study of sin and virtue; that her various other writings are significant advances in the understanding of the relationship of the individual person to his or her universe and in the understanding of medieval medicine; that her collection of her hymns and songs is a significant one that is only recently being thoroughly studied; that she corresponded actively with the religious and political leaders of her day who were molding the future of Europe in particular and the whole world in general; and that she traveled extensively preaching and prophesying and influencing numerous geographical areas and their peoples, it is a surprise that only recently have her life, writings, travels, and influence begun to receive the proper, thorough, and scholarly attention that are due them. Hildegard is a major writer who has much to offer our modern world. A wealth of knowledge will continue to unfold for those who pursue this exciting scholarship of discovery.

SELECTED BIBLIOGRAPHY

PRIMARY WORKS

Barth, Pudentiana, M. Immaculata Ritscher, and Joseph Schmidt-Gorg, eds. *Lieder: Nach den Handschriften herasugegeben.* Salzburg: 1969.

Fuhrkotter, Adelgundis, ed. and trans. *Briefwechsel: Nach den altesten Handschriften ubersetzt und nach den Quellen erlautert.* Salzburg: 1965.

Fuhrkotter, Adelgundis and Angela Carlevaris, eds. *Scivias.* Corpus Christianorum, Continuatio Medievalis 43. 2 vols. Turnhout: 1978.

Heilkunde: Das Buch von dem Grund und Wesen und der Heilung der Krankheiten; nach den Quellen ubersetzt und erlautert. Trans. Heinrich Schipperges. Salzburg: 1957.

Kaiser, Paul, ed. *Hildegardis Causae et curae.* Leipzig: 1903.

Der Mensch in der Verantwortung: Das Buch der Lebensverdienste (Liber vitae meritorum); nach den Quellen ubersetzt und erlautert. Trans. Heinrich Schipperges. Salzburg: 1972.

Migne, J. P., ed. *S. Hildegardis abbatissae Opera omnia.* Patrologiae cursus completus, Ser. Lat. 197. Paris: 1882.

Naturkunde: Das Buch von dem inneren Wesen der verschiedenen Naturen in der Schopfung; nach den Quellen ubersetzt und erlautert. Trans. Peter Riethe. Salzburg: 1959.

Pitra, Joannes Baptista, ed. *Analecta Sanctae Hildegarids Opera Spicilegio Solesmensi Parata.* Analecta Sacra 8. 1882. Reprint. Farnborough, England: 1966.

Welt und Mensch: Das Buch "De operatione Dei"; aus dem Genter Kodex ubersetzt unde erlautert. Trans. Heinrich Schipperges. Salzburg: 1965.

Wisse die Wege: Nach dem Originaltext des illuminierten Rupertsberger Kodex der Wiesbaden Landesbibliothek in Deutsche ubertragen und bearbeitet. Trans. Maura Bockeler. Salzburg: 1954.

PRINTED BIBLIOGRAPHIES

Lauter, Werner. *Hildegard-Bibliographie: Wegweiser zur Hildegard-Literatur.* Alzey: 1970.

Lauter, Werner. *Hildegard-Bibliographie: Wegweiser zur Hildegard-Literatur. Band II 1970-82.* Alzey: 1984.

FURTHER REFERENCES

Beer, Frances. *Women and Mystical Experience in the Middle Ages.* Suffolk: Boydell, 1992.

Davidson, Audrey Ekdahl, ed. *The Ordo Virtutum of Hildegard of Bingen: Critical Studies.* Kalamazoo: Medieval Institute Publications, 1992.

Dronke, Peter. *Women Writers of the Middle Ages.* Cambridge: Cambridge U P, 1984.

Dronke, Peter. "The Composition of Hildegard of Bingen's *Symphonia.*" *Sacris Erudiri* (1969-70): 381-93.

Escot, Pozzi. "Gothic Cathedral and the Hidden Geometry of St. Hildegard." *Sonus* 5.1 (Fall 1984): 14-31.

Escot, Pozzi. "Universal Proportion in Hildegard von Bingen." *Sonus* 11 (1990): 33-40.

Flanagan, Sabina. *Hildegard of Bingen: A Visionary Life.* New York: Routledge, 1989.

Fox, Matthew. *Hildegard of Bingen's* Book of Divine Works *with Letter and Songs.* Sante Fe: Bear, 1987.

Gies, Frances and Joseph. *Women in the Middle Ages.* New York: Perennial Library, 1986.

Grant, Barbara L. "A Feather on the Breath of God." *Parabola* 9.2 (April 1984): 94-96.

Grant, Barbara L. "Five Liturgical Songs by Hildegard von Bingen." *Signs* 5.3 (1980): 564-73.

Hozeski, Bruce, trans. *Scivias by Hildegard of Bingen*. Santa Fe: Bear, 1986.

Jeskalian, Barbara J. "Hildegard of Bingen, Her Times and Her Music." *Anima* (Fall 1983): 7-13.

Kraft, Kent. "The German Visionary: Hildegard of Bingen." *Medieval Women Writers*. Katharina Wilson, ed. Athens, Georgia: U of Georgia P, 1984.

Newman, Barbra. "Hildegard of Bingen: Visions and Validation." *Church History* 54.2 (1985): 163-75.

Newman, Barbara. *Sister of Wisdom: St. Hildegard's Theology of the Feminine*. Berkeley: U of California P, 1987.

Petroff, Elizabeth Alvilda. *Medieval Women's Visionary Literature*. Oxford: Oxford U P, 1986.

Potter, Robert. "The *Ordo Virtutum*: Ancestor of the English Moralities?" *Comparative Drama* 20.3 (Fall, 1986): 201-09.

Sacks, Oliver. "The Visions of Hildegard." *The Man Who Mistook His Wife for a Hat*. Berkeley: U of California P, 1986.

Schmitt, Mirian. "St. Hildegard of Bingen: Leven of God's Justice." *Cistercian Studies* (21 March 1989): 69-88.

Scholz, Bernhard W. "Hildegard von Bingen on the Nature of Woman." *The American Benedictine Review* 31 (December 1980): 361-83.

Steele, Francesca Maria. *The Life and Visions of St. Hildegard*. St. Louis: B. Herder, 1915.

THE HEADINGS OF THE FIRST PART BEGIN CONCERNING THE MAN LOOKING TO THE EAST AND TO THE SOUTH

109. The Fact That They Who Will Have Committed Murder through the Fury of Anger, May Chasten Themselves by Punishing Themselves by Having Been Restrained with Fasting and Scourging

110. The Fact That He Who Will Have Killed a Man through Greed, May Punish His Body with Fasting and Scourging, Leaving the Company of Men for Some Time

111. The Fact That He Who Killed a Man by Anticipating a Man Wishing to Kill Himself, May Castigate Himself, with Punishments by Worthy Fasting

112. The Fact That He Who Will Have Ignorantly Sent a Man into Death, May Cleanse Himself by Punishing Himself with Fasting, Although with Lighter Things

113. He Who Will Have Killed a Man by Poisoning or by Some Other Manner without the Spilling of Blood, May Afflict Himself through Punishment by Having Been Restrained with Fasting and with Scourging and with a Hair Shirt, also Fleeing the Company of Men for Some Time

114. The Fact That Women Who Will Have Separated Themselves from Conception, May Fetch Themselves Back, Punishing Themselves with Fasting and Scourging

115. The Fact That They Who Will Have Killed the Infants Having Been Born from Themselves, May Afflict Themselves with the Bitterest Fasting, with Scourgings and with the Harshness of Garments in the Narrowness of Solitude

116. The Fact That He Who Casts Himself Down into Death, Destroys Himself Completely without Consolation

117. The Fact That with Judicial Repentance, a Natural Possibility Ought to Be Considered

118. The Fact That God, Who Created All Things, Did Not Wish to Have His Glory Alone, Whose Plans No One Is Able to Fight Against

119. The Fact That against This Fact That Man Was Able to Sin, the Son of God, Sustaining Many Wounds in His Body, Also Drew the Sins of the Repenting Ones to Himself

THE HEADINGS OF THE FIRST PART UNFOLD

THE BOOK OF THE REWARDS OF LIFE BEGINS THROUGH A SIMPLE PERSON FROM THE LIVING LIGHT OF REVELATIONS

1. The following happened in the ninth year after a true vision had shown me, a simple person, the true visions which I had previously labored over for ten years. This was the first year after that vision had shown me *the simplicity of the various natural creatures* with responses and warnings for greater and lesser people. It had also shown me *the symphony of the harmony of heavenly revelations, and an unknown language with letters* with certain other explanations. I had been physically sick and weighed down with a lot of work for nine years after the true vision had shown me these things so that I might explain them. When I was sixty years old, I saw another strong and wonderful vision which I labored over for five years.

2. When I was sixty-one years old, which was the year 1158 of the Lord's Incarnation, while I was under pressure from the Apostolic See and while Frederick was the reigning emperor of the Romans, I heard a voice from heaven saying to me: *From infancy you have been taught, not bodily but spiritually, by true vision through the Spirit of the Lord. Speak these things that you now see and hear. For from the first of your visions certain visions were shown to you, just like liquid milk.*

Others, however, were uncovered for you like sweet and soft food. Still others, however, were manifest to you like solid and perfect food. Speak and write, therefore, now according to me and not according to yourself. And I set my hand to writing down the testimony of that person whom, as I have said in earlier visions, I had privately sought and found. I also had a young maiden assisting me in writing down this testimony. And again I heard a voice from heaven speaking to me and teaching me in this way.

THE FIRST PART BEGINS

CONCERNING THE MAN LOOKING TO THE EAST AND TO THE SOUTH

3. I saw a person who was so tall that he reached from the summit of the clouds of heaven right down to the abyss. From his shoulders on up he was in the serenest ether. From his shoulders down to his thighs he was under the clouds on another white cloud. From his thighs to his knees, he was in the earth's air. From his knees to the calves of his legs he was in the earth. And from his calves down to the soles of his feet he was in the waters of the abyss, standing upon the abyss. He had turned toward the East so that he looked East and South. His face, however, shone with such brightness that I could not look at him whole. There was also a white cloud by his mouth that looked like a trumpet and was full of all sounds sounding rapidly. As this person blew air into this white cloud, it sent out three winds. The first wind held up three clouds: a fiery one, a stormy one, and a light one. The other two winds, however, descended with their clouds down to his breast where they expanded their winds. But the wind that remained in front of his face expanded from the East to the South.

4. In the fiery cloud lived a fiery crowd who had one life in one will and in one union. In their presence was a writing tablet full of feathers, which flew with the precepts of God. As the precepts of God lifted up the writing tablet on which God's knowledge had written his secrets, this crowd looked at that tablet with united zeal. And as they looked at

it, God's virtue was granted them so that they sounded forth like a very loud trumpet with one sound in every kind of music.

5. But the wind that had the storm cloud before it was expanding the cloud along with itself from South to West so that the length and width of the cloud was like a street that could not be understood by the human mind. There was, moreover, a large crowd of blessed in this cloud. They had all the spirits of life and no one could destroy them. Their voices sounded like rushing waters as they said: "We are assigned to dwell in various places according to the will of the source of this wind. But when will we receive our dwelling places? If we already dwelt there, we would rejoice more than we do now."

6. But the crowd in the fiery cloud answered them with the voice of singers, saying: "When the Divinity has grasped his trumpet, he will send lightning and thunder and fire upon the earth. He will also grasp the fire that is inside the sun so that the earth will shake. This will happen when God has decided to reveal his great signs. He will then preach through his trumpet in all the different languages to all the peoples of the world. And those noted by the trumpet will then receive their dwelling places."

7. And the wind above which was the light cloud spread itself out with this cloud from East to North. But immense darkness that came from the West spread out to the light cloud with great density and horror. Yet it was unable to pass beyond the light cloud. And there was a lion in the sun and a capricorn in the moon. And the sun shone above heaven and in heaven and on earth and beneath the earth, and it thus proceeded by rising and returned by setting. But as the sun proceeded, the lion went with it and pillaged many things. As the sun returned, the lion returned with it and sent many back to joy. The moon with the capricorn in it gradually followed the sun by proceeding and returning with the capricorn. And that wind blew and said: "A woman will bear a newborn and the capricorn will fight against the seven stars of the Great Bear constellation."

8. In the darkness there was a large crowd of lost souls who were all stirred up. These souls had turned away from those singing in the South, as they did not want to be friends with them. Their leader was the seducer. They followed the devil because Christ's suffering did not mean more to them than the devil's leadership. And they all cried out with lamentation, saying: "Alas, alas, the devil fled life with disgusting and horrible works and gave us death!"

9. Then I saw a cloud coming from the North that extended itself to the darkness. It had become parched of all joy and happiness since it had neither touched the sun nor shown itself to it. It was full of wicked spirits who wandered here and there. They planned out snares for people, but blushed when they thought about the person mentioned earlier. And I heard the ancient serpent say to himself: "I will prepare the powers of my strength as a fortification and will fight my enemies with all my strength." And he spit out of his mouth a froth of many impurities and blemishes upon the people. He inflamed and mocked them, saying: "Vah! I will make those who call themselves the sun through works of light be repulsive and benighted and horrible in darkness." And he spewed forth a most disgusting mist from his mouth, which covered the earth like the blackest of smoke. Then a very loud and disturbing thunder rumbled from the mist, saying: "No person should adore another God unless he sees and knows him. Why should anyone pay attention to someone he does not know?" I saw in this mist, however, the various images of various sins. I saw seven of them in the following manner.

1
THE WORDS OF WORLDLY LOVE

10. The first image was like a black man from Ethiopia. He was naked. He had his arms around the base of a huge tree with many limbs and branches, all filled with many different kinds of flowers. He picked a lot of these flowers and held them in his hands while he said: "I hold all the world's kingdoms with their greatness in my hands. Why should I be withered when I have all this greenness in my hands? Why should I be old when I could be young? Why should I lose my sight to blindness? If this happened, I would be embarrassed. I will hang onto the beauty of this world as long as I can. I do not understand words spoken about another life when I have never seen it." But after he had said this, the root of the tree dried up and the tree fell into the darkness mentioned earlier. When the tree fell, this image also fell into the darkness with it.

2
THE RESPONSE OF HEAVENLY LOVE

11. From the storm cloud mentioned earlier, I heard a voice say to this image: "You are foolish because you want to live in this world. You do not search for a life where the beauty of youth lasts forever and where old age never comes. You do not have any light; you are surrounded by a black fog. You have the will of a human. You are like a

worm that lives for just a short time until the marsh dries up. Therefore, you have fallen into the lake of destruction with all the flowers you hold in your hands. I, however, am the pillar of heavenly harmony. I provide all the joys in life. I do not reject life, but I do trample all the sins underfoot. Likewise, I despise you. For I am the watch-tower of all the virtues that the faithful have. You, however, run around in the dark and work feebly with your hands."

3
THE WORDS OF IMPUDENCE

12. The second image looked like a hunting dog. Standing on its hind feet, it put its paws on a staff. Wagging its tail, it said: "What good is something that makes a person laugh only moderately. The soul is filled with beautiful air that makes it sound like a symphony. But what human being can be mortal forever? Not one! Therefore, humans should be happy while they can be."

4
THE RESPONSE OF DISCIPLINE

13. A second time I heard a voice from the storm cloud. It said to this image: "You are like the devil. You have the squalid humor of a jokester who should be blown away by the wind. You are like the worms that dig in the earth. When people see you, they agree with you. You rush to greet people, just as a dog does. You encourage people to do whatever they want, but you actually give them bad advice, wounding their souls. You make up your own laws. I, however, wear the girdle of sanctity and the mantle of honesty. I am the honorable offspring of the royal marriage of knowledge and justice."

5
THE WORDS OF JESTING

14. The third image was also like a man, except that it had a hooked nose, hands like bear's feet, and feet like a griffin's. It had black hair and wore a pale garment. It said: "It is more fun to play than to be sad; playing is not a crime. Heaven rejoices in all creatures; so will I. For if I appear sad to people, they will leave me. Therefore, I will not do that. I will, instead, be playful in many different ways so that everyone can be happy with me. God created the air which makes the flowers grow and

which carries pleasant sounds to me. These things are very pleasant to
me; why should I not rejoice in them. People also play with their animals and their animals have fun with them; all this is appropriate."

6
THE RESPONSE OF SHYNESS

15. From that storm cloud I again heard a voice say to this image:
"You are an idolater. You only do your own will. You are like a loud
noise made with a person's hands. You have the will of both a human
and an animal in your various actions. For your actions are like someone
who is dying since you are so determined in your desires and since you
walk down the path of vanity. I, however, am ashamed of such things. I
hide like a Cherubim. And I have learned from God's scrolls and de-
crees. I am alive with the heavenly virtues. For I see with the eyes of innocence and I look for honesty in God's will. You, however, flee God's
will in the blindness of your ignorance."

7
THE WORDS OF HARD-HEARTEDNESS

16. The fourth image looked like dense smoke rising up as high as a
tall person. This image did not have any human members, except very
large black eyes. It did not move up or down but remained motionless in
the darkness mentioned earlier. It said: "I created nothing; I established
nothing. Why, therefore, should I do any work? Why should I wear myself out? Nothing excites me except what benefits me directly. Let God
who created all things take care of these things. For if I flatter someone
and ask them about their work, what good will it do me? I am not going
to do anything, good or evil. For if I am always busy being compassionate, what good will it do me? What kind of life will I have if I pay
attention to all the happy and sad people? I will take care of myself. Let
others take care of themselves."

8
THE RESPONSE OF MERCY

17. From the storm cloud I again heard a voice answer this image: "O
you of stone, what are you saying? Flowering herbs give out an aroma
and a stone glitters; all creation shows its fullness in some way. All the
creatures on the earth minister to humans and by doing this freely they

accomplish good. You, however, are not even worthy enough to have the form of a human. Since you have no mercy you are like pungent black smoke. But I am like the sweetest plant growing in the air. I have moisture and I am green. My veins are so full that I can help others. For I came forth with the *Fiat* that made all creation for serving humans. But you are not like this. I think about what is needed and I do that. I help all the sick get healthy; my words are like salve for pain. But you are nothing but pungent smoke!"

9

THE WORDS OF SLOTHFULNESS

18. The fifth image had a human head, except that its left ear was a hare's ear. And this ear was so large that it covered its whole head. The rest of its body was like that of a worm without any bones. This worm twisted in its hole just as an infant squirms in its clothes. It spoke with a trembling voice.

19. "I do not want to injure anyone by rushing, because then I would be banished and would weep without any consolation from anyone. For if I injure anyone, I will not have any friends. Instead, I will give praise to the noble and wealthy. I will not pay any attention to the holy and the poor since they cannot benefit me in any way. I want to be pleasant to everyone so that I do not suffer. For if I fight with someone, they might hit back with force. And if I injure someone, they might injure me more. As long as I am alive I will remain quiet. Likewise, it is sometimes better to lie and deceive than it is to speak the truth. It is also better for me to gather possessions than it is to do away with them. It is better to run away from the strong than to fight them. Who would win? I might start something I could not finish. The victorious and the wise, however, mock me. But they have only what comes to them; I, however, choose my own house. For those who speak the truth often let good things get away; those who fight are sometimes killed."

10

THE RESPONSE OF DIVINE VICTORY

20. From the same cloud I again heard a voice answering the image: "You began to go astray when you spoke your first lie against God. You did not want to stay close to justice. You have wandered into exile, since your not having any good intentions has deceived people. You are not honest. I, however, hold the sword of God's strongest virtues and

can cut out every injustice. I will strike you in the jaw with my sword. I will harden my heart against you because you are as dust. I will make sure that whatever you want to gather to yourself is not much. For I do not want to live my life in the dirt. I do not want to have anything to do with the emptiness of the world's vanity. I, however, want to arrive at the leaping fountain. For I fight against the devil and I destroy all his spoils with the mysteries of God's Scriptures. I will always fight the devil with the Scriptures. For that reason I will always dwell with the true God."

21. The sixth image had a man's face, except that its mouth was like a scorpion's and its eyes were so distorted that their whites were larger than the pupils. Its arms were those of a human, but its hands were gnarled and had long finger-nails. Its chest, front and back, was like a crab's. Its shins were like those of locusts and its feet were like a viper's. It was tangled up inside a turning wheel so that it held onto the top rim with its hands and the bottom rim with its feet. It had no hair on its head and it was naked as it billowed fiery words from its mouth.

11
THE WORDS OF ANGER

22. "I will cast down and trample underfoot anything that hurts me. Why should I be injured? Do whatever you want to do, but do not make me angry. And do not do anything against me. For I will wound you with my sword and I will beat you with my clubs whenever you injure me."

12
THE RESPONSE OF PATIENCE

23. From the cloud I again heard a voice answer this image: "I proclaimed from on high and my voice reached the earth. I poured out balsam on the earth. You are a fraud. You drink blood. And you are always in darkness. I, however, am the sweet air that brings forth greenery, producing the flowers and fruits of all the virtues. I build all the virtues in people's minds. Everything I begin I complete since I persevere. I will not trample anyone underfoot. I am quiet and no one condemns me. When you build your tower I will destroy it with one word and scatter everything in it. You will be destroyed; I, however, will remain for eternity."

13

THE WORDS OF FOOLISH JOY

24. The seventh image was like a man from its head down to its loins, except that its hands were like a monkey's. From its loins down it was like a she-goat. But its feet were hidden in the darkness mentioned earlier so that I could not see them. It wore no clothes and was naked. It said:

25. "I live a sweet and beautiful life. Why shouldn't I? God gave me this life. So what if I take pleasure in my flesh? Similarly, the wood of a cypress is hard and black at first and then it shines like gold later on. Likewise, I should not be blamed for any filth in my flesh. There are many people alive who are blind and do not know what they are doing. I, however, know life itself and I want to live it to the fullest."

14

THE RESPONSE OF SIGHING FOR GOD

26. From the cloud I again heard a voice answer this image: "Why aren't you blushing, O naked one? Because you live a life that is blind and constantly changes. You violate all justice and truth with your actions. You do not live a rational life. I, however, realize that a worldly life can be as dry as a bog. Therefore, I long for life everlasting. I also draw heavenly harmony to myself, as well as the angels and other spiritual joys. I do not become bored with these because they are my friends. I will never be separated from them!"

15

THE WORDS OF A GLADIATOR

27. I saw that the man I mentioned earlier held a sword in his hand. It had three cutting edges and its hilt had been placed in a sheath. He then started swinging it around as if he were going to cut something. This gladiator said: "I have the greatest zeal possible against the North and everyone who dwells there. Who can conquer me? No one! For I have no material in my make-up; no man brought me forth from a woman. But I judge everyone's works. God formed man from the slime of the earth when he completed all his works. But I see into man, just like looking into a mirror."

16
THE FACT THAT THE UNFAITHFUL ARE NOT KNOWN, AND THE FACT THAT THE WORKS OF GOD REMAIN IN LIFE

28. I then heard a voice from heaven say: *Who dwells in every creature? Who is able to count God's works? And how many people dwell on God's earth? Who are they, and what sort are they? How many argue among themselves and spread the blackness of schism, so that they seek their god in the North and pay heed to him there, and so that they shatter and destroy all the righteous things created by God, according to their own perverse wills? They pull everything apart when they say in their hearts: "This life is good; that life is evil." They think they know more than God. But they do not know what they are doing. For God's works, which are done by people, still remain with the infinite. Ezekiel's words show this when he writes about the four animals.*

17
THE WORDS OF EZEKIEL

29. *Their faces were like this: each of the four had the face of a man, but on the right side was the face of a lion, and on the left side the face of an ox, and finally each had the face of an eagle (Ezekiel 1:10).* This means the following. God's work is man and this work is from God. *The face of a man* stands for piety, which gives man sensibility. *The face of a lion* is the virtue by which God gives man rationality. It is *on the right* since piety and God's virtue, which are like wings, reveal divine inspiration by understanding the greatness of good works. *The face of an ox* proclaims God's sacrifice by which he shows man how to offer sacrifice to himself. It is *on the left* since some sacrifice fails whereby one victim is accepted and another one is rejected. Similarly a person who offers his will to God meditates on both earthly and heavenly matters. For during sacrifice God draws a person to himself and then breathes into the person so that the person can make himself a sacrifice to God. *The face of an eagle*, however, prefigures the knowledge of God that gives man the potential for knowledge and knowledge itself according to God's will. This eagle is above all the other virtues since it causes man fear, it brings him life, and it does not abandon him. For it inspires all things, sees everywhere, and appears in man, like the stars in the firmament.

18

THE NUMBER OF THE CHOSEN AND THE DAMNED ARE KNOWN TO NO MAN

30. Although man has a lot of knowledge, no person can count God's works nor know the number of those who will possess heaven. Just as God's works are innumerable, so also are those who inherit heavenly mansions through their good works. Similarly, those who have been seduced by the devil's temptations are innumerable and will dwell with the devil.

19

GOD ALONE KNEW ALL THINGS

31. God, however, knows the number of all things. There are many, many secrets in God which he reveals to no one except partially and according to what pleases him and what he wishes. For he alone knows all things and holds all things together. And he preserves all things according to the plan of his grace. Even this present vision that you see bears witness to this.

20

WHY GOD MAY BE CALLED A MAN

32. For the person who was so tall that he reached from the summit of the clouds of heaven right down to the abyss stands for God who is rightly called man since every power and all things which live come from him.

21

THE WORDS OF ISAIAH

33. He is also the person the prophet speaks about: *The Lord goes forth like a hero, like a warrior he stirs up his ardor; he shouts out his battle cry, against his enemies he shows his might (Isaiah 42:13).* His knowledge is so great. Before the beginning of time, the Lord's very great power gave life to every kind of creature. And the life that he made prospered and multiplied in the various creatures. He created all good things wholly according to his plan and he commanded the beginning of all the virtues since nothing can be found lacking in him. He

also fought strongly against his enemies who suffered from pride. Pride tries to climb first when it sees a flight of stairs and to sit first when it finds a chair. The work of pride is plotting and it causes things to be destroyed. For *the warrior stirred up ardor* in the fullness of his work, which means, of course, the burning fire in the angelic order. He cast out the enemy when the enemy tried to cover heaven with the darkness of evil. As a result of God's very great strength and the joy of his victory, rejoicing rose up when the angels cried aloud, saying: "Who is like God?" They also cried aloud like a strong wind that one was about to fall. Then the angelic army rejoiced since nothing had been destroyed in heaven. The ancient enemy fell into darkness, void of light and the joy of life. And the angelic army placed its arrows and javelins against the will of the enemy.

22
GOD WILL DESTROY THE ANCIENT ENEMY COMPLETELY

34. This person also conquered his enemies through another work of his, clearly man whom he created. With strength he fought anew against the javelins and wickedness of his cunning enemy as he carried his banner into this battle—"The Word that was made flesh." He will persist with this battle until the number of brothers, of course, of the blessed, is filled. With the strongest of fighting he will fight against this enemy just as he had fought him earlier in heaven. He will destroy him completely since his enemy stood leisurely among sin and sat among deception and wickedness. Whoever does not want to live like this is blessed and his blessedness will not fail.

23
MAN MAY IGNORE WHAT MAY ALSO BE ABOUT TO BE BEFORE HIM

35. This person was so tall that he stretched from the beginning of creation to its end. This is because man will be able to speak right up to the end of his time, although he may not know what came before him or will come after him. For God has neither a beginning nor an end.

24

WHAT MAY HAVE BEEN BEFORE THE BEGINNING OF THE WORLD, GOD KNEW

36. From his shoulders on up this person is above the clouds in the serenest ether. This means that before the beginning of the world he alone knew all things in the solitude of his divine clarity. God is above all things and in all of the most excellent of things. Neither the angels nor the souls of the just can bring God to an end. All living things proceed from God. He does not have a beginning, but remains alone in himself. He lives in himself and he knows in himself. God is he who lives and who is capable and who knows. All his works have become distinct and made perfect with these three powers. In him all his works have the potential of perfection.

25

THE FIRE OF GOD IS WORKING

37. God is eternal. And fire is eternal. And God is here. He is not a hidden fire nor a silent fire, but an effective fire. God is beyond the mind and understanding of all creatures. In the clarity of his mysteries and secrets he disperses everything and rules over everything, just as the head rules over the whole body. For God makes life rational when eyes see, ears hear and noses smell; and he speaks reasonable words. God is, therefore, the head of all the faithful. Nevertheless, he does not reveal everything that is concealed in the mystery of his divinity since the mystery of life is concealed in him. Likewise also by decision *he makes his ministers flaming fire (Hebrews 1:7)*. For any decision is made before it is acted upon, as it is in God. He also used fire and water to examine before the law, as before his shoulders, men who came before the law since they had not been examined by any other laws. He then cleansed them according to the law with various harsh tribulations and finished this process when he became a man. He destroyed the devil with his power and purified people mercifully from their sordid sins with his true justice. As the prophet says: *His dominion is vast (Isaiah 9:6)*.

26

THE WORDS OF ISAIAH

38. This means as follows. Justice appeared through a man by God's power when God became a man whereby, like the strength of his shoul-

der, he destroyed the devil's work and ruined hell and whereby he preached baptism upon earth through his apostles. God perfected justice for the sake of people who, formed from the slime of the earth, had become mortal. For man, when he was still like the bud of the first flower, was seduced by the devil who slit open his entrails and belched forth all his filth. At the same time, he marked all his children when he sowed them passionately with poisonous seed. God, however, formed a body in the purity of the Virgin through the warmth of the Holy Spirit without the poisonous seed of a man. Therefore, when God became man, he cleansed men of all the poisonous filth of the devil because this man who had no sin of the world saved sinners whose sins had been wiped away.

27
ANCIENT MIRACLES MADE MANIFEST THAT WERE HIDDEN

39. From his shoulders down to his thighs he was under the clouds on another white cloud: this is because from the beginning of creation to the beginning of truth when *truth arose from the earth (Psalm 85:12)*, he held many miracles in the shining light of his honor in the mystery of his Divinity. He revealed some things through miracles but kept other things hidden. In ruling over and protecting holy souls, God's will is bright and clear in the mystery of spiritual life. It is impossible, however, for the human mind to understand God's miracles.

28
THE OLD LAW AS THE SOUND OF THE WORD

40. But nevertheless he, as from his shoulders down, founded a special cohort of men. He did this when he joined the old law to himself which was like the sound of the Word but was not the Word. The sound of a word is heard before the word is understood. Similarly, the old law was like the sound or shadow of the Word until the Word, Christ, of course, appeared.

29
ALL THINGS ARE CARRIED BY GOD

41. From his thighs to his knees, he was in the earth's air, since as all fleshly things come from the thighs and are supported and carried by the

knees, so also all creatures are supported by God. They are nourished in the fiery warmth and moisture of the air into which all living bodies are brought. In the same way a new people, rising up in chastity and coming to lasting comfort after suffering various things while on earth, is granted the sweetness of miracles and virtues. For when the Divinity joined the Virgin through the breath of the Holy Spirit, the Word became known to humanity. Through the Word the Divinity revealed the new law to humanity when the sound and the Word turned into one thing, making the old and new laws complement each other.

30

THE SOULS OF THE HOLY DO NOT YET HAVE THE FULLNESS OF JOY

42. The old law was hidden; the new law, however, appears openly. Similarly the souls of the holy ones who had returned from their dwelling places on earth did not have the fullness of joy in the old law since they had not yet seen the Father's face completely. They could not see the Father's face completely since a part divided in half cannot be seen completely. When, however, they had been made whole and received their dwelling place, they looked at that which is whole completely. But they were not changed in any way, just as the new law revealed completely what was hidden in the old law without the old law being changed in any way.

31

THE VOCATION OF THE NEW PEOPLE DOES NOT FALL TO THE GROUND IN TRIBULATION

43. From his knees to the calves of his legs he was in the earth. As the knees carry a person and the calves give strength to his feet, so also God carries and strengthens all things and gives the earth strength since he sustains and gives strength to its creatures. For the earth is like the knees and calves of its creatures. Like the axis of a wheel, it carries some creatures. It makes water flow here and there. For if the earth had not been placed between the air and the water, air could not rise above water. But as a knee is sometimes bent but held back by the calf, so also the earth is sometimes led the wrong way by some of its creatures when it does not administer its office righteously. The earth, nevertheless, does not falter because God's power restores it to the righteous way. So also the calling of the new people, having heard the Gospel and been

strengthened by it while they were traveling around the earth, will suffer many trials and tribulations when their knees will have been shaken by the Antichrist. But having strength from its calves, this new people will not fall upon the ground since these people know in their heads that God will help them. Earlier, these people had turned toward sin while they were on earth and had turned to other things in their passion, just like their knees were bent. Similarly, the Church, having been turned around by the new law but failing in its strength, will be bent by the evil destroyer but not be overcome since the Church receives God's power and thus remains invincible.

32
MANY THINGS ARE NOT KNOWN TO MEN

44. And from his calves down to the soles of his feet he was in the waters of the abyss, standing upon the abyss. This means that God's strength and his wondrous life are hidden, as it were in the soles of his feet. They are hidden, of course, in those mysteries which ought not be known by man. He is in the waters of the abyss because many things which are not known are on high and cannot be known by men. For God has all things on earth in his power and rules over and judges these things. He also discerns the judgment of lower things: there is nothing which is not in his power. He stands strongly on his mysteries, just as a person rests on the soles of his feet, resting as God did on the seventh day from all his work.

33
NO MAN IS ABLE TO KNOW THE END OF THE SON OF PERDITION

45. Similar to standing on the soles of one's feet, the calling of the new people, which did not lose its strength to the Antichrist but preserved it right up to end of time known by God and not men, will remain in these wondrous things right up to the newest day. Just as no one can look into the abyss, so also no one knows what will happen after the end of time. Wisdom has spoken about these things.

34

THE WORDS OF WISDOM

46. *Heaven's height, earth's breadth, the depths of the abyss: who can explore these (Sirach 1:3)?* This means the following. The planet of the earth is stirred up with fire and wind and air, but all creatures are sheltered on it. For heaven with all its splendor is on the highest part of this planet. What man can go beyond heaven with his own power? Further, the breadth of the earth is covered with flowing water. The middle of the planet is covered with those things which flow above the abyss. But no one can understand this. The abyss with all its strange things is at the end of the planet. And who can stretch to this end? No one, except God who created it. Man lives on this planet and is surrounded by it, but cannot understand all of it. For creatures live in the power of God just as a heart lives in a person. A little part of a person can be compared to the whole person. Similarly creatures are little but the power of God is great and incomprehensible. All the creatures that are in heaven and on earth and in the abyss cannot understand God nor distinguish him nor enclose him within limits. But all wisdom is from God. God predestined all things with his wisdom and distinguished all the things he created on this planet with his wisdom. He gave all things the taste of heaven and surrounded them with the circle of his royal care. He transformed the earth so that it serves the needs of all creatures. He penetrated the abyss like a manager who does not allow any of his things to be lost. But wisdom is also the eye of God which foresees and contemplates all things. Before his eye wisdom is a most loving friend full of love whom God wants to care for all things. Wisdom also calls people to the height of heaven since man's knowledge makes him master of all creatures. Man is like the eye of wisdom. But man is also like the breadth of the earth because he has the power to desire and to choose. In what way? Because man chooses, he may choose wisdom. As long as he desires help with his will, help will be given him for if he calls upon God, God will help him. However, if he chooses the devil, the devil will greet him with evil ideas. Man can also desire and choose to taste reasonably, but whatever he desires or chooses, he does not do by his own power but by the power of God who created him. As man can do many different things, he can also have many desires and make many choices to demand many things. And as the devil deceived Eve, Eve likewise seduced Adam many times with many suggestions. Man can become like the depth of the abyss when he turns away from good and chooses evil. At such time, the devil supports his desires. And God allows this to happen. When,

however, man entwines himself with good desires so that he can do the good things which he has sometimes passed over, not because he has given up good things completely but because he sometimes neglects them, God then does not allow him to be destroyed because he still desires good. The devil, however, does not trust man completely, even when he fulfills the desires of his flesh, because the devil recognizes that man does not want to give up God. This man, however, is standing upon the abyss since he is like a storm which sometimes brightens with the sun and sometimes wraps itself up in black clouds. Who has questioned man's disdain? Who has questioned why man, created above all of God's works, abandoned God and imitated the devil who had lost all his glory when he was opposed to God because of his pride? Who has questioned whether man perished? Who can measure the destruction caused when man abandoned God and chose the worst tyrant, clearly the devil, rather than God? God sees and judges these things.

35
THE WONDROUS REFORMATION OF MAN

47. This man turns toward the East so that he looks East and South since at the beginning of the world God commanded his creatures to come forth like the shining sun. God not only brought them forth but also multiplied them, as if they were in the South, not only when he redeemed man to his original state after he had rushed away from God toward evil when he fell from his good beginning but also when he gave the great virtues of holiness to man.

36
NO ONE IS LIKE GOD IN HIS WORKS

48. His face, however, shines with such brightness that you can not look at him whole because the holy Divinity burns so brightly with every kind of goodness and justice that no one can look at it. For there is no other God except the one God. No one can perform works like his since God alone can do such wondrous and incomprehensible things. He is also the very fire which makes the angels burn and live. And he is the light from which the mysteries proceed that have the life of the miracles in them. This life is in God. For these miracles are without number in heaven and on earth and in the abyss.

37

ALL THINGS ARE OBEDIENT TO THE ORDER OF
GOD

49. There is also a white cloud by his mouth that looks like a trumpet since the divine and sweet order found in all things that the Divinity brings forth proceeds according to the divine will, like sound from a trumpet. The trumpet is full of all sounds sounding rapidly because all things, reasonable or unreasonable, obey the divine order in full subjection. They obey God out of honor and praise since he created them. For God is good and all things that come from him are good.

38

CONCERNING THE THREE WAYS OF JUSTICE IN
THE THREE ORDERS OF THE BLESSED ONES

50. As this man blows air into this white cloud, it sends out three winds since God, passing through the hidden order of his will with secret inquiry, made the three ways of justice come to the three orders of the blessed. The first wind holds up three clouds: a fiery one, a stormy one, and a bright one. This means that one way of justice is in the glory of the angels, burning with love of God and not wanting anything else than what God wants, just like the fiery cloud. Another way is the work of men, which is stormy and which has many limitations and tribulations, just like the stormy cloud. The third way holds the white and undefiled virginity of the incarnation of the Lord, like the light cloud, because justice is the foundation and sustenance of the blessed. For God, bringing forth all things according to the mystery of his will, wrapped the spirits of his blessed with righteousness. He also supported those falling into stormy works lest they perish completely. He chased the works of darkness away with the light of virginity and with the incarnation, and he revealed what is righteous. The angels remained in the love of God, but man, removing himself from God, has been brought back to his earlier glory and been made holy by holy works which he performed in holiness. The blessed labor in the flesh now, but at the time of the newest day they will rejoice in symphony with every kind of praise. The flesh restrains the spirit while it is in the flesh, but later the flesh will be subjected to the spirit so that man can be completely holy.

39

THE ANGELS WERE ALWAYS BROUGHT FORTH TO THE WILL OF GOD

51. The wind with the fiery cloud above it remains in front of his face since the justice of God's will and his glory cause the glory of the angels who are inflamed with God's love and who aspire to the highest things to endure. For the angels who look at God's face always act according to his will and do not draw back from him.

40

GOD KNEW THE WORKS OF THE HOLY ONES

52. The other two winds, however, descend with their clouds down to his breast where they expand their winds since justice marches in two different directions for people with one direction being toward the old law and the other toward the incarnation of the Son of God. Justice comes about through the good works of people at which time it enters God's deepest knowledge where it is spread out among wondrous things, because God knows about the works of the holy and does not forget them. As part of his divine plan, God rewards the holy and spreads out their good works in infinite praise of his own glory.

53. But the wind that remained in front of his face expands from the East to the South because justice, shining in God's presence in the glory of the highest spirits who stood firm in the truth from the beginning, holds firmly onto the righteous actions of people. The reason for this is that God gave the power of reason to both the angels and people and also gave each person angelic protection. God did this both in the Old and New Testaments, but he united angel and man with greater love in the New Testament than he did in the Old Testament. For an angel was like a voice to man in the Old Testament, but in the New Testament an angel was joined to man as a voice is joined to the Word.

41

THE BLESSED SPIRITS ARE UNANIMOUS

54. In the fiery cloud lives a fiery crowd who has one life in one will and in one union. This is because the protection for blessed spirits lives and burns with fiery glory and honor. Their glory is so great it cannot be described; their number is so large that no one knows what it is unless

God knows in his great knowledge. And all the things that they wish and God wishes have been joined as one. Nevertheless, they are in one union in unanimity just as a body, having individual members, is one body. And so they are one life in unanimity.

42

GOD PUNISHES MEN THROUGH HIS ANGELS

55. In their presence is a writing tablet full of feathers, which flew with the precepts of God. The precepts of God lift up the writing tablet. This means that the tablet before them is full of the mysteries of divine judgment. It also means that the tablet is made manifest by God's will whenever he wants it to be. On the tablet God's knowledge has written his secrets which the crowd looks at with unified zeal. This means that God has other mysteries in his secret counsel, which the blessed pay attention to most zealously. For when God sees men worshipping idols and others breaking his laws, he often stirs up the feathers of the winds and sends lightning flashes and thunder upon the earth. He terrifies people with hunger, pestilence and war and thus sends the whole world into terrible commotion.

43

THE PRAISES OF THE ANGELS IN THE JUDGMENTS OF GOD

56. As the angels look at the tablet, God's virtue is granted them so that they sound forth like a very loud trumpet with one sound in every kind of music. This means that when they contemplate God's will, they also receive God's virtues as they bring praises to God unanimously with strength and with the fullness of all the different kinds of joy. They speak nothing but the praises of God for all his judgments which are true and just, as John also heard in his Apocalypse and has written down.

44

JOHN IN THE APOCALYPSE CONCERNING THE SAME THING

57. *Yes, Lord God Almighty, your judgments are true and just!* *(Revelation 16:7)*. His knowledge is so great. O Lord, you Lord have spoken through fear; you God have spoken through love; you the Omnipotent have spoken through the understanding of all things. "Your

judgments are true and just" seeing that your true fear conquers all fear, your true love binds all loves, and your true omnipotence overpowers all powers. When a person interprets the law to suit his own purpose, as God interprets the law for himself, then you God exercise your just judgment in such a way that he knows he cannot do anything against you. Also when a person puts the love of his own flesh before your just love, he then tramples love underfoot in very bitter sorrow because he can never be consoled unless through you, God. When a person breaks your laws in sin by worshipping idols instead of your name, he then fights against righteousness with your enemy who prevailed upon man from the beginning. He places no value upon you. But then you send lightning and thunder upon the earth as well as diseases and war so that man may know that he cannot do anything without you and knows your judgments are true and just.

45

GOD OUGHT TO BE PRAISED BY ANGELS AND MEN

58. The hosts of angels also praise the good works men do. Praising often, they never cease to praise these works for a moment or an hour. Nor do they ever stop giving such praises. God wants to be praised by the angels because this multiplies their glory and it is pleasing to him. Similarly he also wants the works of holy people to be carried to him and to be made manifest to him by the praises of the angels. And he wants the good works men do to be praised openly to him by the angels. Since man is sustained by God's help, God wants to be praised by men, just as he is by the angels, so that even their glory may be increased.

46

THE SECRETS OF GOD ARE UNKNOWABLE TO MAN

59. God created all things rightly. It has been said that the mysteries of God shine in his sight and are beyond the comprehension of man's knowledge. This has been said by the angels, by spirits, by ministers, by those who speak forth, and by those who rejoice with joy. His mysteries are unknowable to man because of their quality and type. Although man's knowledge is like a mountain since his knowledge enables him to rise up right below God, no man nevertheless sees the top of the mountain nor even the higher part of the mountain, which is God's knowledge. Neither can man climb it. Nor can he know the mysteries of God, nor the secrets of those who always stand in the sight of God. Some of these who are always in God's sight have been named by the prophets

and other holy ones who see through the power of the Holy Spirit. Others, however, have not been named because they only spoke moderately when they were touched with divine inspiration, as Paul the Apostle has written.

47
THE HIDDEN WORDS OF PAUL

60. *I heard words which cannot be uttered, words which no man may speak (2 Corinthians 12:4).* This means the following. As man's heart, infused with many great miracles, might be comforted and might bring the virtues abundantly to others, so also man's heart anticipates the words concealed from him through his foreknowledge of what has been hidden from him. What is hidden from him is through whom, or by whom, or how they came about, or what type there were, or by what means. As the Divinity cannot be seen by men, so also no man can bring forth the mysteries of God with his voice or through his praises. This is because these words are concealed completely in the secrets of the spirits who are alien to man while he is in the flesh.

48
CONCERNING THE GOOD OF PERSEVERANCE AND HOLINESS

61. But the wind that has the storm cloud before it expands the cloud along with itself from South to West: this is because justice, testing the stormy works of men with many tribulations, leads them from the South when they burn there with perfect faith to the end of perseverance. This is just like when men, fighting against the devil, persevere in good and live in holiness with God. This cloud is like a street that cannot be understood by the human mind: this means that the spreading out and the diffusion of good works and the embracing and choosing of the virtues is so great that the spreading out of their good works exceeds the capacity of the human heart.

49
CONCERNING THE MANSIONS OF THE BLESSED

62. There is, moreover, a large crowd of blessed in this cloud. They have all the spirits of life and no one can destroy them. This means that in the blessed mansions of the souls that their good and holy works have

built, the souls of the holy live blessed lives. There are so many that no one can count them, except God.

50

THE SOULS OF THE HOLY DESIRE THEIR OWN BODIES

63. Their voices sound like rushing waters because when they praise, they sound like one sound and like the spiritual breath of one will, like the water of salvation. And according to the will of God, they proclaim they had just recently dwelt in their bodies that, although they have already turned to dust, they want to fetch back so they can rejoice more fully.

51

THE SOULS WILL RECEIVE THEIR BODIES AT THE END OF THE WORLD

64. But from those who burn in God's sight with his love they receive the answer that they will not be able to receive their bodies back before the last judgment or before the trembling of the elements when a tremendous fire will purge the elements while God reveals his great power. For God's voice will call all the dead to rise, whether they be damned or saved. The dead will rise with their bodies for all eternity because their bodies will be changed to an unchangeable life when they rise again, although some will receive death and others will receive blessed life.

52

THE JUSTICE IN CHRIST FIGHTS AGAINST THE DEVIL

65. And the wind above which is the light cloud spreads itself out with this cloud from East to North. This means that justice, bearing the white works of virginity in Christ that go back to the time of the origin of truth, fights against the evils of the devil. Justice could not do this completely before Christ. For just as man lives first in the flesh before coming to the spiritual life, so also the old law was first revealed bodily in holiness and was then made alive in Christ and in the Church. Holiness rose up in life and utterly ground down the ancient enemy whom the old law could not fight against.

53
THE DEVIL WILL NOT PREVAIL AGAINST CHRIST AND THE CHURCH

66. But immense darkness that came from the West spread out to the light cloud with great density and horror. This means that all the diabolical iniquities and evils have gathered together to oppose the works of Christ and the Church with great and general unfaithfulness. Yet this darkness was unable to pass beyond the light cloud. Although the evil attack the faithful with many hardships, they are not, however, strong enough to conquer or darken the works of the faithful who shine in Christ.

54
THE INCARNATION SHINES FORTH AS THE SUN ILLUMINATES THE WORLD

67. In the light cloud, the sun and moon appear, which stands for the hidden mystery of the purest incarnation in the whiteness of Virginity. As the sun lights up the world, so also it stands for the Church which imitates Christ in the regeneration of baptism, just as the moon follows the sun. There is a lion in the sun, clearly the hidden mystery concealed in God. This is a shining miracle, one that God wanted a man to do, namely the Son of God taking on flesh from the Virgin. Thus with the strongest strength of the Divinity, a man appeared as a lion, coming forth in a way that no one else has ever done.

55
THE SIGN OF VICTORY IN THE CHURCH

68. And there is a capricorn in the moon, that is, in the Church. The Church has carried the sign of victory over the ancient serpent from all different regions, for the devil has been conquered. The sun shone above heaven and in heaven and on earth and beneath the earth. This means that the mystery of the Son of God having been made incarnate is above all heavenly mysteries. He also is in other mysteries that are known only in heaven. The heavenly mystery of the incarnation brought many miracles to the creatures of the earth and it penetrated the abyss with the splendor of its power. And the sun thus proceeds by rising because this mystery brought forth virtues which had not been seen before. And the

sun returns by setting when it twists the crookedness of sin into nothingness with its knowledge.

56

THE INCARNATE WORD OF GOD, EXISTING AS ONE WITH THE FATHER, TAUGHT BAPTISM

69. When the sun proceeds, the lion goes with it and pillages many things. This is because when God made his hidden mystery manifest, the incarnate Son of God appeared with him in the flesh and in him in wondrous Deity since they are one. And he destroyed many of the deeds of the devil when the devil flew out of the faithful. When the sun returns, the lion returns with it because when God's same hidden mystery brought forth his mystery of judgment, the incarnate Word of God who exists with God, remains with God, and exists united to God, judged the evil works of humans when he fulfilled the old law in the new law. And having accomplished its work, the lion brings many back to joy by teaching the triumph of the restoration of the baptism of truth in the regeneration of the spirit and water.

57

THE FAITHFUL FOLLOW CHRIST TEACHING HEAVENLY THINGS

70. The moon with the capricorn in it gradually follows the sun by proceeding and returning with the capricorn since the Church, having overcome death, follows God's mystery with a glorious victory by proceeding to spiritual things and going back to worldly things. For the faithful followed God's Son in all his ways when he taught them and conversed with them about the things of heaven. They handed over their bodies to many different punishments just as Christ had done.

58

THE FAITHFUL ONE FOLLOWING CHRIST DESTROYS THE WORKS OF DARKNESS

71. And that wind blows and says: "A woman will bear a newborn and the capricorn will fight against the seven stars of the Great Bear constellation." This means that through divine inspiration justice reveals that the Church wins a glorious victory over the devil through the good and holy works of its members. For every faithful person, renounc-

ing himself and following in Christ's footsteps, destroys the works of
darkness and unites himself with God.

59

THE SOULS SEDUCED BY THE SERPENT LAY THE BLAME OF ADAM UPON THEMSELVES

72. In the darkness there is a large crowd of lost souls who are all
stirred up. These souls have turned away from those singing in the
South, as they do not want to be friends with them. Their leader is the
seducer. They follow the devil because Christ's suffering does not mean
more to them than the devil's leadership. This is because there are a lot
of unfaithful souls in the punishments of Hell. When they had been in
their bodies, these souls despised the words of the celestial cities. They
did not want to be friends with those who had performed good and just
works, but they were always panting for evil. Whence the souls who
imitated the ancient serpent who has been destroyed and lost from the
Son of God remain in the unhappiness of death with the devil because
they had not sought life. And they all cried out with lamentation, saying:
"Alas, alas, the devil fled life with disgusting and horrible works and
gave us death!" This means that they suffer many tribulations from hissing animals and bring upon themselves the torment of Adam and the
darkness he brought upon himself when he disobeyed God's commands
and rushed into death. These souls are punished since they disregarded
and mocked the light of faith that they saw and the works of justice they
heard about. They chose the devil as one greater than God.

60

NO HOPE IN HELL

73. Then you see a cloud coming from the North that extends itself to
the darkness. It has become parched of all joy and happiness since it has
neither touched the sun nor shown itself to it. This is the other type of
unhappiness and infernal torments that, proceeding from the devil, joins
the darkness with its punishing torments. In this kind of cruelty there is
no hope for joy or salvation since the true sun does not cheer it with its
joy or infuse it with the clarity of its brightness. The earthly sun does
not stretch out to it with its brightness either.

61
THE WICKED SPIRITS FLEE GOD

74. This cloud is full of wicked spirits who wander here and there. They plan out snares for people, but blush when they think about the person mentioned earlier. This means that the diabolical spirits are filled with the unhappiness of countless evils as they run around. And they bring forth a lot of wickedness. Being ashamed of God, they flee since they are not blessed in any way and do not want to be. They are in the damnation of everlasting destruction.

62
THE SNARES OF THE DEVIL AMONG THE CHOSEN

75. But you hear the ancient serpent say to himself that he will prepare the powers of his strength as a fortification and will fight his enemies with all his strength. This means that the devil brings forth the snares of his faults through the exultation of his pride when he deceives God's chosen by harassing them. He does not allow them to have any peace and quiet. And he spits out of his mouth a froth of many impurities and blemishes upon the people. He inflames and mocks them because by vomiting the filth of his many evils from the jaws of his perversity he seduces people and brings heresies to them, causing some of them to worship idols and others of them to travel the most crooked of ways. And he says that he will make those who call themselves the sun through works of light be repulsive and benighted and horrible in darkness since he strives to make God's chosen ones who shine in holy works be noxious and sordid in obscure actions. He makes the fame of the chosen stink in the presence of the living.

63
THE DEVIL LEADS TO IDOLATRY

76. And he spews forth a most disgusting mist from his mouth, which covers the earth like the blackest of smoke, since he sends out strong temptations to unfaithfulness throughout the whole world with the darkness of his perversity. Then a very loud and disturbing thunder rumbles from the mist, saying: "No person should adore another God unless he sees and knows him. Why should anyone pay attention to someone he does not know?" This means that through unfaithfulness evil persuasions trample upon men when they worship no God except the idols

which they see and know. Such evil persuasions turn man's reason away from the true God who is invisible to human frailty in the brightness of his Divinity.

64

THEY WHO WISH TO BE BLESSED ADORE GOD

77. Those who wish for the highest blessedness adore the living God who gives life to all creatures and who dwells in the heavens. And they do not adore anyone else than he who, remaining in heavenly glory, distributed all things rightly, as the psalmist David speaks.

65

THE PSALMIST CONCERNING THE SAME THING

78. *Our God is in heaven; whatever he wills, he does. Their idols are silver and gold, the handiwork of men (Psalm 115:3-4).* This means the following. *God* is that life which is hidden with no beginning and which is also ended with no failure. And he *is our God,* who, existing as life, gives out unfailing life to his own. He also *is in heaven,* of course, in the brightness that no mortal man can understand. He is the life that is the source of all life. For God lives and he gives life to his own and he has a mansion for them to live in. Who can do this other than God? For whatever God planned, he accomplished. But men begin many things in their mind which they never accomplish. God also placed all creation perfectly in the mind of man. These creatures are not raised up in another life, but only in the life that God has given them. The unfaithful with their idols of unfaithfulness promise a life that God did not give them. For the idols which man makes do not live, but they are only made from and formed out of silver and gold. Man contaminated his own mind, the silver, and his knowledge, the gold, with the work of his own hands. Because the devil denied God from the beginning, he sends his inspiration into copper. The devil says he is God in these idols, and so he sounds forth from these without the sight of seeing, the wisdom of hearing, the knowledge of smelling, the life-giving quality of the air and without the breath of breathing life. But the devil cannot do anything in these idols so he confuses himself as he begs to be mocked in these idols which have no potential in them, just as man also does not. The devil rejoices only in the seduction of man. For if the devil had power in men's deeds as he wished, he would be able to change their actions into something else, just as God does. God changed the slime of the earth into some-

thing else when he formed man from the slime. Similarly, when man reckons his works before God as if he does not know that God exists, he is then made like the idols because he trusts them completely. Without the grace of God in his work, man is judged as dead. Those who place their hope in idols will dwell with the devil in the outermost darkness.

66
EVERY VICE IS IN UNFAITHFULNESS

79. You see in this mist, however, the various images of various sins. This means that every sin and its results are found in unfaithfulness, for he who does not have faith is without any good. Consider seven of these sins in this way; you will see their fullness with their various changes. They will not be shown to you in various forms, but their manifestations will be shown to you since the devil, having his many javelins of perversity, strives to send many souls into the lake of destruction.

67
CONCERNING WORLDLY LOVE

80. The first image stands for worldly love because the ancient seducer, pouring the love of worldly things into men for the first time, also led them to other sins. This first image is like a black man from Ethiopia. This means that entwining himself fully with fleshly desires, man desires to have no brightness nor any clarity. He is naked. He has his arms around the base of a huge tree with many limbs and branches. This means he does not wear any garment of blessedness, but he understands the strength of vain glory in his works and in his footsteps which have certain sins, just like the branches which stick out from their protection. And this tree is filled with many different kinds of flowers because in vain glory and in the various sins that spring from it, all the vanities of vanities reach out into the world. He picks a lot of these flowers and holds them in his hands because when man reflects on the vanities in worldly love, he desires things, and when he comes upon them with great delight, the flowers, he brings them to himself according to his own will. This sin spoke about this earlier. The root of the tree dries up and the tree falls into the darkness mentioned earlier. When the tree falls, this image also falls into the darkness with it. This means that vainglory, rebelling completely, falls into the darkness of unfaithfulness where the devil dwells. All who choose the world and despise eternal life fall with vainglory at the same time, and they are not able to keep vainglory from falling with them. But although vainglory may fall, it

nevertheless does not believe that it has fallen because it has attached it-self so strongly to worldly things that it does not know anything about heavenly things. Heavenly love responds to vainglory, just as you heard earlier.

68
CONCERNING IMPUDENCE

81. The second image truly signifies impudence, which leads men away from honesty. It accompanies worldly love in this place because when men choose the world and cling to it, they most often live accord-ing to their own will. This image looks like a hunting dog because a man who is impudent follows every wish and pleasure as he catches and holds onto many things, as a dog catches many things. Standing on its hind feet, it put its paws on a staff. This means that it has placed its hind feet on the earth, knowing nothing about heavenly things. It has placed its front paws, however, as if it were meditating about heavenly things while it was on a good journey. It is moving toward the legal precepts that have spiritual support from below when it speaks emptily with a soul wavering only occasionally toward spiritual things. But it does not obey the precepts because it does not have any stability in its mind since it thinks only about empty things. It tells itself about beautiful things some of the time and about tumultuous things at other times, according to whatever excites it. The dog wags its tail. This means that it searches around for men to encourage it in its impudence, as it was revealed in the words this sin spoke earlier. Wherefore also, this sin is seized by the voice of true discipline as shown in the words spoken by discipline earli-er.

69
CONCERNING JESTING

82. The third image signifies jesting. Dragging after impudence, it follows men from heavenly things to various and dissimilar speculative things since it is like the pipes and music of impudence. When the wea-riness and boredom of impudence have touched the souls of this type of person, this person plays some more jokes, just like drawing in another breath. This third image is like a man, except that it has a hooked nose. This means that this sin, thinking about the knowledge of good and evil and following the desires of the eyes and of the flesh, draws people to itself. And with silly foolishness and knowledge, like the hooked nose, this sin says that God does not exist. It has hands like bear's feet, and

feet like a griffin's. This means that it causes people to have filthy ways and to perform unclean works. It follows in the footsteps of no one when it commits robbery since it can steal from anyone through the deceit of its trickery. For men are more soiled by this sin than they had ever been cleansed by any good deed. It has black hair and wears a pale garment. This means that it blackens all the origins of its works with the blackness of vanity. It also surrounds itself with mild joy since it readily adapts to each person's ways so that, drawing the person to itself in this way, it plays with the person, as it spoke about earlier. But the voice of shyness, fighting against it, cries out in opposition and tries to persuade men to be honest.

70
CONCERNING HARD-HEARTEDNESS

83. The fourth image, which follows after jesting, shows, however, hard-heartedness. This is because when a man has become exhausted from jesting, he becomes bored and gets hard-hearted since he has not been touched by heavenly dew. This is also true because he has not plowed his mind with the precepts of the law nor with the plow of the Scriptures. Therefore, nothing restrains him. This image looks like dense smoke rising up as high as a tall person. This means that there is no refinement, but only firm, evil, wickedness in hard-heartedness. It is the same size as a person since there is no evil below or above it. A person does not understand this about his own work because both small and large evils attract a wicked person. This image does not have any human members, except very large black eyes because this sin hardens people so much that they do not wish to know the image of God nor recognize it in other people because without kindness they lack any kind of mercy and goodness. Such people are very abusive and forget about God. They look for someone to praise, but then praise them with the poison of envy, which is like the poison of a snake. It does not move up or down since hard-heartedness does not strive to obtain higher things that might melt its evil ways for the sake of God. Nor does it bend down lower which might make its hardness soft for the sake of man. Nor does it turn toward other creatures to turn away its worthlessness for the sake of these other creatures. It remains motionless in the darkness mentioned earlier since it perseveres with its abusiveness and does not want to do anything else than afflict people. For it is like a piece of lead which has been thrown into rushing water: it lies on the bottom and does not move any place else. It flees from the right hand of the Lord who knows how to make all creation useful to people and who makes people into crea-

tures of peace. God placed man on earth as if he were an elegant stone that reflects any other creature that looks into it. This means that man is above all the other creatures. Therefore, hard-heartedness should not be allowed to harden itself against God or man. For this is the worst evil of all evils. It spares no one and shows no mercy. It despises men and draws back from God. It does not rejoice with men nor does it encourage humans to do good deeds. It is very hard and despises all things as was seen earlier when it spoke. True mercy answers hard-heartedness and warns it to do good.

71

CONCERNING SLOTHFULNESS

84. The fifth image reveals slothfulness. It follows hard-heartedness. It is like filthy envy; it is like little worms coming out of the earth. For when a hardened person does not seek anything good, this person turns to slothfulness. As a result, he does not desire honor or holiness but gets bored and forgets about honesty. Nor does he want to struggle against these sins. Instead, he attracts them to himself through his slothfulness. This image has a human head, except that its left ear is a hare's ear. And this ear is so large that it covers its whole head. This means that foolish men are foolish enough to think that they are excellent. They love their leisure and do not provide themselves with anything good, but hearing evil things, they trudge on slothfully, muttering degrading comments. They spread these comments around as they cover the true intentions of their heart with crookedness. The rest of its body is like that of a worm without any bones. This worm twists in its hole just as an infant squirms in its clothes. This means that through this sin of weariness and slothfulness men change the trust that they should have in God's help for helping people into the filth of their own will, just like an earth worm. Entering into the secrets of their knowledge and covering themselves with foolishness, they trust more in the softness of their flesh than in the divine strength. They do this to prevent having to lift themselves up to the honesty of the virtues. Instead, they can remain slothful in the sluggishness of neglect and the foolishness of worthlessness. Divine victory responds to this sin and urges people to fight against the devil.

72

CONCERNING ANGER

85. The sixth image truly proclaims anger, which is a neighbor to slothfulness since slothfulness deserves reproach. Also reproach kindles

the fire of anger so that anger can inflame and consume the reproaches. This image has a man's face since anger rises up in man and causes him to be evil. Except that its mouth is like a scorpion's: this means that it is like a crushing murderer who causes death with poison. Its eyes are so distorted that their whites are larger than the pupils. This means that the disease of an angry intention is greater than the righteousness of tranquillity. When a person is angry, he does not think about himself or others, but turning away from justice as if he were blind, he sends out storms of rage. Its arms are those of a human because anger is not associated with the fear of God but rather is associated with man's power to know evil since the devil influenced what he wanted to do. Man, however, brought about his wantonness by thinking and considering and doing so that his wantonness is openly visible. Irrational animals are sometimes too noisy when they are trying to attack something else because they do not have the ability to think. Then again they sometimes make a lot of noise when they are afraid that they are going to be attacked by something else. At other times they attack and kill something else because they are hungry. Man, however, uses the wickedness of his anger to attack his friends as well as his enemies. He brings evil to another person in proportion to the amount of good that person does. But its hands are gnarled and have long fingernails. This means that man leans forward and stretches out greedily when he attacks the works of others with great frenzy. Its chest, front and back, is like a crab's because an angry man does not know about peace, the law, and the righteousness of established institutions—all the things that might bring stability to him. In addition, his rage and his violent impulse of provocation cause him to be satisfied with neither spiritual food nor with the commandments of God. He hurls all just and righteous things away from himself as well as the moderation and gentleness of agreeable motives. Such a person rushes backward through the winding ways of evil and walks backward to the devil, just like a crab. Its shins are like those of locusts and its feet are like a viper's. This means that man shows vain glory in his shins and envy in his walk since he leaps over justice with the vain glory of pride and tears many things to pieces with his envy. This image is tangled up inside a turning wheel because man does not walk along the right path since he rests in his own particular will and follows his own heart. So that it holds onto the top of the rim with its hands and the bottom rim with its feet: because man does his work boldly with the exaltation of the freedom of his will whereby he places his footsteps on what he has worn out with his own freedom since he does not reach out to justice but rather to wickedness. It has no hair on its head since anger causes man to be without the honor of good fame and a healthy mind. His anger does not allow him to think about what is good and just. Whence also this image is naked because such a man does not wear any garment of correction and also because he sometimes shows the abusiveness of his anger. This image billows fiery words from its mouth since man speaks burning and fiery words with the vengeance of wickedness when he is angry and when he forgets about God, just as this sin showed in the words it spoke earlier. Divine patience refutes him, however, because of his stubborn fury. Jacob spoke in a similar fashion to his two sons who had slaughtered men in their fury.

73
THE WORDS OF JACOB

86. *Simeon and Levi, brothers indeed, weapons of violence are their knives. Let not my soul enter their council, or my spirit be joined with their company; for in their fury they slew men, in their willfulness they maimed oxen. Cursed be their fury so fierce, and their rage so cruel! I will scatter them in Jacob, disperse them throughout Israel (Genesis 49:5-7).* The angry and hateful who are wicked are *the weapons of violence.* They are always fighting against God and destroying those who are just with their evil words when they speak their evil words against the just. But the just have not thought carefully enough for they have broken the Lord's law and have not built upon the rock where the blessed stand in order to proclaim the wonders of God. Indeed, there are many different avenues and buildings for the desires and works of the blessed to use according to God's law. In addition, the honor of the just does not appear without being tarnished in the zeal of those who think they can do whatever they want and who seek to entrap others with their deceitful snares. The honor of the just cannot be in the midst of such people without being crushed. The glory of the just, however, can be in the angels and with the angels of God and with those who contemplate the face of the Divinity in a mirror. The just cannot go with those who destroy the virtues of the blessed with bloody deceit or with those who use their treachery to penetrate the fortifications that the blessed doctors built to protect the chosen. In their madness they have spoken evilly with the devil when they are opposed to God and wage a stubborn battle against him. Their indignation is inflexibly evil since they will not forsake their evil; they want to continue in their state of destructive damnation by doing evil. Wherefore, the angry and hateful will be divided up by the people who crush them because just as a snake tries to hide in a cave, they are also so exhausted by being under attack that they can hardly draw a deep breath. They will be scattered among those who pro-

claim God, not in order that they may share in their happiness, but in order that the chaff which is blown away from them may be separated out. Since they do not follow God, he hands them over into a state of oblivion where they will have neither worldly prosperity nor spiritual happiness. Just as the passions of their desires have blown them around like the wind, so also they can have no rest. Nor can they be with those who serve God.

74
CONCERNING FOOLISH JOY

87. The seventh image truly signifies foolish joy. It follows anger because it is, as it were, the revenge and cooling off stage of anger. For when a man's anger has passed and he is happy, he disgraces his enemies whereby they, seeing that he is happy, suffer even more gravely from the insult he has given them. This image is like a man from its head down to its loins. This means that people should apply their knowledge of good, which they should also change into heavenly inspiration, to their desires of the flesh which are full of vanity. In this way, they will perform holy and useful deeds and will show restraint. But they sometimes pervert their good works with foolishness since acting like animals, they often do beastly things that are not in agreement with what they are. From its loins down it is like a she-goat since men of this type, being forgetful, often suppress their powers of reason and act like animals when they change rational acts into unstable ones. Neither do they try to be discreet nor to discipline their modesty by being reasonable. But its feet are hidden in the darkness mentioned earlier so that you cannot see them. This means that since they are entangled in changing vanity, they do not test all of their actions to see if they are just, for when they cover their perverse actions with darkness, they are not open to the honesty of the faithful and the things they have hidden completely are not holy in any way. It wears no clothes and is naked because when man is not surrounded with spiritual joy, he is naked in God's presence since he is unstable and does not seek heavenly inspiration. When man covets earthly and fallen things, he does not care for eternal things, as this image showed in the words it spoke earlier. But the sighing of God, as mentioned above, responded to foolish joy and warned people to turn away from the temporal thing of the world and to turn toward the eternal things of heaven.

75

CONCERNING THE ZEAL OF GOD

88. The fact that, however, you see that the man I mentioned earlier holds a sword in his hand. It has three cutting edges and its hilt has been placed in a sheath. This is the fact that God openly shows his zeal marching in from three directions. And God rooted faith in his own strength since he held the sins of men in check with the open blows of divine punishment before the law and under the law. He does not stop doing this even now after the law of the renewal of baptism. Bringing faith with the health-giving virtues, he washes away men's sins with his zeal. He then starts swinging his swords around as if he is going to cut something, because the zeal of the Lord examines both the chosen and the damned with his justice, for the zeal of the Lord says that he fights against the devil and all his followers. No one will be able to overcome the zeal of the Lord because it does not have any substance like the union of a man and woman produces, but existing in God, it judges all things justly in God. For the zeal of the Lord judges all the actions of man and examines them most carefully. Indeed, it suffocated Sodom and Gomorrah with wind blowing the sulphur of fire. These cities sinned in the depravity that came from the throat of the devil when he was a snake and mocked the nature of man. But on account of the devil's own disobedience, it also changed the puffed up pride of a woman into something else, namely by this deed all the sins of the fall became bitter salt. It also struck down the Israelite people when they abandoned God and adored Baal. Being scattered, they became exiles, a people in the service of the gentiles, since they disowned their rightful inheritance. For God discerns whatever ought to be discerned and divides whatever ought to be divided. He also divided pride into two parts and allowed it to rise up again. When pride has not sought anything from God and has selfishly gathered all the things it wants, the zeal of the Lord casts it down from the beginning to the end. But it also burns up luxury with the fire of Gehenna and imprisons impiety with a punishment appropriate to it. In addition, it throws vain glory down harshly, which is the heart of pride, and the fire of sin, which is the heart of luxury, and unfaithfulness, which is the heart of impiety, since they have been withdrawn from God for a long time. The ones who do not want to know God, he does not reward since they do not seek him. But some people caress certain faults of sight, which they nevertheless do not let settle into their lives. They expand some faults, but they do not do this lightly and do not enlarge them into more serious sins. Some people, however, think

about certain faults in their minds and speak about them, but they do not make them part of their actions. The zeal of the Lord does not destroy such people completely, but it eliminates these desires from them with various punishments. He who, however, does not desire life, let him seize the words of the zeal of the Lord, and let him store these words in the innermost cubicle of his heart.

89. I then saw a crowd of wicked spirits among the ones whom the zeal of the Lord had cast out of heaven with righteous judgment and whom Lucifer had brought to his place of punishment. This crowd was spread out among the people of the earth and it heaped its wickedness upon them. The crowd of these spirits was and is so large that it cannot be counted; at least the number is not known by anyone except God. These spirits are the enemies of men so that each one of them, in proportion to its wickedness, ambushes and snares men. Some of them cry aloud that Lucifer should not be subjected to anyone as Lord. They show men how to love the world and urge them to love it eagerly.

76
THE PUNISHMENTS OF THOSE WHO HAVE LOVED THE WORLD

90. And behold, I saw two fires, one of which had a pale flame and the other a red flame. The one with the pale flame did not have any worms; the one with the red flame was full of worms, some of which were like small snakes while others had a pointed face and pointed tails, but all were without any feet. The souls of those who had loved the world while they had been in their bodies were being punished by these two flames and were being dashed about by a flame on each side. They were especially distorted by the heat of the red flames. The souls of those who had been incessant in their love of the world were being dashed about by the pale flame. And the souls of those who had clung to their love of the world completely were being punished by the red flame. And the souls of those who had had two false pretenses in their faithless customs, so that they had praised what displeased them and had censured what had pleased them as if they wanted to make the things they freely were doing annoying, were being tormented by the worms that had the form of snakes. The souls of those who had taken delight in their choice of worldly love were being tormented by the worms that had the pointed face while the souls of those who had failed somewhat in their love of the world were suffering in the pale fire; the souls who

had sinned more seriously were enduring the red fire with its worms. I saw and knew these things through the living Spirit.

77

CONCERNING THE PUNISHMENTS OF CLEANNESS

91. I heard a voice from the living light saying to me: *These things which you see are true, and as you see these things, so they are, and there are more things. For the torments of these punishments cleanse these souls who, living in this changing world, have earned in a non-changing way the cleansing of their sins through punishment. But these torments have not cleansed them from the death which comes to the body; these torments do not prevent them from being weighed in the world by the divine scourges of the merciful God. But these torments will cleanse them unless they are snatched away from these punishments by the labors of men or by the virtues of the holy ones which God works in those men when they call upon the piety of divine grace.*

78

WHAT KINDS OF SOULS MAY BE CLEANSED?

92. The souls of those who have been counted and who have remembered blessedness cleanse the stains of their sins and cross over to coolness while those who have forgotten will remain in the forgetfulness of other punishments.

79

HOW MEN AVENGE WORLDLY LOVE IN THEMSELVES

93. Let men, however, who sweat in worldly love, if they want to overcome the wicked spirits who placed worldly love before them and if they are eager to flee from the punishments of the world that you see, punish themselves with sackcloth and scourges. And let them fast on plain bread and plain water according to the extent that they have sinned by choice, will, time and conversation, and according to the extent that their true teacher in his humanity made public repentance prescribed by priests. This is so because whoever wants to repent justly ought to be presented to his judge who will punish him in proportion to his sin. The judge, however, is the very priest who serves in the office of my son.

For when the mind of men feels guilty, let it tell its sins to the priest, just as it was shown in the law when the lepers showed themselves to my servant Moses. For this reason, sins should be confessed to the priest since the mild fear of confession was revealed in the sweat of my son and repentance was revealed in the drops of his blood.

80
ATONEMENT COMING FROM THE PRIEST

94. The atonement that comes from the priest is recommended because atonement cannot be brought to souls by torments unless that atonement is brought about by some precept of a judge.

81
CONCERNING WORLDLY LOVE

95. Worldly love, however, does not fear God or choose him, but it attracts to itself all the things that it finds pleasing. It boldly makes excuses before God for each and every thing that it seeks in creatures, saying that these have been created for its use. In addition, it does not fear God whom it ought to fear, but it follows its own particular will rather than God's. It does not choose God because it does not want to give up its desires of the flesh. It does not restrain itself out of love of God, but it embraces the world completely. Solomon, steeped with the spirit of wisdom, spoke, however, against this love, saying:

82
THE WORDS OF SOLOMON

96. *Fullness of wisdom is fear of the Lord; she inebriates men with her fruits (Sirach 1:16).* This means that the first aspect of wisdom is fear of the Lord, just like the dawn comes before the sun. For when man realizes that he has been created by God, he begins to fear God. What is truly feared is honored, and what is honored is loved; and if it is loved justly, it is also honored justly. Therefore, let man who realizes he is from God be faithful in his works, even as faith is protection for the holy, and let him have faith in God seeing that it saves him. Let him desire to be saved eagerly. And let him do this in faith, in which wisdom is fulfilled. For man has been tormented with sins. Let him, therefore, practice wisdom which will enable him to cast off his sins and to remove his torments of sight, hearing, taste, smell and touch, just as a

blacksmith files his molds in order to make them perfect. O how great is wisdom! Through it man begins to throw off the powers of the flesh so that he can do what is necessary to cast off sins! Whenceforth the fear of the Lord is formed in the faith of the holy who accomplish their works with wisdom. Similarly, wisdom did all of its works well at the beginning of creation. But the fear of the Lord is also in chosen women who are holy since God created women in such a way that they fear him and his strength. It is fitting that a woman should always be timid. She is, as it were, the house of wisdom since the things of this earth and of heaven are perfected in her. For on one hand man proceeds through her; on the other hand, however, good works appear in her with chaste modesty. If she did not have fear, she would not be able to cultivate chaste modesty because likewise without fear a snake bites everything it can. A timid woman, however, gathers the merits of good works and holy virtues to her bosom and does not stop until she has finished many good things. Thus the fear of the Lord is believed to be in chosen women who were chosen for their holiness and justice and because they performed virtuous works. The fear of the Lord is also thought to be with the just who fulfill all of God's laws and commandments. And it is found in the great miracles of the faithful who die on behalf of God. They light up the whole world, like the sun, with their good and holy works. They cannot do these things, however, without the fear of the Lord, but they are fulfilled faithfully through him. Worldly love does not have any fear of the Lord. These things, however, have been spoken concerning the atonement for the cleansing and saving of souls, and they are faithful things. A faithful person pays attention to these things and remembers them well.

83

THE PUNISHMENTS OF IMPUDENCE

97. I then saw some other spirits in the crowd that I mentioned earlier. They were crying aloud with the great clamor of a dancing soul, saying that Lucifer deserved the honor which God had taken from him. These particular spirits, however, bring impudence to men's minds and they encourage men to seize impudence. I also saw a large, red fire. This fire was surrounded with such dense air that its flames could not erupt into that air. This fire contained a lot of fiery worms that made a lot of noise with their hissing and movements. The souls of those who had sinned through impudence while they had been alive were being twisted in such a way in this bitter fire that they could find no air-hole in the density enclosing this fire. The sides and feet of these souls were be-

ing attacked by the worms. Because they had sweat with the zeal of impudence while they had been alive, they were burning in this red fire. And because they had imitated certain customs with the impudence of their wills, they suffocate in this fire. And because they had impudently twisted the sides and feet of their bodies here and there so many times, their sides and feet are attacked by these worms.

84
THE SINS OF IMPUDENCE ARE DESTROYED THROUGH SUFFERING

98. I saw and knew these things. And I heard a voice from the living light, which I mentioned earlier, say to me: *These things are true. Those who have sinned through impudence while they were alive are purified by such punishments. But if those entangled by this fault are anxious to avoid the evil spirits who lead them to this sin and if they want to avoid these torments, let them abstain from food and drink and let them scourge themselves. They should do this in proportion to their sins and equal to the judgment of the judge who presides over them.*

85
IMPUDENCE IS THE VANITY OF VANITIES

99. Impudence is not very stable, for it changes its mind to suit whatever it wants to do. Nor does it honor God with joy. Rather it takes delight in whatever it chooses to do. Therefore, it is the vanity of vanities. It will not hold anything back, because when one vanity has passed by, another follows quickly. Those who are impudent will be so in eternity as well. For when a person acts out the desires of his flesh freely, he is practicing vanity. This is because when he is a boy, he loves games; afterwards in his youth he embraces lasciviousness; then later he understands more perfectly and thinks about what is good and evil. At this point in his life he will be bored with the things of his boyhood and youth, as if he had never enjoyed those things. When he gets old, he becomes very dry; he will then find it hard to breathe and will beat his breast as he remembers his younger life, the younger life he can no longer have. All such things with man and in man are vanity. For the forest grows and dries up, the flowers flourish and fall down, the grass grows and is cut down. What more is there, therefore? What man sees now, he will not always see; while he laughs now, he will weep later. As a result of all of this, things are empty because they have fallen, failed

and died. They die in order that they may not live in this world. They also fall from a noble state into an ignoble one, from riches into poverty.

86
THE STRENGTH OF HOLINESS IS UNFAILING

100. Kings and leaders who were previously honored are no longer noticed because they were not heavenly kings and leaders. Those who were of lesser order and without riches rise up from that order and poverty as if they were ascending Olympus, but then they fall back down. The strength of holiness, however, which is the source of all good things and which brings forth all good things, will not fall down, but it will have eternal life. These things, however, have been spoken concerning the atonement for the cleansing and saving of souls, and they are faithful things. A faithful person pays attention to these things and remembers them well.

101. I saw other spirits in the crowd that I mentioned earlier. They proclaimed that Lucifer had been worthy of salvation and of the honor of the virtues. And they pretended that they knew the indescribable song of the blessed spirits who are before the throne of God. And they convince people that they can persist in such vanity since they have spoken and done these things with a jester.

87
CONCERNING THE PUNISHMENTS OF JESTERS

102. I also saw a black cloud that had fire in it sending forth a lot of smoke into the air. In this fire and smoke and cloud, those guilty of jesting vanity while they were alive were being punished. They endured the fire because of their choice of this sin. They endured the smoke, however, because of the zeal with which they committed this sin. And they endured the cloud because of the variety of ways they had committed this sin. And I saw and knew these things through the living spirit.

88
THE REPENTANCE OF JESTERS

103. I again heard the voice from the living light, which I mentioned earlier, say to me: *These things that you see are true, and as you see them, so they are. If those who continue committing this sin while they are alive want to cast off the influence of the devil and to avoid the*

punishments for this sin, let them fast in proportion to the number of sins they committed and for the same amount of time they sinned. By fasting they can avoid a more costly judgment from the righteous judgment of their judges.

89
CONCERNING THE SQUALID WAYS OF JESTERS

104. Through his squalid ways a jester makes men play, just as they want and choose to do. The evil spirits want to mock the heavenly harmony, but they will not prevail. Therefore, through a jester they mock and assault various people; they mock them with lies when they cannot make them play games with the truth. Harmonious praise, which is proper to God, cannot, however, end since it is unfailing in the fullness of truth. A jester questions his own soul to see where he can soar and what he can do. When he looks at himself in the mirror of knowledge, he becomes vain and lies. The sound he makes while on earth pleases him no matter where he goes.

90
WHATEVER IS SOUGHT WITHOUT GOD WILL PERISH

105. The sons of men are indeed vain when they search so many times to do greater things according to their own will. They forsake the truth that God reveals to them, and they build up a false prophet in false divines, just like they build mountains. They seek out a gossip who prophesies through signs. And when they have done this, they recognize lies as the truth, deceiving themselves and others as well. For whatever is sought without God and is found without God will be destroyed. Further, when they look around and find jokes and dancing in their veins and blood, they will be mocked as if they were worth nothing. They will diminish when they are mocked, as the glow of the ashes of a fire does. These things, however, have been spoken concerning the atonement for the cleansing and saving of souls, and they are faithful things. A faithful person pays attention to these things and remembers them well.

106. After this, I saw some more of the evil spirits in the crowd that I mentioned earlier. They cried aloud: "It isn't allowed, is it, that anyone may be like God?" These evil spirits show hard-heartedness and they convince men to have a mistress and not to be merciful, things they cannot have and do in heaven.

91

THE PUNISHMENTS OF HARD-HEARTEDNESS

107. Behold I saw a dry well that was wide and deep. Its bottom was seething pitch. The pitch has a wide hole in it through which fiery smoke and fiery worms rose up into the well from below. Sharp and fiery spikes were tossed around in the well, as if by the wind. The souls of those who had been hard-hearted and were without mercy while they had been alive sat on the bottom of the well. They were afraid that they would fall through the hole in the bottom of the well into the fire below. They suffered greatly from the smoke and worms and spikes. They sat on the bottom of the well in the seething pitch and were afraid that they would fall into the fire below because they had been unholy to others. They suffered from the smoke because they had fled from God in their wickedness. There were attacked by the worms because they had brought inhuman sorrows to others, and they were attacked by the fiery spikes because had been hard-hearted and showed no mercy. I saw and I knew these things.

92

THE REPENTANCE OF THE HARD-HEARTED

108. I again heard the voice from the living light say to me: *These things that you see are true. If those who were so hard-hearted while they had been alive that they showed no mercy to other unworthy people want to shatter their hard-heartedness and to avoid the punishments that you have seen, let them fast and scourge themselves. Let them do this in proportion to their sins and in proportion to the judgment brought against them.*

93

HARD-HEARTEDNESS, THE WORST OF FAULTS

109. Hard-heartedness is the worst sin since it shows no mercy. Neither does it think that charity is necessary nor does it do any good works. Hard-heartedness was strong in some tyrants who, although they saw the wondrousness of God, nevertheless would not set their own peculiar wills aside; they put their own mind and heart before the will of God and fought against him. But just as God, seeing the evil of the first angel and the foolishness of the first man, destroyed their peculiar wills, and just as God terrified Pharaoh when he struck down the first born of

Egypt, so even now God confuses hard-heartedness so strong that it refuses to be softened by the precepts of the law or by the judgment of rational people. Wherefore, God removes anyone who might help the hard-hearted and plunges them into confusion, just like Pharaoh. These things, however, have been spoken concerning the atonement for the cleansing and saving of souls, and they are faithful things. A faithful person pays attention to these things and remembers them well.

110. Behold I saw more of the spirits in the crowd. They cried aloud that Lucifer was their Lord. They led people to sloth and encouraged them not to fear God or to care about people.

94

THE PUNISHMENTS OF SLOTHFULNESS

111. I then saw a black cloud that was filled with strong winds, the uproar of thunder and rain storms. The evil spirits that I mentioned before threw fire around like rain drops. The souls who were so slothful while they were alive that they did not serve God vigorously were buffeted by these storms and were burned by the fire that the evil spirits threw around. They were buffeted by these storms because they had not been frightened with fear of the Lord while they had been alive, and they felt the pain of the fire because they had been slothful in heeding the warning of justice. I saw and knew these things.

95

THE REPENTANCE OF SLOTHFULNESS

112. Again I heard the voice from the living light speaking to me: *These things that you see are true; and as you see them, so they are. If those, however, who chose slothfulness and do not serve God vigorously or faithfully do not want to be mocked by these evil spirits and if they want to be absolved from these passions, let them chastise themselves by wearing a hair shirt in proportion to their sloth. Let them scourge themselves, fast, and feed the poor. And let them follow the orders of their leader.*

96

SLOTHFULNESS DOES NOT SHINE WITH THE FEAR OF GOD

113. Slothfulness does not shine with the fear of God, nor does it burn with the fire of the uneasiness of honor, for it has covered over its knowledge with faults while it is alive. Knowledge is the breath of life in the soul that has been rewarded with grace. But sloth does not want to seek grace by doing good works. It has covered over its knowledge while it is alive when with great unhappiness it neglects the faith that it ought to have as its support and in which there is the hope of eternal life. This is the result of its not filling the thundering trumpet with good works and its not breathing forth uplifting devotion to God. These things, however, have been spoken concerning the atonement for the cleansing and saving of souls, and they are faithful things. A faithful person pays attention to these things and remembers them well.

114. I then saw some more of the spirits in the crowd that I mentioned earlier. They shouted against the army of God: "What power do you have over us? None." And with a lot of anger they looked at young women, saying: "These women are suitable for the propagation of the world, just as the earth is suitable for sprouting seeds. Let's hurry up and seduce them before they gather warriors against us." These evil spirits cause anger and fury and other evil things of this kind in people; they encourage them to murder.

97

THE PUNISHMENTS OF ANGRY ONES

115. I saw turbulent air that was seething like fire. Under it there was a wide, black lake full of filthy rottenness containing snakes with only one eye on their face and with their tails thrashing around in this rottenness. The souls who had had anger and who had not forsaken it while they had been alive were tormented by this filthy rottenness and by these snakes and were burned by the fire in the air. Because they had shown never ending anger with steadfast hatred, they were tormented by this dirt and the snakes of this lake, by the dirt on account of their anger and by the snakes on account of their hatred. They suffered from the fire in the air because they had filled up their anger with fury.

98
CONCERNING THE SAME THING

116. The souls who sometimes had anger without hatred and who did not have habitual anger while they had been in their bodies were, however, moving around this place, separated from their bodies. They saw the fierce punishments in this place and were frightened by them. But since they had not had long standing anger, they were not touched by these punishments. Since they saw them, however, they repented of their anger and escaped from these punishments quickly.

99
THE PUNISHMENTS OF MURDERERS OUT OF ANGER

117. I also saw a great fire that had various fierce punishments of both burning and cold. The souls of those who had murdered in this world with the fury of anger were punished here. They suffered from the fire because of their murdering out of anger. They suffered from the cold because of their blindness when they did not think about what they were doing. They suffered from the snakes because of their rashness in not fearing the image of God.

100
THE PUNISHMENTS OF MURDERERS OUT OF GREED

118. I also saw another fire that had two large and horrible snakes in it. These snakes blew their blasts on both the fire and the souls being tormented here. The souls who had committed murder out of greed while they had been alive were burning in this fire and were tormented by these snakes. To be sure, they endured the fire because of their murdering and the snakes because of their greed.

101
THE PUNISHMENTS OF THOSE WHO STRUCK DOWN LEST THEY MIGHT BE STRUCK DOWN

119. I then saw a wide and deep pit that was full of boiling pitch and sulphur and that had frogs and scorpions lying around in it. The frogs

and scorpions struck terror into the souls of those being tormented in this pit, but they did not injure these souls. The souls of those who had murdered someone attacking them were in this pit. They suffered in this pit because of the type of murder they had committed. They were stained by the pitch because they lacked self-restraint when they defended themselves. They were tormented by the sulphur because of the indignity they inflicted upon those they killed. They were afraid of the scorpions because they had been in a hurry to defend themselves when someone attacked them, saying in their hearts: "Let me strike you down before you strike me down." They were horrified by the frogs because they had murdered with bitterness in their hearts.

102

THE PUNISHMENTS OF MURDERERS OUT OF IGNORANCE

120. I also saw fiery air stirred up by wind. It surrounded the souls of those who had committed murder through ignorance and for no reason. They were in this fiery air because they had contaminated the air with murder. They were buffeted by the wind because they had thought what they did was unimportant.

103

THE PUNISHMENTS OF POISONERS

121. Thereupon I saw a great rotating fire that contained horrendous snakes who had mouths and tails very agitated by this fire. The souls of those who had struck down people with poison or by some other means than the spilling of blood while they had been alive were in this fire. They burned in this rotating fire since they brought death to others by concealed means. They were tormented by the mouths and tails of these snakes because of the poison they had used to kill others.

104

THE PUNISHMENTS OF THOSE WHO HANDED THEIR INFANTS OVER TO DEATH

122. I saw a very strong fire burning next to a well of clear water. Some of the souls burned by this fire had snakes around their middle, like girdles. Others, however, breathed in some of the fire and blew it out again, as a man draws in a breath and lets it out again. Further, evil

spirits hurled fiery stones down upon them. All of the ones in the water of the well contemplated their punishments, as if in a mirror, and then were afflicted more and more from the well. These were the souls of those who, while they had been alive, had dried up their ability to have children and had killed the infants already born to them. The souls of those who had destroyed their ability to form children burned in this fire on account of their sin, and they suffered from the girdling snakes on account of their inhumanity. The souls of those who had killed their own infants were punished in this fire because of their wickedness. They drew the fire into themselves and vomited it forth again because of the inhumanity of their murders. They suffered from the fiery stones thrown by the evil spirits because of the hardness with which they had done this. Because they neglected to think about what they did, they bear the same punishments; they look into the water of the well not to find consolation, but to suffer more greatly.

105
THE PUNISHMENTS OF THOSE WHO KILLED THEMSELVES

123. I could not see the punishments of those who had taken themselves into death too early, but I knew that they were in the pit of Gehenna. They were tortured by robbers because they had killed themselves, and they were submerged in the pit of Gehenna because they had not repented for what they did.

106
CONCERNING THE PUNISHMENTS OF THESE EXCESSES

124. I saw and knew these things through the living spirit. And I heard the voice from the living light say to me: *These things that you see are true, and as you see them, so they are. Wherefore, let the people who have bound themselves to the sin punished above strive to punish themselves for their excesses while they are still alive so that they do not suffer worse punishments in the future. If those who had anger with hatred on a regular basis want to cast off the evil spirits who brought this anger to them and if they want to avoid these punishments, let them wear a hair shirt, flog themselves, and fast.*

107

CONCERNING THE ATONEMENT OF ANGER

125. If those who were truly angry without any evil hatred want to make amends for this, let them wear hair shirts and scourge themselves and fast in proportion to the weight of their sins and according to the recommendation they receive from the spiritual advisor of their souls.

108

ANGER IS THE WORST FAULT

126. Anger is the worst fault and is, as it were, the heart of the devil. Sometimes anger hides itself in the grotto of a dove and then attacks a man in his own familiar territory where it destroys the protection of his understanding. It flees the blessing of Abraham who in all his good will obeyed every command of God. Many offspring proceeded in blessing from Abraham. The angry man gnaws away every virtuous grain and devours everything that is germinating. Anger is similar to a stubborn thief. It gnashes its teeth at people because of their worthy gifts from God. For anger instigates controversy wherever it can, and it casts its lot not only in incest, but also in the breaking of all the laws of God. Anger is like a dragon that burns up everything wherever it goes. And it is like a thief who steals things, for anger seizes whatever it can snatch and steal. In anger, wisdom is unwise, and patience strains with impatience, and moderation rushes with the lack of moderation. Anger is also the bitterness that vomits forth the goodness and sweetness in the precepts and laws of God. It is the murderer who divides body and soul and does not allow them to be together. It is also a hard and immovable rock because it grinds away all good and every justice, whence it is in hell since it wants to agitate the things of heaven. When it has overcome a man, it leads him beyond itself and it overcomes him with such great madness because it thinks about neither earthly things nor heavenly things while it grinds away and scatters about the one who was made in the image of God. It draws great torments to itself. Wherefore, let men who have been unjust in any kind of murder punish their bodies. Let them suffer the bitterest of remedies with harsh torments so that they can snatch their souls back by means of the punishments mentioned above.

109
REPENTANCE CONCERNING MURDER OUT OF FURY

127. If he who cast out the soul of a person from his body through the fury of anger wants to punish himself for this so that he will not suffer the torments mentioned earlier, let him make himself thin with fasting over a long period of time. Let him scourge himself. And let him avoid the brightness of light for a time since he made the air foul by his pouring out blood. Let him do this according to the orders of the one presiding over him.

110
REPENTANCE CONCERNING MURDER OUT OF GREED

128. If he who separated the soul and body of a person because he was kindled with greed wants to avoid the torments mentioned earlier, let him also fast and scourge himself severely for a long period of time. Avoiding the companionship of other people, let him live a solitary life in the forest for a period of time. And let him do this with impartial justice.

111
REPENTANCE CONCERNING MURDER OUT OF NECESSITY

129. If he who truly killed a person deliberately because he anticipated that that person was going to kill him wants to shake off the punishments of this sin, let him chasten himself righteously in proportion to his excess after he has already lessened the excess a good deal.

112
PUNISHMENT OF MURDER OUT OF IGNORANCE

130. If the person who murdered someone out of ignorance shrinks back from and wants to avoid the torments for this sin as mentioned earlier, let him fast, but for a shortened time since according to justice he had not willed to commit this murder.

113

REPENTANCE CONCERNING MURDER FROM POISONING

131. If the person, however, who murdered someone by poisoning without spilling any blood wants to tear himself away from the punishments of that sin, let him fast and scourge himself severely for a long period of time. Let him also wear a hair shirt and cover himself with ashes as he flees the companionship of other people to live a solitary life in the forest for a time.

114

REPENTANCE OF THE ONE RECEIVING AN ABORTION

132. Let the women who have crushed and scattered about the result of their conception, clearly the material of a human form, fast and scourge themselves harshly in true repentance so that they may free themselves from the punishments for this sin mentioned above.

115

REPENTANCE OF THE MOTHER KILLING THE INFANT BORN FROM HERSELF

133. In order to escape the damnation of death, let those who have killed the infants they had given birth to and thus have sinned more bestially punish themselves with the bitterest of fasting, the harshest of scourgings and the roughest of garments, all in the confines of solitude, so that they can achieve salvation in the future.

116

THE MURDERER OF HIMSELF DESTROYS HIMSELF COMPLETELY WITHOUT CONSOLATION

134. He who murdered himself is excluded from any good since he did not precede his death with any repentance. For when he killed himself this way without cleansing himself with repentance first, he destroyed himself totally and without any consolation.

117

IN REPENTANCE A POSSIBILITY OUGHT TO BE CONSIDERED

135. However, in any just repentance it should be considered that man is naturally weak. Therefore, that person is blessed who repents his own sin and then brings his repentance before the one who judges both the living and the dead, for repentance that is started in this life through contrition brings eternal life with glory.

118

GOD THE CREATOR DID NOT WISH TO HAVE HIS GLORY ALONE

136. God created all things and made all living creatures. He finished all his work completely and distributed it before the beginning of time. But he did not want to have his glory alone, so he distributed it among his creatures so that they could rejoice with it, just as a hen gathers her young under her wings. However, the first angel fell and destroyed himself; he then made the first man fall as well. With the fall of man all elements became confused. When Abel was killed, the elements were covered with his blood as the earth drank it up. For the devil had said to himself: "I will accomplish my wish among the creation of God; I will be able to do more through man than I can through myself." But God in his great wisdom looked inside himself to discern how he might redeem man who had perished. To be sure, the wisdom of God is so great that no creature can penetrate it. In his wisdom God arranged for his Son to be born from the Virgin so that he might redeem man. No one is able to fight against God's wisdom.

119

WITH HIS SUFFERINGS, CHRIST ALSO DREW THE SINS OF THE REPENTING ONES TO HIMSELF

137. To counter the fact that man was able to sin, the Son of God was very gentle as a boy; to counter the taste of the flesh of man, he took on weariness in his youth; to counter the gluttony of greed in man, he accepted hunger; to counter the sins of injustice, he was surrounded with sadness; to counter the tyranny of the unholy, he suffered many reproaches; to counter the evil of murder, he suffered on the cross; and to

counter the sins of death which had buried man, he died on the cross so
that he might snatch man away from death. For in all his sorrows, he
took on all the sins of those who had repented and had not denied him.
Wherefore, he is called the angel of great wisdom because he is all just
and merciful.

120
A MURDERER IS TO INQUIRE AFTER REPENTANCE IN THE WOUNDS OF CHRIST

138. While all sins are dangerous and evil, murder is, nevertheless,
the worst evil of all evils because man has no fear of God in his heart
when he destroys what God made in his image. Therefore, a person,
separated in this way because he did not think that God was important
when he committed the murder, should seek the repentance that Christ
achieved through the piercing of his side and his various other wounds.
Christ alone suffered his blessed passion so that he might redeem man
who had fallen and had been destroyed. Christ did not need help from
any other person when he did this. These things, however, have been
spoken concerning the atonement for the cleansing and saving of souls,
and they are faithful things. A faithful person pays attention to these
things and remembers them well.

139. I also saw some more wicked spirits in this crowd. They beat
their breasts and bowed their heads sorrowfully as they cried aloud:
"Lucifer is our Lord. Who is stronger than Lucifer and can attack us?
We will make him our Lord. We will be able to do our own will through
him." These have foolish joy and are encouraged with this so that they
might despise established justice.

121
CONCERNING THE PUNISHMENT OF FOOLISH JOY

140. I saw a wide marsh that poured out the foulest smoke. This
smoke spread out like a fog over the marsh. The marsh contained a multitude of worms bubbling forth. The souls of those who had discredited
themselves with foolish joy while they had been alive were afflicted
with this smoke and were pressed down by its fog as they were tormented by the worms in the marsh. They were immersed in the marsh because they had had foolish joy while they had been alive in their bodies.
They suffered from the smoke of the marsh because they had neglected
God's law through their foolish joy. They were covered by the fog of the

marsh because they had chosen impiety as they did these things. They were tormented by worms because they had spoken words with this same foolish joy. I saw and understood these things.

122
CONCERNING THE REPENTANCE OF FOOLISH JOY

141. I again heard the voice from the living light say to me: *These things that you see are true, and as you see them, so they are, and there are more things. But if the men who fail with foolish joy strive to overcome the evil spirits who urged them on to this sin want to flee from this joy, let them restrain their flesh with scourging and fasting in proportion to their sin and according to the wishes of the one who presides over them. For foolish joy does not love truth and takes away everything which delights in truth. It says that its distorted will is not harmful, but it does not know God, and it sharpens its tongue against God.*

123
THE WORDS OF A PSALM CONCERNING FOOLISH JOY

142. It has been written likewise: *The teeth of the sons of men are spears and arrows, their tongue is a sharp sword (Psalm 57:5).* This means the following. The sons of the flesh who sprang from the flesh in sin have a certain power in their flesh, just like the teeth. This power is a hardness against the desires of the soul. Just as some men are armed against others so that they will not be wounded, so also the flesh, armed firmly and unjustly with foolish joy, fights against the will and happiness of the soul. Likewise, the flesh speaks words evilly against God and contrary to the salvation of its own soul, just as poisonous arrows wound souls by thrusting in and penetrating the souls with their javelins of sins so many times. They even turn their power of reason around to evil; they sharpen their power of reason, like a sword, with unfaithful words. Playing around and joking, they pretend to be refined and gather many followers this way. But after seducing their followers, they then wound their souls.

124

THEY WHO ARE NOT CLEANSED FULLY IN THE WORLD, HAVING BEEN SEPARATED FROM THEIR BODIES, ARE WEIGHED MORE FULLY

143. Let those who want to lift up their souls to God refrain from these sins so that they do not wound their souls seriously. Let them repent of their sins while they are able. The souls of those who do penance while they are in this world are, nevertheless, not cleansed fully. After they have died and have been separated from their bodies, they will be judged to determine the punishments they deserve. These things, however, have been spoken concerning the atonement for the cleansing and saving of souls, and they are faithful things. A faithful person pays attention to these things and remembers them well.

THE FIRST PART ENDS

THE HEADINGS OF THE SECOND PART BEGIN CONCERNING THE MAN LOOKING TO THE WEST AND TO THE NORTH

1. The Words of Gluttony of the Belly

2. The Response of Abstinence

3. The Words of Bitterness

4. The Response of True Bountifulness

5. The Words of Impiety

6. The Response of Piety

7. The Words of Falseness

8. The Response of Truth

9. The Words of Strife

10. The Response of Peace

11. The Words of Unhappiness

12. The Response of Blessedness

13. The Words of Immoderation

14. The Response of Discretion

15. The Words of Destruction of Souls

16. The Response of Salvation of Souls

17. The Words of the Lion with Roarings

18. The Fact that God, Opposing Himself to the Darkness of the Diabolical Snares, Brought Forth All the Tools of the Old and New Testaments

19. The Fact That in the Strength of the Son of God There Is That Protection Which Has Not Yet Been Made Manifest to Anyone

20. The Fact That the Mysteries Which Had Been Hidden in Old Prophecy, the Teachers Now Strain to Uncover, and They Will Not Cease from This

21. In Order That the Secrets of the Old and New Testaments May Be Made Strong, Let Them Be Displayed to the Faithful

22. The Fact That the Protection of the Prophecy of the Old Testament Was Gathering Strength

23. The Fact That in the Old Law, the Earth Was Being Sanctified Bodily; in the New, However, Heaven Was Being Made Bright through the Son of God

24. The Fact That the Old Were Clinging to Fleshly Things in Circumcision; the Faithful Truly Serve Zealously in the Baptism of the Spirit

25. Paul to the Same Thing

26. The Fact That Rationality Discerns All Things Which Have Been Given by God

27. The Fact That Rationality, Flourishing in the Old Law, Declared Future Holiness in Christ

28. The Fact That Rationality Manifests God and Man in the Son of God, Who—Having Been Made Incarnate While Knowing No Loss of Divinity—Remained in Those Who Look at Him with a Pure Heart

29. The Fact That the Prophets, Foreseeing the Incarnation of Christ as in a Shadow, Were Speaking Nothing More than What They Were Seeing and Knowing

30. The Fact That the Holy Spirit so Steeped the Rationality of Man that the Prophets Brought Forth the Miracles of God both through Vision and through Wisdom and through Knowledge, as if in Another Life

31. The Fact That Rationality Stands Whole in the Wisdom of God, Although It More Often Leans to the Flesh

32. The Fact That the Mysteries of the Old Testament Prepare Wise Men against the Devil; and They Will Not Cease from This until They May Satisfy Their Own Hearts

33. David to the Same Thing

81. The Fact That Immoderation, Wishing to Be in Excessiveness, Will Be Scattered Like Dust

82. Likewise concerning the Destruction of the Souls of Those Men Who Had Held God—as if God Were Not—in accordance with Contempt, and Thus Had Sent Themselves into Destruction, and Why This May Be

83. How Men May Tear Themselves Away from the Devil and Destruction

84. The Fact That When the Servants Are Allowed to Know All the Hidden Things of the Lords, They Wish to Dominate over Them

85. The Fact That Man May Know God in the Purity of Faith, and He May Cast the Diabolical Illusions from Himself

THE HEADINGS OF THE SECOND PART UNFOLD

THE SECOND PART BEGINS

CONCERNING THE MAN LOOKING TO THE WEST AND TO THE NORTH

1. I then saw the man I mentioned earlier turn toward the West so that he looked both West and North. On each shoulder he had a wing that covered his arms and he also had a wing on his back and on his chest. All of these wings were raised up, as if ready for flying. The tip of the wing that was on his back was, however, bent toward his left wing, but it was not bent at all toward his right wing. The tip of the wing that was on his chest was divided into two parts with one part curved back to the left wing and the other to the right wing. He also had a book in the middle of each wing. The book that was on the left wing had two pages, one colored green and the other silver. On the green page there was written: "Noah entered the ark as the Lord had commanded him. What is the reason the Lord did this? He began to rebuild man in water and

then he had him reborn in water." On the silver page there was written: "God wrote his Law on a stone tablet since man had no softness for divine reason. Later he wrote in softness, as it were in a fleshly heart." The book that was on the right wing also had two pages, one colored sapphire and the other gold. On the sapphire page there was written: *The Lord has sent word against Jacob, it falls upon Israel (Isaiah 9:7).* However, on the gold page there was written: *"In the beginning was the Word, and the Word was with God (John 1:1).* In the beginning the Word of God created all things, and later he bent himself back upon his own deeds." The book that was on the wing on his back was like marble and stone colored white. On it the finger of God had written: "The prophet prophesied to men through vision, wisdom and knowledge. And the Spirit of God breathed into that root to make it live, from which God made a man rise up even from mud. These are the miracles of the Divinity that God performs in men by foreseeing, by writing, by playing a lyre, and by sending angels with wings of prophecy." The book that was on the wing on his chest was all black and was full of stars. It had white letters on it, drawn from the depth of the other books, that philosophers and wise ones, using these books, had brought together. They had prepared for God the streets of justice in the West and in the North, just as a person draws water from a well and does not stop until his vessel is full. Similarly, God made all creatures in the beginning and did not stop until he had completed his work entirely.

2. As I mentioned earlier, from his shoulders down to his thighs this man was under the clouds on another white cloud. This white cloud was filled with the souls of the just. I heard a voice in this cloud that sounded like thunder. It thundered softly: *Give praise to the king ruling all things and glory to the living God.* Then all these souls rose up in a procession of life. They proceeded and did not turn back, just like the wheel of life goes and moves and does not turn back. But in a more secret place in this cloud, there were the souls of holy ones who were hidden very carefully, as if in a clear mirror. These souls had been decorated with all different kinds of precious stones and with every type of embellishment. They also played trumpets and lyres, playing all the different kinds of music. They echoed the sounds of the sea and of many waters and said: "How long will we continue and when will our time come when our works, which are seen in heaven before the face of God, restore our dwelling places in the presence of God so that we may see the face of God without the covering of Moses?" The following divine answer was given to them: *This will not be before the four winds have intermixed themselves in turn and have been blown together in turn,*

before the head of the ancient serpent has been ground away and destroyed, and before the sun with the lion has gathered together all its winged creatures. These souls of the just knew and heard the holy ones of God who were hidden. They saw them, as it were in a bright mirror. They eagerly awaited the answers that had been given them and were hopeful while the lion roars aloud until every schism in the world is erased.

3. And behold, just as I had seen various other sins in this cloud, I now saw eight other sins in various images in a similar manner. I saw a certain image, like a serpent, lying on its back in the darkness I mentioned earlier. Its eyes burned like fires, its tongue stuck out of its mouth and the end of its tail had been cut off. Its body was all black with lines of pale and poisonous color descending from its head all the way to its tail. Its belly had been slit open and in it there appeared the image of a man, lying on his back as if in a cradle. He had a hat on his head, which was like a helmet that had been lifted on high. Under his hat he had white hair that reached down to his shoulders. He was clothed in a fine white garment of silk and wore a mantle that was the same color as the serpent.

1
THE WORDS OF GLUTTONY

4. This image said: "God created all things. How then can I be spoiled by all these things? If God did not think these things were necessary, he would not have made them. Therefore, I would be a fool if I did not want these things, especially since God does not want man's flesh to fail."

2
THE RESPONSE OF ABSTINENCE

5. Again I heard a voice responding to these words from the cloud that reached from the South to the West. It said: "No one should play a lyre in such a way that its strings are damaged. If its strings have been damaged, what sound will it make? None. You, gluttony, fill your belly so much that all your veins are bloated and are turned into a frenzy. Where then is the sweet sound of wisdom that God gave man? You are mute and blind and you do not know what you are saying. Just as heavy rains destroy the earth, so also excess meat and wine lead man into blasphemies of mockery. I, however, saw a beautiful form in the mud as

God put man together. I am, therefore, like a soft rain so that man does not have to sprout weeds. I draw moderation out of men so that their flesh does not revolt and burst, having been flooded with more life-giving food than it needs. For I am a lyre sounding praises and piercing the hardness of heart with good will. For when a man feeds his body moderately, I reverberate like a lyre with his praises in heaven. When he feeds his body temperately with moderate food, I sing accompanied with musical instruments. You, gluttony, do not understand what you do not know, neither do you seek to know and understand. Sometimes you fill your belly gluttonously, and then your belly churns around until you vomit froth from your mouth. But I encourage moderation in food so that a person is neither hungry nor too full. Thereupon I sound praises with my lyre and sing accompanied with my musical instruments. O all you faithful, restrain yourselves from gluttony. The belly of the ancient serpent gulped many things down from Eve, and it vomited forth many filthy things through Eve."

3
THE WORDS OF BITTERNESS

6. The second image was like a leopard. It said: "I consider courage and victory as worth nothing, and I do not want anyone to resist me. I consider the Scriptures and faith as burdensome and harmful to me. I will chew through these things."

4
THE RESPONSE OF BOUNTIFULNESS

7. I heard the voice from the storm cloud answer this image, saying: "You are dangerous, detrimental and a very cutting exasperation. You do not want to respond to God or his precepts, but you instead want to stay bitter. But I am bountiful in rain and dew and in ointment and medicine so that I bring about pleasant things in the rain, joy in the dew, mercy in the ointment, and consolation for all sorrows in the medicine. I will remain this way in all these things and I will reign like this for eternity. Your material is, however, for Gehenna, the place from which you have risen."

8. The third image had the form of a man, except that its head, which stuck out from its body between its shoulder-blades, was like the head of a wild beast rather than like the head of a human. It had large and fiery eyes and a mouth like a leopard's. Lines of bluish-green descended from

its jaw to its chin. The head of a serpent descended from each side of its mouth which shot out flames. Above its knees, however, it stood with the rest of its body erect. It covered its head with a pitch-black cloth, as a woman does. The rest of its body was clothed with a very black garment with woven sleeves hanging down from it. It spoke as follows:

5
THE WORDS OF IMPIETY

9. "I do not want to obey either God or man. For if I were to obey either of them, he might order me to do something best for him and not for me. He might not think about my good, but might say to me: 'Go away.' This, however, cannot be. For if anyone injured me, I would return that injury a hundred-fold. I will act in such a way that no one will dare to resist me. For I do not want to lie under anyone's feet. I will do whatever is for my own good, as anyone who is not a fool does. If God wants me to do what pleases him, I will not do it unless it also brings good to me."

6
THE RESPONSE OF PIETY

10. I heard a voice answer this image from the storm cloud, saying: "You are diabolical and cruel and you are very wicked. For if God were to allow you to do all the things you want to do, who would he be then? If God were to give good things to you for the evil that you do, where would the scepter of his power be? When you undertook evil, God cast you out as a piece of lead into the inferno where all the creatures there can persecute you. Where, therefore, is your power now? You are full of darkness, blasphemies and misdeeds. What do you eat? Confusing things. Where do you dwell? In that place where everyone is against each other, where there is always unhappiness, and where the murderer who poured out blood is."

11. The fourth image was surrounded with such intense darkness that I could not distinguish any of its members, except that with difficulty I could distinguish that it had the form of a deformed and monstrous man. It stood on a dry, hard, black foam that sent forth many flames of fire and spoke as follows:

7
THE WORDS OF FALSENESS

12. "Who speaks everything truthfully? If I were to speak truthfully to others about their prosperity, I would offend myself. For lifting up another makes me fall down. I prefer to speak puffed up words that will give me honor. What I cannot have in one hand, I will demand with the other. For if I were to be truthful, I would not be able to require all the things I want. When I attend to my business, I discover things that are unsuitable to me, and so I say whatever I want to. For many truths are so immovable that they are not able to move even themselves; they have been tied, as it were, to a tree. They bring about only what they see and hear. Therefore, many are poor and needy and deprived from these truths. What I, however, demand falsely, I acquire. When I want to be nobler and richer than others, I speak more nobly and richly than they do. This is better than being tied to a tree. But I often speak the things that I do not see and hear. Thus I turn away from many evil things, but I also pass through many evil things. If my speech were to be only one way, I might be condemned. Therefore, I multiply my stories so that I cannot be overcome by any one of them. This is more useful to me than being pierced by javelins and swords. I never come across the noble and rich without some business to do."

8
THE RESPONSE OF TRUTH

13. I again heard a voice responding to this image from the storm cloud, saying: "O serpentine and hellish tongue, you are without any of the greenness of the grace of God. You bring forth the flames of injury and deception. No amount of evil is sufficient for you since you sprang from evil; you are the daughter of the devil. Your ways are unjust and you do not know where you are going. The murmuring and deceptive suggestions of the devil are like breasts for your sins, and you yourself suck the breasts of a harlot from whom you receive some of her wages so that you can rid yourself of honor and blessedness and honesty. I, however, am like a pillar in all the ways of the Lord; I am a good trumpet sounding the justice of God. I count all God's works, what they are and how many they are. And I reveal his works with truth. As a result, I am an advocate in the palace of the king and I am in all his honor. I also wear earrings and bracelets. I shine with all the embellishments of God because I speak the truth through the justice of God. Heaven and earth

and all the other creatures are truthful. The waters that flow under heaven and on earth as moisture persevere in truth. You, however, o perverse one, are the worst vermin. You will be trampled under foot like stinking dirt."

14. The fifth image also appeared in the form of a man. He had black curly hair and a fiery face. He was clothed with a cloak of many colors that had openings near his shoulders so that he could stick out his arms. In his left arm he held an ax that he had drawn close to himself. In madness he cut his hands often on this ax so that his garment was steeped in blood.

9
THE WORDS OF STRIFE

15. He said: "I cannot stand or suffer from such excessiveness because anyone can shake out his coverlet and then burden me with it, just as a little she-ass is burdened supporting a sack when it is young. As long as I breathe and live, I will not allow anyone to strike me with the madness of his will. I will hold back all my things so that they cannot trample me under foot, as they do the earth. I will injure them more than they injure me. I never get weary doing these annoying and outrageous things to them since I can tear their hearts to pieces with them."

10
THE RESPONSE OF PEACE

16. I heard a voice from the storm cloud answer this image, saying: "O harsh and fiery heat of outrage, you are a bloody criminal and are like grinding teeth. You seethe from various injuries as you pour out your blood. You want to walk wherever it pleases you. But you also carry great rage in your mouth and use it to shatter many. You disgrace those who eagerly follow gentleness. For you destroy good advice and quiet minds; you bring an end to these things with your deception. You see the dwelling place of peace as worth nothing; you do not desire peace or want it. You hide yourself in a cave like a serpent. You wound everyone with javelins since you are like a snake who kills people by striking them. Therefore, you are the shadow of death, the worst of poisons and quick destruction for people. I, however, exist like medicine for everyone; I anoint what you chase; I heal what you wound. I do not place any value in disruptive wars or in the babbling of those who cry aloud because I am a mountain of myrrh and frankincense and all the

other aromas. I am a pillar of cloud on the highest mountain because I attract all good things and proceed above all the heavens. Whence also I will fall upon you, and I will attack you severely without end; I will not allow you to have any peace."

17. The sixth image was like a leprous man. He had black hair and no clothes. He covered himself with the side leaves of certain herbs, and he beat his breast with his hands.

11
THE WORDS OF UNHAPPINESS

18. He said: "What salvation do I have, unless tears? What life do I have, unless sorrow? What help comes to me, unless death? What answer will be given to me, unless destruction? For I do not have anything better."

12
THE RESPONSE OF BLESSEDNESS

19. I heard a voice from the storm cloud answer this image, saying: "You are a glutton for punishment and you do not desire anything else. You should call upon God and seek his goodness. You look at yourself with an evil eye because you do not trust in God. You seek nothing from God and, therefore, have nothing. I, however, shout to God and receive an answer from him. I beseech him and in his goodness he gives me what I want. I seek from him and I receive from him. For I am venerable joy and I play the lyre in God's presence when I give him all my works. Because of my faithful hope in him, I sit by his bosom. You, however, do not trust in God and you do not desire his grace; therefore, all evil rushes to you."

20. The seventh image was like a wolf who crouched down. He watched carefully so that he might gulp down anything he could snatch.

13
THE WORDS OF IMMODERATION

21. He said: "Whatever I want to seek, I will snatch; I will hold nothing back from myself. Why should I hold anything back from myself and then have no reward? Why should I renounce what I am? Each type should be allowed to proceed according to its type. If I have to live

in such a way that I am afraid to breathe, what is my life worth? I will laugh and enjoy what I can. When my heart rejoices, why should I limit it? When my veins are full of pleasure, why should I cut them? When I know how to speak, why should I be silent? For every movement of my body is my salvation; I act according to the way I was created. Why should I change myself into something I am not? Every creature comes into existence with its own nature and acts according to that nature. I will do the same."

14
THE RESPONSE OF DISCRETION

22. Again I heard a voice from the storm cloud answer this image, saying: "O watcher of snares, with your snares you bite into all the things that are honest and rational since you are like a young animal who knows no moderation; you act like an unclean animal. All the things that are in God's plan act accordingly. The stars twinkle from the light of the moon, and the moon glows from the fire of the sun. All things are subordinate to greater things and do not surpass them. You, however, do not contemplate either God or his creation, but you walk as if you were an empty husk of grain blown about by the wind. I, however, walk in the light of the moon and sun, and I think about God's plan. I rise up with these in honesty; I value charity fully. For I am a leader in the palace of the King, and I know all his secrets. I do not, however, reveal his secrets, but I do understand and choose them; I shine with them like a ray of the sun. You, however, are maimed with disease and are like a cadaver full of worms."

23. The eighth image was like a tower with a slate roof on top of it. It had three windows in it. Under these three windows there were the two arms of a man sticking out and reaching above the slate roof. These arms were covered with darkness, as if with sleeves. The hands were uncovered, but were, nevertheless fiery.

15
THE WORDS OF DESTRUCTION OF SOULS

24. It said: "What merits and wages do I earn? Fire. I and the material I am made from do not want that. I flee from such bright things and refuse to follow bright works. I do not even want to be embellished with bright things since I am the one who plunders souls. This is my joy since

the one I came from wants me to do these things. And I speak evil things."

16
THE RESPONSE OF SALVATION OF SOULS

25. I heard a voice from the storm cloud answer this image, saying: "You are like an arrow from the devil, flying through the dark as a snare and wounding the blessed with martyrdom since they do not agree with you. Since they do what you reject, you want to destroy them, but you are not able to. For the blessed rise up with the flag of faith among the multitude of the angels. They rush against you and, like a great thirst, want to overcome you, just like a stag wants to drink water from a fountain. For they baptize you and bring you the seven gifts of the Holy Spirit who appeared in the humanity of the Savior as if in a flood of water. These things will destroy you since you are against God. I, however, am like a building built out of good materials. I am the tower of Jerusalem in the works of holy ones. I raise up the ones who repent through the ram that hung on the thorns, revealing Christ. I hold simple ones firmly through the faith of baptism and the innocent ones through the anointing of the Holy Spirit, because through the whiteness of virginity which flowers in the flesh of Christ like a lily, I am restored to salvation and become a companion of God."

17
THE ROARINGS OF THE LION

26. Behold there was a lion standing by the man whom I mentioned earlier. This lion had turned against these sins and cried aloud, roaring into the wind: "O devilish sins, I will destroy you by boiling you in a pot placed on a fire. I will bring you to your end because you have always striven to fight against me and the justice of God."

18
GOD BRINGS FORTH THE TOOLS OF THE OLD AND NEW TESTAMENTS AGAINST THE DEVIL

27. I again heard a voice from heaven saying: *God uses many signs and a variety of punishments to oppose the darkness of the snares of the devil. He calms down the turmoil of the sins that have sprung up in such a way that they cannot resist the blessedness of the highest city.*

Looking out from heaven he has protected his faithful with holiness.
Therefore you see that the man I mentioned earlier turns around to the
West so that he looks both West and North. The reason for this is that
he, a strong warrior who stands against the devil bravely, always knew
in his own ancient counsel that he brings all the tools of the Old and
New Testaments and all the power of good words against the darkness
of falling ruin and against the foolish coldness of ignorance.

19

IN THE STRENGTH OF THE SON OF GOD THERE IS UNFAILING PROTECTION

28. On each shoulder he has a wing that covers his arms. This means
in the strength of the Divinity and in the humanity of the Son of God,
there is protection that never fails and never ends since God watches
over all things in his Divinity and through the humanity of the Son of
God. But God also hides those works that, hidden in his ancient secret
counsel, he has not yet planned to reveal to anyone. For although God
works new miracles everyday, there are, nevertheless, many things hidden in his own secret counsel that he has not yet revealed. Likewise,
they cannot be understood by man before God manifests them in various
works.

20

THE HIDDEN THINGS OF THE PROPHECIES ARE REVEALED THROUGH TEACHERS

29. He also has a wing on his back and on his chest. These are the
mysteries that before the nativity of the Son of God, as it were, on his
back, had been hidden in the obscurity of old prophecies by his own
hand for their protection. These are the mysteries that the teachers of
truth now try to uncover since God has willed that they be revealed now.
With the profound wisdom necessary to protect spiritual things, the
teachers now reveal the mysteries of the New Testament, as if from a
well. And they will not stop doing this, just as God did not stop before
he had finished his work in six days. At any rate, they will never be
strong enough to empty this well.

21

THE SECRETS OF THE OLD AND NEW TESTAMENTS OUGHT TO BE PUBLISHED; THEY OUGHT TO BE MADE STRONG; LET THEM BE DISPLAYED

30. All of these wings are raised up, as if ready for flying. This means that all the secrets of the Old and New Testaments are being shown to the faithful so that they can be made manifest and can be strengthened.

22

THE PROTECTION OF THE PROPHECY IN THE OLD TESTAMENT WAS GATHERING STRENGTH

31. The tip of the wing that is on his back is, however, bent toward his left wing, but it is not bent at all toward his right wing. This shows that the prophecy in the Old Testament was protected by the strength of its own secrets and by the integrity of its own words. This is so since the prophecy and the law are one, and they provide for the physical needs of the living. But they do not strain the right side of spiritual things because that side does not yet worship the one who sends forth heavenly rewards.

23

SANCTIFICATION IN THE OLD AND IN THE NEW TESTAMENT

32. The tip of the wing that is on his chest is divided into two parts. This means the protection of the secret profoundness is found in the Old and New Testaments when the teachers of truth, both in the prophets and in the Gospel, multiply the mystical mysteries with mystical words. As a result, the earth is sanctified outwardly and inwardly through the purification found in the Old Law. In the New Testament, however, heaven is made bright with many and various signs of righteous and spiritual justifications through the Son of God.

24
CONCERNING CIRCUMCISION AND BAPTISM

33. One part curves back to the left wing and the other to the right wing. This means that the Old Testament leaned toward the defense of earthly things; the New Testament, however, eagerly desires the protection of heavenly things. While the old clung to fleshly matters such as circumcision, the faithful truly serve with zeal through the Son of God in the baptism of the spirit. But the old have not been justified through their observing such matters; the faithful, however, have truly obtained the highest reward of unworldliness through the faith of Christ, just as Paul the apostle also says:

25
THE FACT THAT MAN IS NOT JUSTIFIED FROM THE WORKS OF THE LAW

34. *Nevertheless, knowing that a man is not justified by legal observance but by faith in Jesus Christ, we too have believed in him in order to be justified by faith in Christ, not by observance of the law (Galatians 2:16).* This means that the grace of God comes to people through the Holy Spirit. Since the fall of Adam had mortally wounded the souls of the just, the finger of God wrote out the law for them through Moses. Violated flesh was not able to free violated flesh since it had been violated. As a result, the Lord anticipated through the law of Moses that men should sacrifice goats and bulls in obedience to him, just as they could discern in his mystery that they should sacrifice themselves to God by mortification of their body, similar to the way they sacrificed their beasts to him. When, however, the most immaculate and cleanest of men offered himself through his blood and death as a sacrifice to God, all people were cleansed. Therefore, let men know that they are not justified through the works of the fleshly law when they observe it. The blood and ashes of their own breasts could not justify or free them, but the justice of the truth of the Son of God that shows them the way to salvation was able to do so. For through the faith of the Son of God, those who believe faithfully in him also served. As a result, the faithful believe in him faithfully. He is the way and the truth, clearly the way in faith and the truth in belief. They believe in him so that they can be justified through the faithful works performed out of their love of the Son of God and not from their deeds done unwillingly through bitterness. For good works bring one to heaven by turning aside evil works since

Christ anointed people through his repentance when he saved them through his actions. Christ was a clean and fattened sacrifice offered for people who believe in him. The old law did not justify or free people completely, but it showed the way since it was a voice heard before the Word. But the Word is the Son of God who gave the new law in truth.

26
RATIONALITY DISCERNS ALL THINGS

35. He also has a book in the middle of each wing. This means that along with the power of divine protection, there is the power of reason which, according to God, produces, dispenses and discerns all the things that God has given since there is nothing that the power of reason cannot penetrate and keenly analyze.

27
FUTURE HOLINESS IS DECLARED IN CHRIST

36. The book that is on the left wing has two pages because the power of reason, flourishing in the old law with divine protection, brought forth two revelations of righteousness. One page is colored green and the other silver. The green is the justice in the material of the work of God, which God brought forth. Just as the earth brings forth all greenness, so also the Old Testament showed every seed and flower of future fairness. This is also made manifest in the silver foundation of pure knowledge that declared the future pure holiness of Christ. You see the words mentioned earlier that were written on the green colored page. They demonstrate the flowering revelation of divine learning. Because Noah obeyed by building the ark, the one who had no beginning or end also restored those perishing in water by having them be reborn to life later through baptism. The words mentioned earlier that were written on the silver colored page make manifest in the purity of the true knowledge of revelation that God showed the hardness of men in the old law since they were hard and not soft toward him. Later, they softened their hearts toward him when they clung to his divine words in the new law.

28

THE SON OF GOD WHO DWELLS IN CLEAN HEARTS KNOWS NO LOSS IN THE INCARNATION

37. The book that is on the right wing also has two pages. This means that the power of reason in the New Testament, protected by the highest blessedness, gives two demonstrations where the one Lord, God and man, in the Son of God is made manifest. One page is colored sapphire and the other gold. This means that virginity, the sapphire, showed forth in Christ when he, born from a virgin, taught chastity so that everyone who wants to imitate him may choose chastity. In addition, a golden brightness shines from him when the faithful believe that he is true God born from God the Father and that he formed all things with the Father. For at the time of the beginning of creation, the Son of God was already complete; he was before all other creatures. He did not lessen himself in any way when he made all the other creatures. He who was not made, made all things. Nor did he suffer any loss of divinity when he was made incarnate. You saw the words mentioned earlier that were written on the sapphire colored page. These words make manifest that the Virgin gave birth to a pure man in pure virginity when the Lord of all sent his own Word on a sweet mission to all those who believe. He remained among those who strove to look at God with a pure heart. The words written on the gold colored page show that the Son of the world, appearing in the world openly in revelation and in the signs of many miracles, declared that he is the leader who came as the Son of God. Clearly he was the leader who brought forth all creatures and who chose a Virgin from among those creatures to be his mother.

29

THE PROPHETS CONCERNING THE INCARNATION OF CHRIST, CLEAR AND WHITE

38. The book that is on the wing on his back is like marble and stone colored white. This means that the power of reason, protected by the strength of the prophecy that prophesied the coming of Christ in the future, foresaw his incarnation, as if in a shadow. A person who sees someone's back does not see his face and wonders what his face is like. Similarly, the prophets prophesied the coming of the Son of God, but they did not know him in the flesh yet. They also had a certain hardness, like the solidity of marble, because having been filled with the Holy

Spirit, they did not cringe before anyone but always stood firm with the integrity of truth. They did not cut their words here and there either since they accepted what they said from no one other than the one who is complete integrity, namely God. They were like stones because they persisted with rigor and did not give any ground to anyone else. Nevertheless, they acted in the whiteness of simplicity since they spoke nothing other than what they saw and knew. Similarly, an infant does not speak anything in its simplicity other than what it sees and knows.

30

THE PROPHETS BROUGHT FORTH THE MIRACLES OF GOD THROUGH WISDOM AND KNOWLEDGE

39. The finger of God had also written on that book the secrets he wished to reveal. This means that the Holy Spirit steeped the power of reason of man as he prophesied. The Holy Spirit also did this through a vision when the prophets, inspired by the Holy Spirit, saw into the distant future through the Holy Spirit. Certain ones said many things with wisdom since the omnipotence of God touched their minds when they brought forth many, many significant things, just as wisdom also built all things. Certain ones said many things when the Word of God looked and blew into their knowledge as they spoke about hidden and obscure things. For the Spirit of God breathed into the root to make it alive, from which God made a man rise up even from the mud. And the Spirit inspired that life and made it never ending, of course, the soul which has no end. The Holy Spirit also illuminated the prophets with its breath so that they brought forth the miracles of God into another life, just as the mud was changed into another life of flesh and blood. These were the miracles of the Divinity that God brought forth in wondrous ways through the prophets when they spoke, foreseeing what they foresaw in the Spirit, writing what they handed down from memory by command of God, and playing a lyre since the power of reason, inspired by the Holy Spirit, came in measure in voice and words for praising God, thereby praising God with these things. God also did this in men by sending them angels with wings of prophecy. As previously mentioned, the prophets, lifted up in the spirit of prophecy, showed many miracles just as the cherubim had. The prophets knew and brought forth the mysteries of God because God in his secret judgment worked where he wished and how he wished and in whom he wished.

31
RATIONALITY STANDS IN THE WISDOM OF GOD

40. The book that is on the wing on his chest is all black and is full of stars. This means that the power of reason stands completely in the profound wisdom of the protection of God so that it does not divide itself with contrariness, although men have many diversities in their ways. This also means that wisdom spoke both in the Old and New Testaments, making them unified. The wing is black because the power of reason in humans more often leans toward the flesh and often wonders what and what kind of things it speaks from. But the wing, nevertheless, shines in the light of the stars since men have faith and intelligence. Through faith men believe in God whom they cannot see. They also understand the miracles of God, which is difficult to do for those who have been created by God.

32
THE MYSTERIES OF THE OLD AND NEW TESTAMENT ARE PREPARED AGAINST THE UNFAITHFUL

41. This book has white letters on it, drawn from the depth of the other books, that philosophers and wise ones, using these books, had brought together. This means that the power of reason is in the bright goodness of God and brings out into the open and confirms the mysteries that have been gathered together in the Old and New Testaments. These mysteries prepare the faithful and wise men when they gather catholic doctrine together so that the righteous can fight against unfaithfulness and the devil himself. They do this from the Scriptures which they desire to explain; they do not withdraw from doing this. They then fill up the conscience of their hearts with these mysteries. Similarly, God does not stop doing his work until he has brought it to perfection. For when they look into and sift out the Scriptures carefully, they worship God and esteem his name. They also seek to honor God, as David the Psalmist says.

33

DAVID TO THE SAME THING

42. *All the nations you have made shall come and worship you, O Lord, and glorify your name. For you are great, and you do wondrous deeds; you alone are God (Psalm 86:9-10).* This means that God made all creatures; he also allowed man to perform works, for men work, form and order. They work within creation. Everyone forms what he wishes, but is not able to give a spirit to what he has formed. What each person presides over, he gives commands to. Because God created man and brought him to life with the breath of his spirit, all the tribes born from Adam, existing as creatures of God, will come to God according to his will. Those who adore the Lord seek his presence when they call upon his name and when they know him because they do not want to be separated from him, just as a son cannot ignore who his father is. Therefore, they glorify the name of God when they cry out to him and call upon him for help. But some people hold their work as equal to God's. They even call their work their God. This is caused by the counsel of the devil who inflates them to such ideas. They think that the name of God glorifies them; they do not know God. They want to have God when they cannot have God. Therefore, the old and new law have been given to man so that he can know God by believing in him, by seeing him and by attending to him. Wise philosophers have drawn out wisdom from these two laws. They never cease filling their vessels with what is pleasing to God. Actually, all the things that God has made are pleasing to him. The Lord is great in his wondrous things, in his celestial virtues and in works that shine with beauty. God made Noah enter the ark, he showed Abraham many good things, he also gave Moses the law, and he led those who believed in his Son back to life: these are all wondrous things. He did all these things so that the faithful would always think about them with devotion and so that they would never stop searching their profoundness since they came from God. God alone made these things. All good rises from him and returns to him. The faithful should contemplate the profoundness that when God created man, he made him like a wheel in the spirit of life so that he rolls back to God.

34

THE FACT THAT VERY MANY BEFORE THE LAW ARE BLESSED IN THE LAW AND IN BAPTISM

43. As I mentioned earlier, from his shoulders down to his thighs this man is under the clouds on another white cloud. This white cloud is filled with the souls of the just. This reveals that the whiteness of the miracles of God holds the souls of those who serve God, because this whiteness reaches out with the strength of the leader of all creatures in the incarnation of the Savior of men who became incarnate in glory. Those who were before the law, those who were in the law, and those who have been baptized have obtained the highest blessedness through the redemption of the Son of God. So they now rejoice in that mansion that God provided for them at the beginning of time. Through faithful works, faithful men prepare rest for their souls in this dwelling place of blessedness where they can rest happily after the life of their flesh has been consummated. In the place of blessedness, you can also hear the voices of the angelic celestial hierarchy glorifying the ruler of all things and the one living in the ages of ages. And so the souls of the just are lifted up into joy. They proceed from life to life and do not shrink back from this since they will remain in their new life eternally. Similarly the wheels of life, signifying the Divinity of the coming of the Spirit who, in turn, signifies baptism, rush to instruct and cleanse men. They do not stop doing this since no other teaching will help lead men to life. These souls threw their idols away while they were alive. They left their own lands and came with Abraham. They gave up the offices they held on earth. As a result, they are like exiles from their earthly ignorance. But entering into the mansions of God, they present their merits and receive many rewards.

35

THE SOULS OF THE PERFECT, WHO HAVE BEEN SEPARATED LIKE ANGELS FROM MEN, TAKE DELIGHT IN JOYS

44. But in this whiteness of blessedness, the souls of the more perfectly holy are rewarded with more secret joys. These are the ones who had been contemplatives while they had been alive. These souls have been embellished with all the heavenly virtues and with total holiness. They now praise God with the lofty sound of trumpets. This sound com-

es from the mouth of the prophets, the wise and the chosen of God. The works of the Holy Spirit are innumerable in men. They also exult God with lyres in complete joy; they make a sound so wondrous and inexplicable that the human heart cannot grasp or understand it. Because they worked with fire and water in the holiness of baptism and because they moved some with these works, they therefore sound like the sea and rushing waters that send forth a multitude of wondrous sounds. They are the ones who had lifted themselves above their fleshly desires and their intentions in their hearts while they had been alive. They had cast their earthly desires aside, as if they were not even human. They had separated themselves from other people, like angels from men. They dedicated themselves to matters of heaven with their watchful works, and they looked at God through the windows of faith with the simple goodness of an infant. And they persevered in these matters without wavering.

36

THE SOULS OF THE HOLY ONES DESIRE THEIR BODIES TO BE RESTORED TO THEMSELVES

45. They also voice their desire for the time when their works will be seen openly in the presence of the living God and when their bodies in which they did these works will be restored to them. They long for this so that they can see God after the difficulties which had covered their faces before Moses have been removed from them. The works of these holy ones, done through the inspiration of the Holy Spirit, shine like heaven in God's presence since they were done with God and in God. As a result of their good works, God gives these souls a cooling rest. But he will not give them the fullness of joy until the fullness of people has entered into the last day. At the end of the world God will join the bodies and souls of the holy with their works, and their heavenly work will lead them before the face of God where they will see him fully. But because the body had done these good works with the soul, when the soul is separated from the body, it cannot have the fullness of God since it cannot see the face of God fully without the body. Therefore, when the body and soul are rejoined, God will uncover his face so that the holy ones may see him fully since the body and soul which had worked together have been rejoined. The holy ones now, however, cry aloud with a strong cry since they find it difficult to wait to receive their bodies. They plead for the images of their bodies, just as a hungry boy asks his

father for bread to whom his father responds kindly, giving it to this son quickly.

37

BEFORE THE HOLY ONES MAY RECEIVE THEIR OWN BODIES, THE WORLD WILL BE SHOOK VIOLENTLY

46. They are also told that before they can receive their bodies again, the world will be shook violently and will be changed into another world. The ancient enemy and his strength will be crushed, and the true God, existing also as man, will gather all his chosen members so that they can receive the wholeness of their bodies at this time.

38

THE HOLY ONES KNOW THEMSELVES FROM THEIR WORKS AS COMPANIONS IN THE HOLY SPIRIT

47. The souls of the blessed who have already been rewarded will know these newly chosen of God as companions since they performed their various good works through the inspiration of the Holy Spirit and since their good works were diverse because of the warm touch of the Holy Spirit. They hear their voices as they sing songs of joy and they see them in the purest piety of thought and contemplation. The newly chosen souls will listen to the divine answers given to them from above, just as those supporting them do, while God's strength lifts up his strong precepts and checks all the rashness of the devil at the end of the world so that their bodies can be restored to them for eternal blessedness and glory.

39

IN UNFAITHFULNESS THE DEVIL PUTS FORTH DISAGREEABLE THINGS

48. Just as you saw various other sins in this cloud, you now see eight other sins in various images in a similar manner. This means that in the dark unfaithfulness where you had previously seen the snares of the devil, you have also often looked at the signs, raging through the four parts of the world and through the four elements, which disturb the earth's orbit and which attack and harass those who should be able to serve God

quietly. For the devil, showing his weaknesses and strengths, as if he were God, endlessly sends unpleasant things to men. He also does this for a long time; nothing else prevails more fully.

40

THE ANCIENT SERPENT WISHES TO DRAW ALL THINGS TO HIMSELF

49. You see a certain image, like a serpent, lying on its back in the darkness I mentioned earlier. This means that the devil, the ancient serpent, in the darkness of his worthlessness uses his appetites and desires against heavenly things when he tries to convince people to descend from heavenly desires to earthly things. Its eyes burn like fires since the devil's intention sends the flames of deception into the fire of hatred. Its tongue sticks out of its mouth since falsehood proceeds from his fierce bite. The end of its tail has been cut off because his will is unable to bring his work to completion. He wants to draw all things into his lake of destruction except that the divine will prevents his doing this. Its body is all black because he uses all his efforts to advise men to forget about God. Lines of pale and poisonous color descend from its head all the way to its tail. This means that Satan's ways have the paleness of death and shake out the poisonous commotion of humanity through gluttony as humans begin on their destructive path with the devil and are led into the perversity of destruction with him. Satan's ways lead to the worst of ends because just as the beginning of the devil is evil, so also is his end.

41

CONCERNING THE GLUTTONY OF THE BELLY

50. Its belly has been slit open. This means that the devil's mouth lies open ready to devour souls. In its belly there appears the image of a man, lying on his back as if in a cradle. This stands for the gluttony of the belly. Because the devil first prevailed upon men to sin with gluttony, he can more easily and fully snare men with other sins. This image of a man lies down as if resting, lying down in ignorance through the appetite of gluttony, so that the devil can draw man away from the desire to be in paradise. For man was first seduced by the serpent with food. He has a hat on his head, which is like a helmet, that has been lifted on high because gluttony lifts up its own will with empty power in the minds of men. When men have their bellies filled, they begin to be

proud, as if they were overflowing with good things. Under his hat he has white hair that reaches down to his shoulders because holding out the whiteness of abundance with the power of his strength, he despises everything without any bashfulness and does not want to be under any-one else's power. He is clothed in a fine white garment of silk since he is entangled in the pleasure of precious and delicious feasts. He wears a mantle that is the same color as the serpent since he surrounds himself with the fleshly desires of various sins. The wickedness of the devil pro-duces these sins so that he can turn men away from salvation through an abundance of food and drink. This sin also revealed this through the words it spoke earlier. But this sin can be resisted with abstinence, and man is warned not to clothe himself with foolishness.

42
CONCERNING BITTERNESS

51. The second image stands for bitterness. It follows after gluttony of the belly because after a man has burdened himself with gluttony, he runs into bitterness and discomfort from the over-abundance of food, just as winter follows summer. This image is like a leopard since its works are harsh. It imitates a wild animal, existing with two natures. It is also most bitter in its words and in its works, as shown earlier in its speech. It is scolded loudly with the words of true bountifulness. People are encouraged to be generous. There is great hardship when people turn away from God and return nothing to God for all the things God has giv-en them. Therefore, O illustrious and wise ones, prepare your souls for God.

43
ISAIAH TO THE SAME THINGS

52. Isaiah, inspired through me, shows this to you when he says: *If you bestow your bread on the hungry and satisfy the afflicted, then light shall rise for you in the darkness, and the gloom shall become for you like midday; then the Lord will guide you always and give you plenty even on the parched land. He will renew your strength (Isaiah 58:10-11)*. This means as follows. The soul has breath and desire and will, and it is joined to the flesh that sprang up from the earth. When the soul has moved the flesh, that is, when it has made it living, it knows the sins of the flesh from which the flesh sprang up. But when the flesh has been perfected, the soul is hungry for dutiful action, clearly so that it can do good. Let man rise up quickly with the breath of the soul by

which he can stretch to God. Let him ascend quickly with the desire of the soul by which he can embrace God, and let him hold strenuously onto the will of the soul by which he can love God. For the soul understands many good and evil things, as man reveals through his actions. It is like the wind that blows over the grass; it is like the dew that falls upon the grass; and it is like the air bringing the rain that makes things grow. Therefore, let man pour out his will by desiring good things. How? The wind is like help for those who suffer; the dew is like consolation to the desolate; and the air bringing the rain will restore the needy and fill them up with teachings, just like those who are hungry. When man yields his soul to these, he looks keenly into the powers of his own soul. When you have done these things, o man, and when you have redeemed with good conviction your soul that was afflicted by demons and men and that was chained and imprisoned with sins, and when you have filled your soul up with good intentions, then your light will rise up out of the darkness of your sins to the source of justice. You will walk in good and holy ways so that you will stop sinning and begin to do good works where the darkness of sin does not darken the light of holiness, but where those who are unwilling also serve. When those of your group fail by doing nothing, just as the day fails after midday, so also your sins will fail. The Lord of all and the God of all creatures will give you the grace necessary for you to resist your enemies. He will do this for all eternity so that your enemies may no longer dominate you, but that you may trample them underfoot, like a little stool under your feet. He will fill your soul with heavenly joy and light, just as shown by the clear day of good deeds. He will free your bones, of course, the bones of your limbs that have done good and holy works from corruption, of course in the future resurrection, so that no mortal things will survive but holy and incorruptible ones will be called forth one after the other.

44

CONCERNING IMPIETY

53. The third image stands for impiety. It walks after bitterness because where bitterness is in the minds of men, impiety joins it. This image has no joy and is unshaken by the good things of the Lord, but because it is so strong, it tears all good things into pieces. This image has the form of a man, except that its head which sticks out from its body between its shoulder-blades is like the head of a wild beast rather than like the head of a human. This is because ruling over men and beginning with its own peculiar knowledge, it acts and bites openly like a

beast. It is also deceitful, concealing things in human beings, for it rejects true teaching and goodness and obedience and subjection, which are in God, and it lacks the beauty of justice in all things. It has large and fiery eyes and a mouth like a leopard's because being very harsh with its anger, it tears to pieces and dismembers everything it can. It does not want grace or mercy and it discerns no wisdom with discretion. It tramples the holy and just under foot everywhere. Lines of bluish-green descend from its jaw to its chin since in grinding its teeth and in biting it holds onto its very foul and bad will that stretches out to foolishness. This is the result of its working under the illusion of deception without the honor of God. The head of a serpent descends from each side of its mouth because as a result of its despising God and man, it never stops biting, but always finds something new to bite with its serpentine ways. It shoots out flames from its mouth since it shoots arrows into men by making them furious in many different ways. Above its knees, however, it stands with the rest of its body erect. This means that it uses its strength to worship idols when it causes men to rage with impiety, similar to idols. It also deceives men in such a way that they think they are just and doing acts of justice. It covers its head with a pitch-black cloth, as a woman does because with harshness it binds men's minds with the dark and clinging vine of fickleness. The rest of its body is clothed with a very black garment because it is clothed with the error of most wicked cruelty, which makes it lack the whiteness of life. Its garment has woven sleeves hanging down from it, but its arms are inside its garment. This means that its works are completely useless. Withdrawn by their own strength, its works do not appear to anybody who is good. This sin spoke accordingly earlier. The virtue of piety responds to this sin and shows that its speech is always evil.

45
CONCERNING FALSENESS

54. The fourth image stands for falsehood. It follows after impiety because when a man is impious, he approaches falsehood. He builds each and every lie zealously and casts truth away. This image is surrounded with such intense darkness that you cannot distinguish any of its members because falsehood is in darkness and does not have the righteousness of good works in it. It has no righteousness, but only the darkness of death. With difficulty you can distinguish that it has the form of a deformed and monstrous man. This means that lacking the beauty of truth and the attractiveness of justice in all its words and actions, it does not work with righteousness, but it walks in the darkness of

death so that it moves with both certainty and uncertainty. It does not have the carefulness of charity, in which God is found, but rather the unfruitfulness and deceptiveness in which it has men continually acting. It stands on a dry, hard, black foam that sends forth many flames of fire. This means that falsehood, disillusioned with words that have no strength, appears dry without any greenness of justice, hard without any sweetness of kindness, and black without any whiteness of the virtues since it has no serenity but only the flame of anger which injures so many, as was shown by the words it spoke earlier. It is restrained by the response of truth who warns it that men may be truthful. People who choose lying not only pursue this sin, but they also struggle with those who are friends to whom they tell a lot of lies. The prophet David, steeped with truth from my spirit, has spoken about this.

46
DAVID TO THE SAME THING

55. *From the womb the wicked are perverted; astray from birth have the liars gone (Psalm 58:4)*. This means that original sin sprang up through food and made man's beautiful and happy nature mortal. For through this food, good knowledge went to sleep and evil knowledge awoke. As a result, liars have been separated from the truth. The nature of man was made repugnant in a poisonous womb because of the mouth of the serpent who deceived a human by asking why she could not eat the fruit. Since our first parents broke the command of God as a result of the advice of the serpent, they died in sin. In addition, their first born sons were estranged from the protection of holiness by their sin of forgetting about God. Therefore, let men abstain from food since the ancient enemy with his gluttonous throat had previously deceived man with food. For when people demand food, they suffer from avarice which makes them fill their bellies with every kind of food and which leads them from the knowledge of good to that of error. And so men have erred from the womb, of course when our first parents committed the first original sin and then became mobile in their giddiness. For after the taste of food, the taste of sin was present. When they had eaten, they spoke falsely since the devil set a great lie in place with the food with which he denied God and his justice. All those who fill their belly in gluttony with the drunkenness of food and wine do the same thing. Through drunkenness the sons of men are liars, valuing truth very little and denying it. Since the temptation of the devil was present from the very beginning of the human race, people speak lies just like the devil and strike themselves and others down. When they are opposed to God

who created heaven and earth, they are in hell, are they not? They are sometimes destructive in life and try to make like they are in heaven, but they have never seen heaven and never will. Whatever is destructive, they say is a great honor. They forsake man with their lying in so many different ways. They also praise a person through illusion while they strike him down with deception. And so they are like those who made a bull-calf on Oreb and like those who said Israel was their God. This is the way men act who lie and say vain things and who promise to give themselves all the things found in creation, according to their own will. But all those who have lied in this way, have died, just as the idols have also died. They are in the north with the north wind and thus will fall.

47

CONCERNING STRIFE

56. The fifth image demonstrates strife. It follows falsehood because when a man is a liar, he runs into strife so that everyone strains fraudulently with fraud and injury toward his brother. He appears in the form of a man. He has black curly hair and a fiery face. This means that man who is rational loves strife more than the rest of the animals who are irrational. Further, he often makes fun of the rest of the animals with his strife. He does this through confused lewdness and through denigrating troublesomeness with his duplicity and with his fiery will whenever he is furious with anger. He is clothed with a cloak of many colors that has openings near his shoulders so that he can stick out his arms. This means that he covers his desires with a variety of other faults. Having no integrity because of the harshness of his madness and having no restraint of righteousness, but only causing raging schisms, he stretches out his arms and acts according to his own will. Whoever is full of strife does not respect the will or usefulness of anyone else, but acts only according to his own will. In his left arm he holds an ax that he has drawn close to himself because with harsh contrariness he thinks about the divisive words he has gathered around himself in perverse ways. In madness he cuts his hands often on this ax so that his garment is steeped with blood. With his cutting and contrary words, he often makes his own works worse when he brings reproach upon himself because of his madness. He also reveals his conscience to others through the guiltiness of his own words. He thus irritates himself because he confuses himself and others with his violent reproaches. He showed this in the words he spoke earlier. But he is resisted by the judgment of the highest peace. Let men be cautious to avoid this sin.

48
CONCERNING UNHAPPINESS

57. The sixth image stands for unhappiness because unhappiness, which turns away from all the good things of God, follows strife. Men who think they are saved run into death when they do not cultivate God. This image is like a leprous man and has black hair. As lepers have been separated from the healthy people of the world so that they are not touched by leprosy, so unhappiness has been segregated from all of God's virtues so that it cannot shine in their brightness. Nevertheless, it is still like a man because when all the other creatures of God are happy, man makes himself unhappy through the suggestions of the devil. And man is filled up with the blackness of overflowing and various evils, like the hair. He does not show any embarrassment because he does not want any wise person to suggest that he reform. He has no clothes but covers himself with the side leaves of certain herbs. This means that lacking the covering of good holiness, he is without the joy of salvation. He is surrounded with the instability of various vanities, and he tries to make himself happy in various ways. But he cannot be happy. He beats his breast with his hands because he blames his conscience when he looks into the innermost parts of his heart where he finds evil works. He has no hope in God, but sighs and suffers many hardships, just as he showed when he spoke earlier. He is refuted by blessedness. Let men be cautioned not to stay this way.

49
CONCERNING IMMODERATION

58. The seventh image truly stands for immoderation, which suitably follows after unhappiness. When a man rebels against the good things of God, immoderation shoots up everywhere it is able. It will not, however, be strong because whatever is against God will not stand but will be destroyed. This image is like a wolf because without discretion, man has the madness of deceit and the rough changeableness of evil. He crouches down and watches carefully so that he might gulp down anything he can catch. This means that bent by his own strength, man leans toward the lower part of the worst ways of his own will. He thinks about the various vanities so that he can draw himself to them. He does this to disturb the honesty of righteous guidance, which leads nowhere, and to fulfill the pleasures of his own desires. Immoderation showed this in his

earlier speech. True discretion answers him. Let men be encouraged to see moderation in all things.

50
CONCERNING THE DESTRUCTION OF SOULS

59. The eighth image stands for the destruction of souls. It follows immoderation because when a person fights against God without any moderation, he brings about the destruction of his soul. He refuses to be with God and gnashes his teeth against him although he realizes that he is the mountain of salvation. He is full of ruins since the first angel built a ruin for himself and for all those who followed after him. He is like a tower with a slate roof on top of it. It has three windows in it. This means that he is great and unshakable in his firmness, just like the tower of destruction where pride, like its top, is secure, like its slate roof, and does not reach to God but only to the sadness of death. He looks out with his senses and intellect and knowledge, like the three windows, to see if he can lead souls to their destruction. With these three powers he denies true faith in the holy Trinity when he does not believe one God to be in three persons and three persons to be in one God. Under these three windows there are the two arms of a man sticking out and reaching above the slate roof. This means that with the prospect of destruction, he has no respect for God's strength, but only for the devil's strength by which man lifts himself up through the faithlessness of evil. Man stretches his evil-spoken words to reach above his security when he has no hope in God but only in empty vanity. These arms are covered with darkness, as if with sleeves. This means that the strength and perversity of destruction died in the obscurity and concealment of robbers when destruction secretly struck down the souls of those who followed him into the place where the works of perverse men are found to have no holiness and where they burn with the fire of bitterness. They do not have any hope for salvation. For destruction seeks nothing; it desires nothing other than to lead other souls to where it is, as it revealed in its speech earlier. But the salvation of souls refutes destruction and warns people not to imitate destruction which places no value on salvation. Destruction itself, however, is in destruction and holds no remedy of salvation in salvation. It fights against God since it wants to cling to the one who has no light but who dwells in darkness. Jeremiah, the prophet, inspired by the Holy Spirit, speaks about this.

51

JEREMIAH TO THE SAME THING

60. *How is it, Israel, that you are in the land of your foes, grown old in a foreign land, defiled with the dead, accounted with those destined for the nether world? You have forsaken the fountain of wisdom! Had you walked in the way of God, you would have dwelt in enduring peace (Baruch 3:10-13).* This means the following. Where did this evil come from since you are the results of the miracles of God and are spoken about as if you were in heaven with all the other luminaries where you ought to see God? Where is this evil from, you who seem to have your mind on earth, the dwelling place of your enemies? For evil desires, the enemies of your soul, spring up in your flesh. Your earth begins to play in fresh greenness and then enters into lust and thereupon rushes into the depth of the sea; these are the squalid, lukewarm and foulest of works in which your mind has grown old in an alien land where your sins are opposed to holiness. Indeed, you do not know God. In your sleep you have been made foul with deadly works that stink with unbelief to God and to all his holy ones. Wherefore also you are ravished along with those who dwell in the torments of hell who did not see the day of faith nor the sun of mercy and who have given up the moon of holiness with all its stars of holiness because they rejected the light of God's grace. You have given up the fountain of wisdom, clearly infinite life with God, which no one will ever be able to drain empty with his knowing or thinking or seeing. For if you had walked along the way commanded by God and followed in the footsteps of Christ, blessedness would shine in you and the honor of the Lord of the Sabbath would lead you to life. You would dwell with the full understanding of peace-giving charity so that God could make you manifest on earth in the presence of men and in heaven in the presence of his angels. And he could show that you were like the light of brightness in holy works; he could have brought you forth like the sweet sound of a lyre. But because you neglected all these things, you fall into ruin. O Israel, you who want to see God in holy works, do not imitate the fallen sons of Jacob who should have neglected the devil, but did not. But imitate all those works perfectly that God put before Adam in paradise, which he also embellished in Adam later, which he made manifest in the circumcision of Abraham in the revelation of the true Trinity, which he showed to Moses in a red flame, and which he, destroying evil works, opened up in the sons of Israel. And climb the ladder of the virtues that Jacob showed, imitating Christ, the Son of God, bringing forth the brightest virtues. Christ weighs out mercy for all

those who seek him, just as he demonstrated when he was in the world according to his will. For he rested like a unicorn on the bosom of the Virgin and then afterwards he ascended like a capricorn the mountain of the virtues and miracles. He thereby overcame the devil completely and lessened the power of the devil.

52
CONCERNING THE LION, THE FORM OF THE ZEAL OF GOD

61. There is a lion standing by the man whom I mentioned earlier. This lion has turned against these sins. This means that the Savior's humanity is in the Divinity's majesty. The Savior, existing as both God and man, pits the strongest strength of his zeal against these sins of the devil. The lion cries aloud, roaring into the wind, because he can destroy these sins with the fire of the Holy Spirit and can cause them to cease to exist since they tried to fight against him. For he cried aloud with the inspiration of the Holy Spirit and steeped his disciples with the Holy Spirit as he commanded them to preach and to give testimony to the new sanctification so that they might release perished souls from the ancient serpent and his evil temptations when the devil tries to rebel against the truth and the salvation of men. The devil tries to resist Christ, the Son of God, with various devices among his chosen. Christ, nevertheless like a very strong lion, leads all the devil's attempts and efforts toward sin to nothing and destroys the devil completely.

53
THE ZEAL OF GOD AFFLICTS MEN WHO NEGLECT HIS WILL

62. Similarly, with his divine power Christ tames and throws down and grinds away the devil and the sins that are with him. Many times with his zeal he uses physical calamities to chastise and scatter the people who oppose him and do not heed his blessed and just warnings. For just as a lion devours other animals with its strength, so also the strength and zeal of God grind away the entrails of the devil. This same zeal crushed the devil's first lie completely with which the devil had built up his reason for his existence. This zeal kills enemies who say that they cannot be anything else by nature and who continuously look to whatever pleases them. Such enemies surround themselves with the sins of the devil, neglecting God's will and rejecting his will as if they did not ex-

ist. Therefore, they are scattered about and ground away with God's zeal, just as those have been dissipated whom Jeremiah the prophet also speaks about.

54

JEREMIAH TO THE SAME THINGS

63. *The hands of compassionate women boiled their own children, to serve them as mourner's food in the downfall of the daughter of my people. The Lord has spent his anger, poured out his blazing wrath; he has kindled a fire in Zion that has consumed her foundations (Lamentations 4:10-11).* This means that women are fragile works who do not have the strong marrow of men; they bend the sadness of their hearts to those works that have not been cooked in the fire of the Holy Spirit, for they boiled their own children according to their own will. Therefore, they burn with carnal desire and their souls will perish when they draw the weaknesses of their boiling flesh to each and every sin. And so their desires, clearly for the same men, are their food when they do whatever they want. They do this with grief and destroy their souls that ought to be counted among the people of God in holy works. Lacking all the good virtues and the holiness of honesty, they say: "What is this that we never see? We hear many things that we cannot understand and that we do not know to be true." When they have said these things with great stubbornness, the joy of life with all its holiness leaves them and all the virtues that should have embellished them are destroyed. The Lord of all then brings his vengeance upon them when he arouses his zeal against them. He does not spare them, but pours out his scourges upon them like a flood. He punishes their evils and scorns them by leading them nowhere. And so he raises his zeal against them by which they should have looked upon God but did not. They puff themselves up with pride when they think they can climb a mountain so high that no one can conquer them. But the Lord digs up the foundation of their pride and destroys it completely. He pulls it out by the root so that it cannot spring up again, demonstrating that they can find no safety in either the beginning or the end of their pride. Those who follow pride on its journey will perish, for they do not have faith in God who created them and who freed them from the devil.

55

MEN WHO PUT THEIR NEAREST ONES IN ANXIOUSNESS, GOD PLACES IN MISERY

64. God also sends his revenge to certain men by means of hidden judgment so that those who have sinned bodily may be punished bodily. Why this should be done, he alone knows since he does not make all his secrets manifest. When certain men cause those nearest them to be anxious by taking away their substance and thereby forcing them into their own service, God often comes forth with his vengeance to strike such people down so that both they and their sons are not happy while they are alive and so that they eat the food of contrition and not the food of exaltation. Because they have been wicked in their perversity, God also completes his judgment of them with righteous examination and righteous judgment. He also consumes their confidence with fire and overturns their strength, scattering about and destroying those fortifications that they trust more than God. Doing all things justly, God judges all things according to their works, for God knows all things, but his knowledge does not destroy anything; otherwise the judge would not be just. But the devil tries to destroy what he sees and knows, in so far as he is able to. God, however, always is and always was and therefore knew all the things that had been hidden. The devil, who had a beginning, saw all the things that had been done, but was not able to contemplate people's hearts inwardly. God understands all things because he does all things, and he did what was pleasing to himself.

56

GOD CREATED NO MAN IN WHOM THERE WILL NOT HAVE BEEN KNOWLEDGE OF GOOD AND EVIL

65. Has there been any person in the world who did not have knowledge of good and evil? No. From the knowledge of good and evil man has love and fear of God, just as he uses a plow to make his land bring forth fruit and just as he avoids and pulls out useless plants so that he is not disgusted with his crop. It is a great testimony and a great thing that heaven and earth are not able to overthrow this; heaven and earth do not do anything other than that which they were assigned. However, he who has the desire of life, let him grasp these words and let him store them in the innermost cubicle of his heart.

66. I saw some other evil spirits in this crowd that I mentioned earlier. They cried aloud with a great clamor, saying: "Why is Lucifer a servant of subjection when he might have been a Lord?" They represent gluttony in men and they encourage them to the gluttony of their belly.

57

CONCERNING THE PUNISHMENT OF GLUTTONY

67. I saw a huge fire that burned fiercely and had a blackness inside itself that burned even more intensely. The souls of those who had chosen the gluttony of the belly while they were alive were being punished in this fire and its blackness. In addition, certain ones of the spirits mentioned earlier shook out various sparks from the fire to injure these souls, saying: "Alas! They chose their bodies more than their souls." They felt the burning of this fire because of their great appetite for food and drink while they had been alive. They suffered from this blackness because of the many evils they had caused with their gluttony. They suffered the sparks of this fire and the sight of these spirits because they had done all these things with overflowing vanity. I saw and knew these things through the living Spirit.

58

CONCERNING THE PUNISHMENT OF GLUTTONY

68. I again heard the voice from the living light say to me: *These things that you see are true. If people who have loved the gluttony of the belly want to escape these infestations of devils and these miserable punishments, let them abstain from food and drink close to the quality and excess of their thoughtlessness and close to the limit set by their teacher.*

59

WHOSE GOD IS GLUTTONY

69. Those who chose the gluttony of the belly often cry aloud against God and strive to provoke him to anger, saying: "Why did God create us for glory and then take it away from us, as if we ought not to have it? Can't we do what brings us pleasure?" It can be said that their belly is their God, for they direct their every thought and concern and desire to filling their belly. Since they act according to their own will, they devote all their efforts to filling their belly.

60
THE WORDS OF MOSES

70. It has been written about this: *Where are their gods whom they relied on as their "rock"? Let those who ate the fat of your sacrifices and drank the wine of your libations rise up now and help you! Let them be your protection! (Deuteronomy 32:37-38)*. Where is the glory the gluttonous had hoped for when they gorged themselves to overflowing at various feasts, which pleased them very much? Their glory is nothing more than the torments and unhappiness of destroyed men who were seduced and led into confusion. Their trust is the food that they consumed immoderately, through which they have the trust of deception. As they persisted eating this unsuitable food, they advised others to do the same, because as fire rises up when it is blown by bellows, so also evil things rise up from the gluttony of the belly. What trust or what victory should come to those who kill and destroy things completely? The devil knows that man cannot live without food and that they should obey the precepts of God. Therefore, he first advises him that the precepts of God regarding food and drink can be broken so that he can deceive him more easily later; whatever the devil thinks is a good idea, he advises man to do. But the wicked spirits have been pruned off and cast into the infernal torments as a result of their wantonness. Nor does anything make them more happy other than the deception of man while man can still do good and evil. After such people are dead, they will not be happy, but will suffer from the afflictions of their punishments. Through idols the wicked spirits wanted men to offer victims and fatten calves and wine at unsuitable feasts because what God said in the Old Testament should be consumed, they give this for feasts. God proclaims that men should abstain from food and from sin, but the devil strongly speaks against this, for abstaining from food does not bring luxury whereas gluttony does. Therefore, let whoever wants to serve God flee gluttony and hold his belly back from gluttony. These things, however, have been spoken concerning the atonement for the cleansing and saving of souls, and they are faithful things. A faithful person pays attention to these things and remembers them well.

71. I heard other spirits in the crowd I mentioned earlier crying aloud: "What is this that God does? And what about the honor Lucifer desired?" They made people bitter and prevailed upon them to be unpleasant both to the precepts of God and to other people.

61

CONCERNING THE PUNISHMENTS OF THOSE WHO HAVE SINNED IN BITTERNESS

72. I saw a very large fire that was black and red and white. It contained many fiery vipers of horror which sent forth a lot of fire from their mouths. The souls of those who had been slaves to the sin of bitterness while they had been alive were punished in this fire and were tormented by these vipers. They suffered from the black flame as a result of the unfaithfulness they had hidden within themselves. They were punished by the white flame on account of the deceit and ridicule they had held for things. They were afflicted by these vipers because they had lifted up the contrariness of bitterness against divine judgment and against human affection in their words and deeds. I saw and understood these things and again heard the voice from the living light say: *These things that you see are true.*

62

CONCERNING THE PUNISHMENTS OF THE SAME ONES

73. If those who fight against God with bitterness do not want to be afflicted by the spirits and punishments mentioned above, let them be servants to those who fast in proportion to their own excesses and according to the order of the judge judging them. Let them do this because they despised God with great bitterness.

63

CONCERNING THE SIN OF BITTERNESS

74. Bitterness rejects God; it does not choose his piety; it does not seek his mercy; it does not love his judgments. But it gnashes its teeth and speaks evil words against the things of God, and it chooses security for itself in all things. It does not know what it should do because it is not guided by the fear or love of God. It does whatever it wishes, but whatever it does not wish, it gnaws away with its wickedness because a bitter and unpleasant person flees from wisdom, leaves blessedness behind, and flees from charity whenever he hates his work and replaces truth with lies. This same person is also involved with the bitterness that sells life to the works of death, that drinks the draught of death, and that

searches for trouble. He does this in the way he snatches each and every thing and in the way he divided and dispenses it according to his own will. Bitterness also kills this man, although it promised to be his defense. Therefore, bitterness does not plant anything that can be reaped in faith, nor does it gather into its barns what God has given to his sons. By doing only worthless labor, it groans horribly. It does not desire any joy out of life, but only embraces sorrowful work that does not embrace God. These things, however, have been spoken concerning the atonement for the cleansing and saving of souls, and they are faithful things. A faithful person pays attention to these things and remembers them well.

75. I saw some other spirits in the crowd. They cried aloud saying: "Lucifer has the potential for greater and more miracles than are in God. We know who Lucifer is; we do not, however, long for the other God." These people are urged on to impiety, which if they choose it, will be to their detriment.

64

CONCERNING THE PUNISHMENT OF THE IMPIOUS ONES

76. I saw a great fire that, overflowing with fiery and seething lead mixed with sulphur, had every type of fiery viper in it. The souls of those who had imitated impiety while they had been in their bodies were afflicted with these punishments. They burned in this fire because of the wickedness of their impiety. They suffered from the seething lead as a result of the burdensome weight of their impiety, and they were twisted with the horror of these vipers on account of the indignity with which they had despised others when they did not want to understand them. I saw and understood these things through the living Spirit. And from the living light I again heard a voice say to me: *These things are true.*

65

CONCERNING THE PUNISHMENT OF THE IMPIOUS ONES

77. If the people who have included impiety in their works are eager to escape from the torments of the dreadful spirits, let them subdue their bodies with fasting and scourgings according to the way shown them by righteous ones since they carried out their many works impiously.

66
CONCERNING THE EVIL OF IMPIETY

78. For impiety does not want to fear God. It does not know the love of God or do anything with divine virtue. But with all its evil works it looks back to the North and it scatters all its works around with its knowledge of evil. In wickedness it winks its eye as it speaks evil words. The prophet David, inspired by my Spirit, has spoken about those who imitate this sin.

67
DAVID TO THE SAME THING

79. *Let their encampment become desolate; in their tents let there be no one to dwell (Psalm 69:26).* This can be understood in this way. In regard to the impious who do not gather good things together but rather scatter them, let their will, which they follow with determination, be destroyed so that it is scattered around completely since they do not want to have a master or anyone else higher than themselves; they do not even want anyone to be equal to them. Whatever they seize, they draw to themselves, and whatever they do not want, they trample underfoot so that they never sing with any spiritual joy. They join forces with other abuses so that they can mock charity, deny goodness and flee blessedness. Let no one dwell in their tents of evil customs because anyone who desires celestial tents should turn away from such evil customs. Blessedness is a stranger to the impious since they do not try to do any good with their eye of knowledge, but they just look back to the devil with their works and despise God. Therefore, God does not acknowledge the works they do or the foundations they build, but he instead hurls these things away as if they were dung. For they forsake the law of God in their thoughts and they do all things only according to their own particular will. As a result, the light of truth is necessarily taken away from them since they do not seek or want it; they walk in the darkness of death through their works. Therefore, they will be punished because they followed the fall of the devil when they forsook God. However, the ones who choose God will draw piety to themselves by which they will cling to God more fully. These things have been spoken concerning the atonement for the cleansing and saving of souls, and they are faithful things. A faithful person pays attention to these things and remembers them well.

80. I saw others in this crowd of evil spirits who cried aloud with a great clamor, saying: "We will see the seat of our Lord, who is Lucifer, above the stars. He will be higher than anything else because he has willed everything. Who can be like him?" These spirits send blasphemies to attack the throne of God and his honor. They are the eye of pride, and they encourage others to trample upon men with lies and blasphemies.

68
CONCERNING THE PUNISHMENTS OF LYING MEN

81. I saw a fire that burned in complete blackness. It contained dragons lying around blowing on this fire with their blasts. Near this fire there flowed a river of very cold water. These dragons, entering the fire now and then, stirred it up completely. Both the fire and the river had fiery air above them that touched them with its fire. The souls of those who had been false with perjury after they had made an oath were tormented in this fire and water; they were shuttled back and forth between the flames of the fire and the coldness of the river as the dragons dashed them about. The fiery air did not injure those who had been false without perjury after they had made an oath, but it seriously injured those who had been false with perjury under oath while they had been alive in their bodies. They suffered in the fire because they told many lies while they had been alive. There were tormented in the coldness of this water since they had sinned so zealously. They were attacked by these dragons because they had done these things so many times. They were severely burned by this fiery air since they had told so many lies under oath and with perjury. I saw and understood these things. And I heard the voice from the living light say to me: *These things that you see are true, and as you see them, so they are; and there are more things.*

69
CONCERNING THE REPENTANCE OF LYING MEN

82. If the men who sweat in falseness want to avoid these wicked spirits and their punishments, let them fast and scourge themselves and wear a hair shirt for a long time according to the judgment of their judge. Let those, however, who want to destroy their lies told under oath and with perjury chastise themselves very harshly with fasting and scourgings and with the roughness of hair shirts for a long time.

70

CONCERNING LYING

83. For falseness does not rejoice in the truth, but rather it exaggerates what does not exist and what cannot exist with exaltation and unjust delight. It does not place any value on the truth, but speaks strange things with lies that people are unaware of. It is anxious to do these things against God and his holy ones in whom God has done marvelous things. This sin is inhuman; when man sins as a result of his desires of the flesh, he is human, but when he lies, he is inhuman. For lies cover themselves with lies, just as a serpent hides in its hole. Therefore, liars turn back from holiness and from the joyful life found inside the gates of the daughter of Zion because they reject the teachings of the Holy Spirit when they follow the works of the devil. Through exaltation liars make themselves like the hills of the world. Thus liars rule the wise and wealthy while they live within time, but they will be counted as worth nothing in eternity. For God is in all things and above all things and he weighs all things as being just or unjust with equal judgment. He weighs out his rewards to each person in proportion to the measure and quality of his deeds. These things, however, have been spoken concerning the atonement for the cleansing and saving of souls, and they are faithful things. A faithful person pays attention to these things and remembers them well.

84. I saw some more spirits in the crowd I mentioned earlier. They cried out against the practice of God with loud voices, saying: "Who are you and where do you come from since you do not want anyone to be like you? We will wear you out for all time and will draw your brightness away from you in order to make our brightness much brighter than yours." These spirits bring strife to people and encourage them to be quarrelsome.

71

CONCERNING THE PUNISHMENTS OF STRIFE

85. I saw a very deep well that had black and fiery fog in it. A strong and fiery wind blew around it. There were snakes with horrible shapes in both this fog and wind. The souls of those who had done their work with strife while they had been in their bodies, having now left their bodies, were punished in these fires so they were blown by the wind into the well only to be lifted again out of the well back into the wind. They were also afflicted by the snakes. Those who had been persistent with

strife in their words but not in their works were punished by the afflictions outside the well and did not fall into the well. But the souls of those who had lived lives full of strife while they had been in their bodies were tormented by the black and fiery fog inside the well. They suffered from the horrible fire in the well because they had been strifeful in their horrible works. They burned in the fiery wind because they had shown impiety as they acted full of strife toward others. They fell into the well as a result of the confusion they caused others by their quarreling with them with evil actions. They were tormented in the well and then in the wind outside the well because they had returned to their impiety after they had insulted others. They suffered from the snakes in the fires since they had been so bold in causing strife. But those who had been strifeful with their words but not with their actions were not punished in the well, although they suffered some of the afflictions caused by strife. I saw and understood these things through the living light. And from this living light I again heard a voice say to me: *These things that you see are true.*

72
CONCERNING THE REPENTANCE OF THE STRIVING ONES

86. Therefore, let those who are anxious to cast away the evil spirits who encourage them to strife and to flee from the punishments of strife that they earned by their works chastise their flesh with fasting. Let them also abstain from fat foods and castigate themselves with scourging as well. But let those who caused strife with their words but not with their actions only abstain from food and drink.

73
CONCERNING THE EVIL OF STRIFE

87. Strife is a restless evil and does not want to be agreeable. It flees patience and does not endure any injury easily. It seeks out quarrelsome men and encourages them to quarrel; it does not allow them to speak peacefully since it is bold and resolute in its speech; it enters each one of them with strifeful works. Men who choose to quarrel imitate the devil who wanted to blacken the beauty of the good angels and to be more beautiful than they are. Therefore, God cast the devil and those who follow him into infinite confusion where they suffer everlasting reproaches, just as David, inspired by me, shows by saying:

74

DAVID TO THE SAME THING

88. *Let my accusers be clothed with disgrace and let them wear their shame like a mantle (Psalm 109:29).* This means the following. Let the wicked who gnaw away at heavenly gifts with biting detraction be clothed with perpetual grief, and let them wear garments of shame since their ideas were so empty; what they wanted to do, they were not able to accomplish. Their brightness was changed into blackness when what they wanted to do was destroyed. In addition, let them be covered with double confusion since they destroyed blessedness and put on unhappiness as well; they have been cast out from glory and have been punished as well. These spirits also encouraged men to tear everything established well and honestly to pieces, to provoke other people to quarrels, to injure their ancestors, and to speak to their ancestors with stubborn boldness, just as it has been written: *Who has appointed you ruler and judge over us (Exodus 2:14)?* This should be understood in the following way.

75

LIKEWISE IN GENESIS TO THE SAME THING

89. What authority or what power established you who are like us, for you rule us as if we are not men and you judge our works as if you are God? What virtue gave you the power to rule us and make us turn like a wheel? For you want to preside over us and say that you are our masters; you call us bent and slow. You order us not to try, but you place many things upon us that you refuse to carry. You also warn us to turn away from many things that you yourself do both secretly and openly. For strife of this kind casts out law and masters from itself; it judges according to a law that was not established righteously, but according to the will and power of the ones who made it. Let those who want to save their souls not walk with strife, but let them walk peacefully with their words and deeds; let them show good will as they work for justice. These things, however, have been spoken concerning the atonement for the cleansing and saving of souls, and they are faithful things. A faithful person pays attention to these things and remembers them well.

90. I saw other spirits in the crowd I mentioned earlier who cried aloud, saying: "We do not want any other God than the one who is Luci-

fer. For he will fight some time or other against the one who says that he is God." These spirits bring a lot of unhappiness to people, and because they think they were born unhappy, they encourage others to unhappiness.

76
CONCERNING THE PUNISHMENTS OF THE DESPAIRING ONES

91. I saw a wide and deep ditch that was full of sulfurous fire and various kinds of snakes. The souls of those were punished in it who had not trust in God fully while they had been alive, but who blamed all the adversities that happened to them on their own unhappy nature. They were in the ditch because they had not trust in God. The sulfurous fire burned them because they had sinned worthlessly in despair. And they were afflicted by these snakes since they thought the adversities that happened to them were the results of their own unhappy nature.

77
HOW MEN MAY BLOT OUT THE SAME SIN BY PUNISHING

92. I saw and understood these things. And I again heard a voice from the living light say to me: *These things that you see are true and as you see them, so they are. If men, however, want to overcome these spirits who bring them unhappiness and if they want to avoid the punishment for the despair of unhappiness that comes from within themselves, let them either seek a solitary life or subject themselves to obedience in the monasterial life.*

78
CONCERNING THE SIN OF THOSE WHO JUDGE THEMSELVES CREATED IN EVIL

93. When certain contrarieties come to some men, they do not trust in God and judge that they are evil and have been created in evil. They say: "God neither wants to nor is able to nourish us since we have been born so unhappy that we cannot be helped." But let those who say such things turn inward and place their hope in God's mercy. Let them sigh and cry aloud that they have sinned so that they can deserve to obtain God's grace. For the nature of man is good, but man turns to contrari-

eties when he allows his flesh to go unbridled, doing whatever pleases it. These things, however, have been spoken concerning the atonement for the cleansing and saving of souls, and they are faithful things. A faithful person pays attention to these things and remembers them well.

94. I then saw some more spirits among that crowd. They cried aloud against the good and just angels of God, saying: "If you weigh out glory and honor for your Lord, we should do the same for our lord!" These bring immoderation to men and urge them to be immoderate in all their actions.

79

CONCERNING THE PUNISHMENTS OF THE IMMODERATE

95. I saw a certain sea that was of wondrous length and breadth. It was all mixed up with sulphur and seethed with fierce fire. The souls of those were tormented in it who, while they had been alive, had been immoderate in words and deeds and in all the movements of their bodies and minds and who did not want to moderate any of these unsuitable things they did. They were immersed in the water of this sea because they had become dirty from their sins. They were afflicted by the sulphur because they had forgotten about God. They were punished in the fire because they had neglected the law of God. I saw and understood these things.

80

CONCERNING THE REPENTANCE OF THE IMMODERATE

96. From the living light I mentioned earlier, I again heard a voice say to me: *These things that you see are true. But if those who are immoderate in everything they do want to flee these wicked spirits who trample on them with this sin and if they want to flee its punishments, let them wear the yoke of obedience and let them abstain from fat foods.*

81
CONCERNING IMMODERATION

97. Immoderation does not dwell completely on earth or in heaven since everything about it is uncertain. It wants to be excessive everywhere and says: "I might have taken possession of these things if I had not examined each one of them." It does not want to be quiet; it rolls out in front as if it were a wheel that had been pushed. As dust is scattered by the wind, it is also dispersed and shows uncertainty to itself. Alas, it can be found in those who dwell on the earth which God made firm above the waters. Alas, it can also be found in those creatures that dwell in the sea with which God has surrounded the earth. The devil makes people be immoderate by leading them into the same fall that he fell. The devil is hostile to men since God made man to resist the devil and to earn heavenly rewards. These things, however, have been spoken concerning the atonement for the cleansing and saving of souls, and they are faithful things. A faithful person pays attention to these things and remembers them well.

98. I saw some other spirits in this crowd who cried aloud with great clamoring, saying: "Who is God? And who are we?" They have contempt for God, as if he were not God. They encourage people not to trust in God, but to reject him in every way. These evil spirits thus lead people to their destruction.

82
CONCERNING THE PUNISHMENTS OF THOSE WHO DO NOT TRUST IN GOD

99. For the punishment of this sin, I saw the pit of hell which had been prepared for the devil. For those who do not trust in God are considered worthy of the punishments of hell. I saw and understood these things through the living Spirit and heard the voice from the living light say to me: *These things that you see are true. And as you see these things, so they are.*

83

CONCERNING THE PUNISHMENTS OF THE SAME ONES

100. If people want to chase away the evil spirits who encourage them to do works that lead to their destruction and if they want to turn back from their destruction, let them trust in God. Let them follow God's laws justly and holily with as good a will as they are able. Let them be watchful with fasting and alms-giving so that they can snatch themselves away from the devil who leads them to their destruction. For whoever does not trust in God does not know what their soul is. Nor does he seek to understand or see God in the miracles God has performed in his creatures. For God, who is of such great height that man cannot look upon him while he is alive, shines forth to men in the great brightness of his own works. He gives people all the things they need.

84

IT IS PROPER FOR THE SECRETS OF GOD TO EXIST

101. Who can do this, unless God? What can a servant bring to his master if he knows about everything his master has hidden? Or what can a maid-servant bring to her lady if she knows all her secrets? If this were allowed, then the servants would be able to dominate their masters.

85

MAN MAY KNOW GOD IN THE PURITY OF FAITH AND HE MAY REJECT THE ILLUSIONS OF THE DEVIL

102. When man does not know himself and the creatures he sees, how can he bring himself to God whom he does not see? But let him know, see, and speak without any despair about God, with the purity of faith since he does not know who God is and that God is able to nourish him. He does not know who God is since he has been submerged in such evil things that he had no joy or life. For the tumult of the devil shows God to men, not as he is, but like a statue. Because of his wickedness man tries to deny the glory of the great blessedness God wants him to have. Let the man who wants to be saved not do this, but let him trust in God and let him cast away the illusions of the devil. Let him wash away his sins as much as he is able through true repentance. After his soul has

left his body, let it be purged gently and let it be quickly snatched away from the punishments it deserves. These things, however, have been spoken concerning the atonement for the cleansing and saving of souls, and they are faithful things. A faithful person pays attention to these things and remembers them well.

THE SECOND PART ENDS

THE HEADINGS OF THE THIRD PART BEGIN CONCERNING THE MAN LOOKING TO THE NORTH AND TO THE EAST

1. The Complaint of the Elements

2. The Response of God to the Elements

3. The Words of Pride

4. The Response of Humility

5. The Words of Envy

6. The Response of Charity

7. The Words of Empty Glory

8. The Response of Fear of the Lord

9. The Words of Disobedience

10. The Response of Obedience

11. The Words of Unfaithfulness

12. The Response of Faith

13. The Words of Despair

14. The Response of Hope

15. The Words of Luxury

16. The Response of Chastity

17. The Words of Zeal of God

18. The Fact That Although the Devil May Not Delay that He Ensnare Man with Faults, He Will Not, Nevertheless, Be Able to Take Away the Glory of God

19. The Fact That God Shows Man that He May Not Fall into the Confusion of Sins

THE HEADINGS OF THE THIRD PART UNFOLD

THE THIRD PART BEGINS

CONCERNING THE MAN LOOKING TO THE NORTH AND TO THE EAST

1. And I saw that the man whom I mentioned earlier turned to the North so that he looked both to the North and to the East. The winds, air and greenness of the earth, which are under the firmament of heaven, covered this man from his thighs to this knees, as if they were a garment. And the fire and light of the air decorated his garment. But the power of the elements worked around the middle of his hip bones and then went back again into this same middle, just like a man who breathes out and then in again.

1

THE COMPLAINT OF THE ELEMENTS

2. I heard a loud voice speaking from the elements of the earth saying to this man: "Hurry. We cannot finish our journey since we have been pushed aside by our master, for men subvert us with their crooked ways, just as a mill stone does. Therefore, we stink with pestilence and hunger after all justice."

2

THE RESPONSE OF GOD

3. But this man answers: "I will purge you with my branches and will torment men again and again right up to the time when they will return to me. At that time, I will prepare many hearts according to my own heart. As many times as you were defiled, that many times I will cleanse you with the torments of those defiled. Who can do less than I do? The winds stink after blowing through the branches and the air vomits forth dirt since men do not open their mouth to righteousness. The greenness also leaves because of the wicked superstitions of the perverse tumults who do everything according to their own desires. They say: 'Who is that Lord whom we never see?' I answer them, saying: Do you not see me through the day and the night? Do you not see me with the sowers and when the seed is bathed with the rain so that it grows? Every creature clearly knows its creator and reaches back to him. Man, however, is a rebel and divides his creator among many creatures. But who made the scrolls with wisdom on them? Seek in those scrolls who created you. As long as a creature has fulfilled your needs out of duty, you cannot have complete joy. However, after creation has dried up, the chosen will see the highest joy in the life of all joys." But in the fog which I mentioned earlier, there were various other faults, seven of whose images I saw in the following way.

4. The first image had, as it were, a woman's face. Her eyes were fire, her nose was sprinkled with dirt, and her mouth was closed. She did not have, however, any arms and hands, but instead on each shoulder she had a wing like the wing of a bat so that the right wing reached to the East and the left to the West. This image had a chest like a man; its shins and feet were formed like the legs and feet of a locust; it did not have a stomach or a back. I saw that its head and the rest of its body were not covered with hair or a garment, unless it was hidden in the

darkness I mentioned earlier. But a very fine film, like a golden circle, stretched from the point of its chin to the top of each side of its jaw.

3
THE WORDS OF PRIDE

5. This image spoke: "I cry aloud from the mountains. Who can be like me? I spread my mantle over the hills and valleys, and I do not want anyone to fight against me. I know that no one is like me."

4
THE RESPONSE OF HUMILITY

6. I heard a voice from the storm cloud which extended from the South to the West respond to this image, saying: "I am a pillar of cloud. Will I suffer any pain if someone strikes me with horrible injuries, when the Creator descended from heaven in order to draw humans back to himself? I dwell on high with the Creator and I descended upon earth with him, and so I dwell to the very ends of the earth. Therefore, I cannot speak passing words falsely. Of course, in order that I may even say this, I am this, but I may not be that. Because I say this, I am not the sun that lights up the darkness, for I pass through the darkness with God. No storm can move me either since I am full of goodness with God." However, I saw a second image who had a monstrous form. Its head and shoulders were somewhat like a man, except that its hands were like a bear's paws. Its chest, stomach and back were beyond being human since they were so gross. However, from its loins downwards it was similar to a man, except that it had wooden feet. Its head was fiery and it shot out flames from its mouth. It did not have on any garment, but it was completely hidden in the darkness I mentioned earlier. Its right shoulder leaned upon this darkness.

5
THE WORDS OF ENVY

7. This image answered: "I am the shepherd and guardian of excess, and I cast out all greenness from men whenever I want to. I also strike down appropriate tongues. I also bite them, as skillfully as serpents that are as plentiful as the sand of the sea. They cannot resist me since I am called Gehenna. And so I draw many to myself and pollute all things that God does. If I cannot have the things that are bright, I value them as

nothing. If those who call me night were to sprinkle water on me, I would quickly dry myself. In addition, I aim my words like hidden arrows and wound the heart of those who call themselves righteous. For my strengths are like the North. All the things that are mine, however, I give with hatred because hatred was born from me and is smaller than me."

6

THE RESPONSE OF CHARITY

8. Again from the storm cloud I heard this response given to this image: "O most filthy filth, you are like a snake that attacks itself, for you cannot sustain anything that is stable and honorable. You, however, are the shadow that is against God and that attacks people through unfaithfulness. You rightly call yourself Gehenna since it holds out excess against all just moderation and tears to pieces everything that springs from wisdom. Neither is Gehenna strong against anything bright. I, however, am the air, I who nourish all greenness and bring flowers to mature fruit. For I have been taught by the inspiration of the Spirit of God so that I pour out the clearest of streams. Of course, I bring forth tears from a good sigh as I also bring forth a good aroma from tears through most holy works. I am also the rain that rises from the dew through which the grass rejoices with rich life. You, however, the most wicked and worst poison, devour these things with your punishments, but you cannot trample all these things under your feet. For the more you rage, the more they grow. Whereas you are mortal, these strengths live on and through God's power they appear like flowers on a vine. You, however, are the most abominable and darkest abomination and the hissing sound of the devil. You do not even want to be any other way and with pride in your mind you say: 'I draw more people to me than there are grains of sand by the sea.' But you will fail, for I make the power of good works equal throughout the day and night. I spread my mantle upon the day and night; I do a lot of good works during the day and I anoint the sorrows of the night. Thus no one can accuse me either way. I am the most prized of friends on God's throne; God hides no counsel from me. I have a royal dwelling place and all the things that are from God are mine. Where the Son of God wipes away men's sins with his tunic, there I also bind men's wounds with the sweetest of linen. You, however, blush because what is the better part is not for you."

9. The third image was in the shape of a man, except that its hands were covered with hair and its shins and feet were like those of a crane.

On its head, however, it wore a hat made from the top of an onion. It was clothed with a black garment. In its right hand it held a small green branch; in its left it truly held certain green flowers that it gazed at with great care. It said:

7

THE WORDS OF EMPTY GLORY

10. "I search for all causes carefully and I am a witness for myself because I understand such things in my righteousness. How then could it be proper that I desert the honesty of what I see and know? For I am confident in my ability to fly through villages and streets just like the birds who live in the forest and sing whatever they wish. I want to learn the songs of the birds and to sound like them. I want to give human sense to the sounds of the birds and I want to make the ways of various other animals be strong with the beauty of maidens. For I give out all my things in such a way that all who see me rejoice in these things and that all who hear me give honor to me in these things; also that all may marvel at my righteousness. For I am like a lyre with wings, a guardian with beasts, and a wise one with men. I also gather all kinds of rich things with praiseworthy joyousness to myself. When I have done all these things, who can be like me? If I do not seek, I will not come upon anything; if I do not search, nothing will be given to me because I will not have prosperity unless I acquire it through my own wisdom and righteousness. I do not place any value on anything that is burdensome and heavy to someone else because I am wise and righteous. But I do want to have my glory. Why should any of this be troublesome to God when I was created to be this way?"

8

THE RESPONSE OF FEAR OF THE LORD

11. Again from the storm cloud I heard a voice give an answer to this image: "Although you do not fear anything but grab each and every thing greedily, you are the worst emptiness of the worst idol. What can man do without the grace of God? Nothing. For when a man turns the wheel of his knowledge toward vanity, God attacks him; when, however, he lights himself up to the good, God helps him. You, however, plot all the things you do, but when you begin to do them, your head is fastened down backwards and your feet are lifted upwards into the air by the judgment of God. You also blush at the water of baptism and do not seek the medicine of God, but you wash yourself with all the evils of

fleeting vanity and do not desire to have anything that is alive. I, however, have the honor of God because I see each and every sin just as it is. I have the honor of God when I look at an office and accept that office, but do not weigh how much power it might have. I breathe in the love of God, I fear his judgment, and I rejoice in his reward. How do I deserve to share in the highest of joys? Of course, by fleeing the foulness of sin, by giving up the pomp of the world, by being careful that the desires of the flesh not burn in me, and by being careful that I do not sin freely. For I will not use creatures according to the desires of sin, but I am full of zeal to be fed by them. Therefore, God will give me my food from the tree of life, which shows that God will never be without good work in man although the devil infects man with many things that are objectionable to God. For God made man good and built his foundations good, which are holy works, so that man could be housed in the tabernacle of God. Let the person who wants to dwell in the house of God think and act accordingly. You, however, o most wicked pest, have no honor of honor."

12. I saw a fourth image. It had the head of a serpent, a furry chest like that of a caterpillar, and shins and feet like those of a viper. Its back, however, and tail and all the rest of its body were like a crab. It moved headlong here and there as if it were being blown by the wind. It was so agitated that it shook all the darkness which I mentioned earlier. It also turned toward the North and poured fire out its mouth.

9
THE WORDS OF DISOBEDIENCE

13. This image said: "Why do you think about the commands of others? When we do this, we neither see nor know who we are. We pay attention to the philosophy of the law and to others who are wiser than we are. Can we, therefore, not do what we know? But we can act only lowly when many masters give us commands according to their will and their wrongdoing. Can we not do what pleases us? What is this? Even if I can see trees full of leaves and can understand the songs of the birds, but masters give me all their commands, I cannot ever know what I might be able to do. What I, however, decide to do for myself, I know how honest and useful it is and I know whose salvation it is. It is far better for me to do what I know than what I do not know, because what I do not know is sometimes more new than useful. Therefore, I will do what I see and touch and understand with my own senses. I will also sort out what will be my salvation among creatures and what will be my en-

emy since God made things obey me and be subject to my orders. Why would God have made these things subject to me if I were to have no power over them? Therefore, I will think about what pleases me in them."

10

THE RESPONSE OF OBEDIENCE

14. From the storm cloud I heard a voice responding to this image: "I who obey God have a certain bondage. But to whom is it and of what type is it? At the time when God created all things with his word, when he said: 'Let it be done, and it was done,' I was an eye and was watching God's plan as all things were created thus. However, when the first angel came to life, he thereupon opposed God. I then said that the works of that one did not have life since he wanted to be something he was not. He also tried to hurt and to oppress me, but he was not very strong. For I existed like the sun, moon, stars, and the foundations of the waters; I am the root of all of God's works, just as the soul is to the body. Just as a man's will accomplishes what he desires, so also I do God's will by doing all the things that he commands. I consulted with God a long time ago and he ordered all the things he wanted to do through me. I sound like a lyre at the command of his word because I obey all his commands. I touch nothing, I wish for nothing, I desire nothing unless it is in God because I came from God, I do things through him, and I do not want to have any other God. You, however, o transgressor of the command of the Creator, in your presumptuousness you say that you are God and, therefore, do not search for the true God. Whatever you wish, you do. Where, therefore, are the heaven and earth you created? Where is the beauty of the mountains and fields you created? You have made nothing but you still deny what God did make. Why? When you spoke those words about yourself and when you decide all things only according to what pleases you, you do not want God who was before time began and who will be after the change to the newest day. Therefore, o worst one, you are like dried leaves and like scales from a fish because you have cast away the good things. Your name is with nothing useful but is with death."

15. The fifth image had the form of a man, with the exception of its head. It was surrounded with the darkness I mentioned earlier from its knees down to the soles of its feet. On its head no other form appeared except that it was completely filled with very black eyes, among which there was one eye, as it were, on its front that burned sometimes like a

burning fire. It had, however, placed its right hand on its chest, it held a staff in its left hand, and it wore a black coverlet around itself.

11
THE WORDS OF UNFAITHFULNESS

16. This image said: "I do not know any other life than the one that I see and touch and stroke gently. What kind of reward will a doubtful life give me? Regarding this, I say: 'This is, or it is not.' And so by seeking and asking, by seeing and hearing, and by knowing, I come to nothing. If I will have occasionally seen anything through a revelation brought to me by some other creature, what will I have? I, however, walk nowhere nor wish for anything, unless I know it well. For when I fly upon the wings of the wind, I am thrown down to the earth. Or when I ask the sun and moon what I ought to do, they respond very little to me. Or when I hear two sounds, I do not know which one is useful to me or praises me. For I do not know the signs. What I see, I know. I also hear many rumors and sermons and teachings, which I do not know. Therefore, I will do whatever I know to be the most useful to me."

12
THE RESPONSE OF FAITH

17. From the storm cloud I again heard a voice giving this image an answer: "O most wicked one, you are the deceit of the devil who denies all just things in his heart. You also signify the very heart of the devil for the propositions of your thinking reach back to the devil who stands on your right side. Whence also your eyes are so hidden that you cannot see the way of salvation, which rises up to heaven and which restrains you, you who are the night, just as the right falls upon the left. The right oppresses you. This oppression should lead to a glorious ascension because evil knowledge is called the maidservant of good knowledge. For evil knowledge does not want to serve with the maidservant, just as the mistress of a household does not want to do servile work with her maidservant; therefore, she holds a name of glory, that of mistress of the household. You are condemned when you judge things by yourself, since you flee from the things that are bright in faith. Your rationalizations always hurl sin upon the men whom you deceive, because you are not able to walk along the ways of the commands of God. I, however, praise God faithfully with the angels when I desire all the things that are of God and when with the Cherubim I write out his judgments that the Cherubim bring forth just as they are in God. But I also judge all things

through the prophets, the wise ones and the scribes. In addition, all the kingdoms of the earth shine forth in me through God's justice. I am a mirror of God because I reflect all the precepts of God."

18. I truly saw the sixth image in the form of a woman whose head was covered with a dark covering in the manner of a woman and the rest of whose body was clothed with a dark garment. Before her face there appeared, as it were, a mountain of burning sulphur. To her right and left side, next to the mountain of sulphur, as it were, were those who sank down into the darkness I mentioned earlier; these made a loud crashing noise in this darkness. But also to her right, clearly next to her back, there was the loud sound of thunder. This image was frightened by all these things and with sighing and shaking, she pressed her arms and hands to her breast and covered herself over completely with the darkness. She said:

13
THE WORDS OF DESPAIR

19. "I have been greatly frightened! Who can console me? Who can help me and rescue me from these calamities that oppress me? The fire of Gehenna surrounds me and the zeal of the Lord cast me down into the inferno. What else is left for me, unless death? I do not rejoice in any good things nor find any consolation in sins; I do not find any good in other creatures."

14
THE RESPONSE OF HOPE

20. From the storm cloud I again heard a voice responding to this image: "O tinder dry wood of the devil, you are the tinder dry wood of sin. You do not know or think about how many good things there are in God. If you look for good things in those who are not with God, no one will help you find them, and if you search for evil things in those who are not with God, no one will judge you. For God created heaven and earth and all things as useful and he put boundaries around hell with his own commands. All good rewards are given by him and all judgments of evil things come from him. Why then do you expose yourself to the destruction where you may not be judged? For evil spirits do not want God nor do they trust him. All creatures rush to follow the precepts of God, but the devil denied them and was then cast into hell; he can do nothing unless by the power of Gehenna. Therefore, no one who wants

to accomplish good can propose destruction for himself since God is the highest good and always rewards the good works people do. I sit on the throne of God with good desire and I embrace all his works in faith; by doing good works, I draw all the earth to myself. You, o mortal and infernal wicked one, do not do these things since you have no trust in the good works of God. What will this bring you? You bring upon yourself many punishments that you do not see, and as a result you destroy your life with childish foolishness."

21. The seventh image had, as it were, the form of a woman who was lying on her right side. Bending her legs, she had drawn them up to herself, just as a man who lies leisurely on his bed. Her hair, however, was like the flames of fire and her eyes were white, just as she had been created. She had white coverings on her feet that were so slippery that she could not walk or stand on them. From her mouth she gave forth a certain panting and a certain poisonous froth. At her right breast she was nursing, as it were, a young dog; at her left breast she was nursing a serpent. She plucked some flowers from the trees and some herbs with her hands and smelled them with her nose. She wore no garments, but was all fiery and because of her burning, she dried out everything lying next to her, just like an open window.

15
THE WORDS OF LUXURY

22. And she said: " I will surround God's image with filth, which is a very troubling thing to God; I can thereby destroy all things. For I am a glorious and high one and I draw all things to myself, as allowed by the nature I was born with. Why should I restrain myself and why should I tear myself away from the favors of a luxurious life and a saving mind? If I accomplish only a small part of what I want to do, is this blameworthy? If, however, I do not do what my flesh demands, I will be angry, sad, deceitful, tormenting, and entangled with unrest. Heaven, therefore, has its own justice and earth seeks its own favors. If the nature of the flesh were troublesome to God, he would do what it cannot accomplish."

16
THE RESPONSE OF CHASTITY

23. I again heard a voice from the storm cloud, as it were, from the diadem of the king, giving a response to this image: "I am not indiffer-

ent, as you are, o filthy one, you who always play with wantonness, for I
do not lie on the bed on which you lie, you who bring disgrace to yourself. I also do not send out poisonous words from my mouth that teach
slippery baseness. Instead, I draw a drink of the sweetest water from the
well of blessing since all my works have the coolness of God. For I sit in
the sun and I look at the king of kings when I perform all my good
works freely. I do not want the tail of the scorpion that wounds you with
uncleanness. I have the joy of honesty and modesty in a pleasant life, for
the pleasant life that I have does not restrain me with the blasphemy of
baseness nor does it wound me with unclean lewdness. You, however, o
most filthy one, are the gluttony of the belly of a serpent, you who
sprang from the ears of Adam and Eve who listened to the serpent and
then let obedience vanish. But I have sprung from the highest Word of
the Father. Therefore, heaven and earth will confuse you when they
have seen you naked in confusion."

24. To the right side of the man I mentioned earlier, I also saw standing an image with the form of a human. It had a fiery face and it was
clothed with a doubly warm garment.

17
THE WORDS OF THE ZEAL OF GOD

25. This image cried out against the faults mentioned above, saying:
"O entrails of the devil and the outpouring of the devil's wickedness that
brought death to the human race, you will be confounded by the blood
of Christ and you will perish in the Alpha and the Omega since you are
the very worst death."

18
THE DEVIL IS NOT ABLE TO TAKE AWAY THE
GLORY OF GOD

26. I again heard a voice from heaven saying to me: *The Creator
who made the world made it firm with the elements and decorated it
with many embellishments when he filled it up with the various creatures for the service of man. But the envious devil did not wait very
long to ensnare man with his most wicked faults in order to dishonor
man. Nevertheless, the devil will not be able to carry the glory of God
away, as it is being shown to you in this vision.*

19

GOD SHOWS MAN THAT HE MAY NOT FALL INTO THE CONFUSION OF SIN

27. For the fact that you see that the man whom I mentioned earlier turns to the North so that he looks both to the North and to the East, this is because God shows man how not to fall into the confusion of the blindness of sin, how to avoid such confusion with strength, and how to prepare himself for the honor of true light since man has both the knowledge of good and evil. For man is able to know what part of the wheel of knowledge declines.

20

THE ELEMENTS SHOW THAT MAN MAY GIVE GLORY TO GOD

28. The winds, air and greenness of the earth, which are under the firmament of heaven, cover this man from his thighs to his knees, as if they are a garment. This is because the flight and breadth of the winds and the sweet moisture of the air and the keen greenness of the trees and herbs, which are contained in the highest things where God works in producing and maintaining these things, all of these exhibit glory when they are fully obedient to God as he produces and maintains them. For God is glorified through the mystery of his creatures, just as a man is honored for his work on a garment. And the fire and light of the air decorate his garment since fire, warming various creatures with its heat, and the light of sweetness, illuminating them, honor God since they adorn him in his power where he is known through the elements and is called omnipotent through them. Just as a man is called lord and king because of the glitter of his garments and because of the diadem on his head, so also God is glorified through the just works of the soul, because as there are the strengths of creatures, so also are there the strengths of the soul. For the beginning of just desires fly into the soul, as it were, the winds; and the taste of good will plays in the soul, as it were, the air; and the perfection of perfect works is green to help the soul, as it were, the greenness of the earth. This is all according to the wisdom of the highest mysteries, as it were, under the firmament of heaven, since wisdom begins to work good things in the soul of a just person and it also finishes these works in the soul. And in these elements, God is, as it were, from his thighs to his knees. When all these things come from

him, they are sustained and brought to perfection by him. Wherefore all these things that come from the thighs of procreation, when good works are procreated in man by God, right up to the knees of strength, when they are strengthened by God, are like a garment of glorification. It is just that man gives the glory of his actions, not to himself, but to God. In addition, the fire of holy ascension by which the faithful soul is enkindled so that it does not become dry and cease doing holy works, and the light of truth where a good reputation is seen and heard in men, are like decorations to this garment, of course, the glory of God. This is because these things are made for the honor and glory of God. The holy soul will give honor and glory to God with the just works it does while it is in the flesh, because the soul does these things with God's help, just as the prophet bears witness, saying:

21

DAVID TO THE SAME THING

29. *I love you, O Lord, my strength, O Lord, my rock, my fortress, my deliverer. My God, my rock of refuge, my shield, the horn of my salvation, my stronghold (Psalm 18:2-3).* This means that my God, through whom I was created and through whom I live and to whom I reach out to when I sigh and from whom I ask for all good things because I know that he is my God and that I ought to serve him since I have knowledge through him, is my helper in all good things since I accomplish my good works through him. I also place my hope in him because his grace clothes me like a garment. And so he is my defender since he protects me from evil when my evil conscience stings me. He gives me counsel so that I do not do evil works. But God is the horn of the salvation of my soul since he teaches me the law through the Holy Spirit. In the law I walk on his paths and take the food of life that is given to those who truly believe. I will have taken this food by the time God receives me into the highest blessedness after I have been sanctified and chosen through all these things. And he will take me to His bosom.

22

CONCERNING THE STRENGTH OF THE ELEMENTS AND CONCERNING THE SPIRITUAL LIFE OF THE SOUL

30. But the power of the elements work around the middle of his hip bones, of course, of the man I mentioned earlier. And then they go back

again into this same middle, just like a man who breathes out and then in again. This is because just as the middle of man strengthens and just as his hip bones carry him, so also the power of the elements, which hold and carry the world, come from the strongest strength of the Creator when they bring warmth, moisture, greenness and firmness to various creatures, when they cause them to germinate and grow, and when they also gather themselves again into the strongest strength of the Creator where they allow creatures to be submissive. For creatures that are under the elements grow and are then killed. When the elements do what they are supposed to do, they bring forth fruit, but when they gather themselves again at God's command, they no longer bring forth fruit. As a man draws in his breath so that he does not falter in what he does and as he gathers it into himself again for the restfulness of a new life, so also these works provide for the life of the soul. For the strength of the spiritual life of the soul is like the middle of the hip bone in the flesh, from which the strength of the virtues, just like the elements, bring forth good; the virtues then return this strength again through contemplation of the words that have been spoken. Similarly, when a man is sorrowful in his heart, he pours out tears to God, but when his sorrow has passed, he once again holds his tears back.

23

THE FACT THAT THE ELEMENTS ARE OVERTURNED BY HUMAN INJUSTICES

31. The fact that you hear a loud voice speaking from the elements of the earth to this man means that the elements bring their complaints to their Creator with great crying aloud, not so that they may be spoken like human complaints, but so that they may show the significance of their anguish. When they were shown the righteous way by their Creator, with certain movements and other motions they were then able to go beyond the things tangled up with their sins. This shows that they are not strong enough by themselves to travel the ways and to fulfill the duties given them by God since they can be overturned by the injustices of other men. As a result, they stink with the pestilence of depraved rumor and with the fame of feeble justice since they do not cultivate them properly. They sometimes also draw the fog of the painful smells of the baseness of men to themselves, therefore communicating their own foulness, because they are with the elements and the elements are with them.

24

THE FACT THAT GOD TORMENTS MEN SO THAT HE MAY LEAD THEM BACK TO REPENTANCE

32. This man, of course, God, answers in such a way as to purge these things with his own judgments and castigations. He answers that men who have been soiled with sin will be tormented with scourges and branches until they return to him repentant. He will bring men's wills back to himself this way.

25

THE FACT THAT GOD WISHES ALL THINGS TO BE CLEANSED IN HIS SIGHT

33. As many times as these elements have been defiled by the depraved acts of men, that many times God will cleanse them by sending torments and hardships to men since he wants all things to be cleansed in his sight. Nothing can bring God to an end, nor can he be diminished in any way.

26

CONCERNING THE FRUITS OF THE EARTH CORRUPTED BY SIN

34. The winds stink of baseness and do not blow pure air, but blow in a heavy thunderstorm. And the air vomits forth dirt because of the uncleanliness of men; it then brings unjust and unworthy moisture that destroys the greenness and fruit that ought to nourish people. Sometimes this moisture is fog and sometimes snow, from which harmful and useless grubs are born that damage and eat up the fruits of the earth. This is because men close their mouths to righteousness and to the other virtues so that they do not have to open their mouths and hearts to truth.

27

THE FACT THAT PERVERSE MEN SAY THAT GOD IS NOT SEEN

35. Those who ought to have greenness have nothing but dry dryness because of the wicked superstitions of the deeds of the devil that come to perverse men who turn everything around and do things only for their

own pleasure and the desires of their own flesh. While men do this, they say in their hearts and with their tongues: Who is that God, or who is able to be God, or what power does he have, he whom we never see but who is always hiding?

28
THE FACT THAT MEN SEE GOD THROUGH CREATURES

36. The Lord answers these, asking them if they have seen him in the light of good knowledge and in the light of the temporal sun when they ought to be doing good things. They are also asked if they had not seen him in the shadows of their heart and in the darkness of the night when they ought to have avoided evil things. And they are asked if they have not known him in the seeds of justice that sprout from the moisture of the Holy Spirit, or if they have not seen him when they sow their seeds in the earth and those seeds are bathed with the dew and the rain so that they grow. What can be made from nothing unless by the Creator of all things?

29
THE FACT THAT MAN DARES TO TEST THE CREATOR

37. Every creature clearly knows its creator and reaches back to him. It knows that God alone created it because he is the one who made all things. Man, however, who is restrained and divided by many vanities, tries to restrain his Creator when he refuses to admit that he can do better things. Man divides God up among many other creatures since through his own will he makes God the cause of each and everything he does according to his own will. As a result, he says that since God created him this way, he is not able to avoid the sin that he wants to do.

30
THE FACT THAT WISDOM DICTATED THE SCRIPTURES

38. But the Scriptures were written with wisdom since God made them. No one would have understood them if God's wisdom had not dictated them. The Scriptures ought to be searched carefully and keenly to see who created man since God is the one who created him.

31
CONCERNING CREATURES AND THE HIGHEST BLESSEDNESS

39. As long as a creature fulfills the temporal needs of men in this world by producing what is usable to men, man will not see the greatness and perfection of eternal joy because the elements have dealings with men and men have dealings with the elements of the world. However, when the world has come to an end so that creatures have fallen into the dryness of failure at the end of time and have realized that they have changed, the chosen will see their Creator and will receive the reward for their good deeds in a life of eternal and complete joy with the highest blessedness. They will then not care about or need the elements or other temporal things because they will be in eternity and will dwell in a blessed life with God, just as it has been written:

32
THE BOOK OF WISDOM TO THE SAME THING

40. *In the time of their visitation the just shall shine, and shall dart about as sparks through stubble; they shall judge nations and rule over peoples, and the Lord shall be their King forever (Wisdom 3:7-8).* This means that those who are just through holy works will receive the brightness of eternity and perpetual happiness. They performed these holy works through their faith in the Holy Trinity on the wheel that Ezechiel saw. God saw them in their holy works and they will see God as well through them. As a result, they will be lifted up on the height and breadth of shining brightness with joy and gladness without being troubled by their fragile flesh. And there, sparkling with their holy works and not weighed down by their bodies, they will be spread out in holiness and will not be hindered by any impediments. In addition, with the just judgment of the Lord they will judge those to whom sins clung, trampling their sins under foot if they had not committed them habitually. And so with righteous and just judgment they will rule over the people who are no longer on earth with their earthly cares and desires. Then with royal honor and immortal domination, the all-seeing Lord will rule over those who have obtained life by means of their holy works and merits; he will do this for eternity.

33

SEVEN FAULTS OPPOSED TO THE SEVEN GIFTS OF THE HOLY SPIRIT

41. But the fact that in the fog which I mentioned earlier, there were various other faults, seven of whose images you now see in the following way. This is the fact that in the thickness of wicked unfaithfulness in which there are many forms and various kinds of evil and unclean faults, there are as many faults with their wicked deeds as there are gifts of the Holy Spirit. These faults try to resist these gifts in every way possible, but they will not nevertheless prevail because God's goodness completely overcomes the devil's perversity.

34

CONCERNING PRIDE

42. The first image stands for pride, which is the source of all faults and material and mother of all other evils since pride caused the first angel to be cast out of heaven and drove man from paradise. Regarding souls who want to return to life by doing good, pride places snares in the purpose of their work and prevents them from receiving the highest reward. For when man is praised often for his good actions, he becomes proud and this cancels out his blessed reward. Pride has, as it were, a woman's face since it turned the thoughts of the first angel who fell from heaven around to foolish ones. With foolishness it also caused the first woman to be cast from paradise; even now it leads men beyond themselves with twisted softness. Her eyes are fire since her intention burns with foolishness. Her nose is sprinkled with dirt since lacking discretion it is filthy with foolishness. And her mouth is closed since she has no fondness for righteous words but in her heart denies God and everything else that is good. She does not have, however, any arms and hands because her strength and works do not have any life but are dead. But instead on each shoulder she has a wing like the wing of a bat because both in heavenly and earthly things she prepares falsely, like the defenses of an empire, since she has no righteous justice but only deceptive and darkened confidence. So that the right wing reaches to the East and the left to the West; this means she is opposed to God in heavenly things and she truly rushes to the devil in earthly things. This image has a chest like a man because its heart is always swelled up with empty greatness. Its shins and feet are formed like the legs and feet of a locust because in its swelled up heart it tolerates its own ways with vain glory

and gives out empty and unstable examples. It does not have a stomach or a back since it does not offer any pasture land that can be used, nor does it give anyone any strong support with which that person could persevere in doing good. The fact that, however, you see that its head and the rest of its body were not covered with hair or a garment; this is because a proud mind doing proud works walks foolishly and naked without the hair of prudence and without the garment of salvation. Unless it was hidden in the darkness I mentioned earlier; this means that no matter what it does, it lies in the perversity of unhappiness. But a very fine film, like a golden circle, stretches from the point of its chin to the top of each side of its jaw; this is because it neither gives honor nor shows care but only shows contempt to anyone who knows God who knows all things. It has done this and has been outwardly foolish from the beginning right up to the present, just as a spring bubbles to the top, when with gnashing teeth and biting it tries to overcome God who is stronger than it is. But just as it fell down prostrate in an ugly manner in the past, so also even now the higher it rises in the thoughts and actions of foolish men, the lower it drags them down. Nevertheless it knew no one was like it, as it said earlier. Humility, however, resists pride and encourages men to shrink back from it.

35

CONCERNING ENVY

43. The second image, however, signifies envy. It accompanies pride since it is the work of pride and the fire of all evil things, for when men are proud, they envy the accomplishments of others and stir up evil. You see this image who has a monstrous form; this means that the devil does all his work out of envy and begrudges men obtaining the highest blessedness, as it has been shown to you earlier. Its head and shoulders are somewhat like a man, except that its hands are like a bear's paws; this means that although a person knows God in his mind, as in his head, nevertheless that person often judges another person not according to the precepts of God, but according to his own envy. Further, on its shoulders of trust and power, it knowingly puts wickedness before justice while showing its arms to be hard with strength. But this image is nevertheless like a man since through the human knowledge that it has, it quietly brings evil to men. But men then go beyond this with their own cruel work of harsh pillaging and bestial greediness when they powerfully and bitterly tear to pieces, trample under foot, and destroy everything they can. Its chest, stomach and back are beyond being human since they are so gross; this is because knowledge and the fishing net and the hard

wood of the customs of envy go beyond men with their great and tortuous wickedness. No righteous teaching, well ordered disposition and proper method for doing things is found in them, but rather only the gnashing of teeth and the bitter tumor of incompetence that digresses without discretion. However, from its loins downwards it is similar to a man, except that it has wooden feet. This means that an envious man who has been bent out of shape with the desires of the flesh turns more to evil than to other things, although he has a greater and deeper understanding than other creatures. In his evil works, man reveals dry and deadly footsteps that do not have the greenness of any usefulness when he does not walk with righteousness either in his own footsteps or in the footsteps of others. Its head is fiery and it shoots out flames from its mouth since man does not follow any established law in his life; he does not even try to be righteous or useful in important or insignificant things. But it is completely hidden in the darkness I mentioned earlier because man hinders the progress of others when he neither seeks out nor examines justice; he instead desires the evil ways by which the devil subjected the world to himself, just as it has been written:

36
THE BOOK OF WISDOM TO THE SAME THING

44. *But by the envy of the devil, death entered the world, and they who are in his possession experience it (Wisdom 2:24)*. This has the following meaning. The devil is opposed to God and wants to divide up God's honor so that he might usurp an equal part of that honor for himself. As a result, God struck the devil down into Gehenna and did not allow him to do what he wanted. When the devil saw that man had been created, he knew God's power but thereupon spread out his envy and asked man why God had given him the command he had received. And so through the evil of envy the devil turned God's work, namely man, away from God and drew man to himself; man abandoned God and joined the devil. In this way through the blowing wind of the envy of the devil's suggestion, death, which destroys all things, came into the world and the devil subjugated the world to himself. The devil showed his power in the world when he caused man, who ought to be like a god in the world, to serve him. Therefore, the devil enters another tabernacle where he exercises his power. All who follow the devil's example walk in his footsteps of evil and oppress others with envy. And so they are at the side of the devil since they cast away the good and just things that they know. They gnaw at and bite the gifts of God that God created and gave to them. As a result, they will have the friendship of the devil in

Gehenna. But the faithful who flee from this evil and embrace God through faith are the sons who will receive celestial wages since they anxiously receive their awaited wages from God after being honorable in their wondrous deeds. Therefore, they will be called to heaven with all their embellishments.

45. The fact that, however, envy's right shoulder leans upon this darkness means that man ought to have righteous trust and power in his good and holy works. When he envies the accomplishments of others, he puts himself above diabolical wickedness; he also puts himself there when he wants to take away from another person what that person has from God. For envy is a plunderer and is like a robber who hides along a road so that he may cheat each and every one who passes along that way and so that he may steal the money each one has. Envy traps men along the way when he takes their possessions from them; he also tears up those who have freely given their possessions to another person when he ambushes that person along the way, just as he has shown in the words he spoke earlier. Charity, however, refutes envy and warns men not to be envious.

37
CONCERNING EMPTY GLORY

46. The third image reveals empty glory. It follows envy as a companion since the disruption of strange things brings about change, for when men envy the accomplishments of others, they desire glory for themselves. This image is in the shape of a man because it has the desires of fleshly concupiscence. Except that its hands are covered with hair; this means that it changes the works that it should direct to the intellect of man according to reason into bestial deeds. And its shins and feet are like those of a crane; this is because reaching out, as on its own shins, to the empty choices that are obstacles from the devil, it sets its feet on uncertain paths. As a result, it puts men who imitate it on empty heights without the virtue of good ways where they act foolish and irrational rather than righteous and prudent. On its head, however, it wears a hat made from the top of an onion, because men who follow empty glory in their minds love earthly and fallen honors. While they are green and useful now, they will later be clothed in dryness, just like the onion stalk. It is clothed with a black garment because empty glory is alive but is surrounded with the darkness of unfaithfulness in the annihilation of death. The fact that, however, in its right hand it holds a small green branch; in its left it truly holds certain green flowers that it gazes at with

great care; this is because men imitate empty glory when they show the deeds they do while they are alive to be full of empty boasting even as they hold the greenness of heavenly things. Some people, however, because they prefer this world, act as if their earthly deeds bloom with earthly things as a result of their own righteousness, and they put all their effort into this because they want all their actions to be glorified with the vanity of boasting. But fear of God answers empty glory and shows that it is detestable.

38
CONCERNING DISOBEDIENCE

47. The fourth image stands for disobedience. It walks after empty glory because it is like a chariot for empty glory and all the other faults mentioned earlier, since it prepares and fulfills all its duties according to the will of empty glory and all the other faults, and since it penetrates them with fire. You see that this image has the head of a serpent because its intention was the same as that of the serpent right from the beginning, namely it persuades man not to be obedient to God. You also see that this image has a furry chest like that of a caterpillar because in knowing man through its own particular will, it strives to lift itself on high; and by not knowing God and because it has tried to satisfy itself by perfecting itself completely, it does not strive to imitate prudence but rather foolishness on high. Its shins and feet are like those of a viper because as a result of men being free to choose their own desires, it directs their footsteps so that they turn away from blessed submission, thus casting the ones who resist God into the shamelessness and temerity of wickedness. Its back, however, and tail and all the rest of its body are like a crab because it also leads self-confidence, which disobedience holds in the hard wood of rebellion, to the same end as disobedience when it persists in doing evil. All the other bonds of its perverse deeds move forward with stubborn boldness and then go back with deceptive craftiness so that it has no stability. But with the worst of pretenses it rejects all the things established by the precepts of God. Further, it moves headlong here and there as if it is being blown by the winds. It is so agitated that it shakes all the darkness which I mentioned earlier. This means that when men choose to be disobedient, they not only stand in rebellion, but they also move from disobedience into rebellion. In the same way, they move boldly from one thing to another, having been stirred up by the deeds of the devil where all the perversities of all the faults have been moved to the commotion of agitation, because through the evil of disobedience, they draw all the other faults to themselves.

But it also turns toward the North and pours fire out its mouth. This is because it reaches to the one in the North who is opposed to God through his bold disobedience. This fault is bold first and then vomits forth the flames of the various other faults with it words which show no obedience to those who are owed reverence. After it burns everyone it can with its words, it reveals itself, as I mentioned earlier. Obedience responds to disobedience and urges people not to imitate it.

39
CONCERNING UNFAITHFULNESS

48. The fifth image manifests unfaithfulness. It follows disobedience because when men have chosen disobedience, they then become unfaithful so that they deny God. This image has the form of a man, with the exception of its head, because although it knows God to be, it refuses to cultivate him worthily because it has changed its mind to unbelief and, therefore, does have the righteous beginning by which it knows God through faith. It is surrounded with the darkness I mentioned earlier from its knees down to the sole of its feet because it is unable to bend toward true faith or to walk in true faith, but it remains unmoveable in the darkness of unfaithfulness when it does not know God inwardly in word and deed. On its head no other form appears except that it is completely filled with very black eyes, among which there is one eye, as it were, on its front that burned sometimes like a burning fire. This means that it does not have prudence of mind, but only the foolishness of human knowledge. With its innermost intentions growing dark from unfaithfulness, it makes known the fullness of its disbelief when, looking around everywhere, it draws all the works of unfaithfulness to itself and when, seeing truly, it neglects and rejects the light of truth. For unfaithful men often say that they have the righteousness of faith, but their actions are filled with the perversity of deceitfulness. Although they cannot hide the depraved intentions of their mind, they sometimes show their intention openly as if it were shining in faith. The deceived then put their hope and trust in them even though they do not have any blessedness or light of life. The fact that, however, it has placed its right hand on its chest and it holds a staff in its left hand means that perverse men, loving unfaithfulness, rest from doing good and holy works because of the concupiscence of their heart. They have an empty trust in the evil actions by which they divide God into two parts when they try to examine God both in the higher and lower creatures in the elements, with these creatures having no true life. And this image wears a black coverlet around itself because it defends itself strongly with the decep-

tion of the darkness of diabolical deceits while it strives to have a blessed life, just as it reveals in the words it spoke earlier. This image is refuted by faith who warns people to avoid unfaithfulness as they reach for God in the mirror of purity. They are also encouraged in the same way by Paul the Apostle, just as it has been written:

40
THE APOSTLE TO THE SAME THING

49. *Let us draw near in utter sincerity and absolute confidence, our hearts sprinkled clean from the evil which lay on our conscience and our bodies washed in pure water. Let us hold unswervingly to our profession which gives us hope, for he who made the promise deserves our trust (Hebrews 10:22-23).* This means the following. Having been warned by the Holy Spirit, let us approach the highest blessedness with a true intention, let us begin good things with peace, and let us finish these things with piety because charity burns in peace and piety beholds God by imitating God in all the things man is required to do. And so with the pure and simple perfection of true faith in our hearts and not with the evil duplicity by which a man chooses one for himself but despises another according to whatever he wishes, let us, with our hearts washed with the rivulets of the Scriptures, cast out anything in our conscience that drives us to evil and let us search in the true words of the Scriptures for who God may be and what his works are. Therefore, let us wash our conscience, which has been covered over with the scales of death through the fall of Adam so that it often denies true faith and all its works. These things, however, cannot be pure in us unless our sins have been washed from us so that our bodies are visibly perfected with the water of baptism. The Holy Spirit washes us and makes us alive invisibly as we are cleansed from the filth of our sins through him and as the unclean dirt of the wretched nature of our body is washed through him. After this has been done, let us hold with firm and sincere faith the confession of that hope which we professed openly in baptism, trusting God and denying the devil. Let us do these things so that we can cast off all the seductive deeds of the devil in order to persevere inviolately in the things that were rooted and strengthened in us when we were signed with the water of regeneration, for we are called the sons of God through sincere justice. Indeed, God is faithful in all his offerings and in all his works; he will give the promised reward of blessed heredity to his faithful and to those who truly believe in him. This is because they will receive from the true Son of God, truly made flesh in the end of ages, a lasting and eternal reward in the fullness of faith.

41
CONCERNING DESPAIR

50. The sixth image signifies despair. It follows in the footsteps of unfaithfulness because it is the kindling wood of unfaithfulness and of all the other faults since it does not have any hope in itself or in others but acts as if there were no hope. You see this image in the form of a woman because failing and weak, it does not give any good and righteous consolation, by which it shows that it is not victorious but has only the vile shaking of a failing woman. Its head is covered with a dark covering in the manner of a woman and the rest of its body is clothed with a dark garment; this means that its intentions are fragile and weak, surrounded with dark desolation and doubt, while the rest of its deeds are truly corrupt; it does not wear any garment of light and joy. Having been weighed down with doubt, it does not have any glory of blessed hope around it. For men who have been deceived by the devil when they have no confidence in the grace of God because of their despair unclothe themselves from all the good of celestial beauty. Before her face there appears, as it were, a mountain of burning sulphur since where men of this type should see true faith in blessed hope, they only see despair, as on the top of the mountain. They have the dryness and stink of foolishness, which draw away the greenness and good smell of the virtues of the soul, just as sulphur makes the body dry and stinking. To her right and left side, next to the mountain of sulphur, as it were, were people; because where people ought to lift up their hearts to the goodness of God, as it were, on the right, and where they ought to spit out evil, as it were, on the left, they hold the wind of elation in their minds with the most fervent and bitter sorrow and contrition of despair, not thinking about the goodness of God and not having any hope, but only accumulating all kinds of evil things in their hearts. These people sank down into the darkness I mentioned earlier and made a loud crashing noise in this darkness, because when despair hands men over into damnation, it brings them disillusionments, harsh punishments and diabolical laughter. But also to her right, clearly next to her back, there was the loud sound of thunder. This means that in that contradiction by which despair displaces God and refuses to look at him, the fall of the first angel led despair into the ruin of many miseries and punishment because it did not seek the mercy of God when it was able to. This image was frightened by all these things and with sighing and shaking, she pressed her arms and hands to her breast and covered herself over completely with the darkness. This means that when men have fallen into diabolical destruc-

tion through despair, they are so frightened that they forget about the works they have accomplished. And so with a desolate sigh and with trembling forgetfulness in which they do not even know themselves, they place the strength and understanding of their works, which they ought to extend to the height of blessed hope, in the sorrow of evil knowledge where they do not have the consolation of good knowledge. They hand themselves over completely to empty unhappiness since they are not willing to rise up to glory, just as despair has shown in the words it spoke above. But hope responds to despair and warns men not to consent in their hearts to despair.

42

CONCERNING LUXURY

51. The seventh image signifies luxury. It follows despair because after men have despaired of having mercy from God so that they no longer hope for the good of mercy, they lay hold of luxury in which they do everything they want, doing whatever their flesh demands in its filth. This image has, as it were, the form of a woman since just as a woman has been made for child bearing, so also luxury exists as the desire and kindling wood of sin. She lies on her right side because she spreads the righteousness of good and pure works under herself. She sometimes calls upon God through the will of the flesh and excuses herself, and she sometimes says that she has willfully repented, which, nevertheless, she has not done, and so she sins more fully with confidence. Bending her legs, she has drawn them up to herself, just as a man who lies leisurely on his bed. This means that she speaks to men seeking pleasure about fortitude, in which she ought to stand erect for God, turning them around and casting them down into the frailty of their flesh. And drawing them to herself through the strength of shameful works, she rests delightfully in her own mind since she is not strong enough to abstain from the concupiscence of her own flesh. Her hair, however, is like the flames of fire because men, living luxuriously, drag the shame that they should change into chastity in their minds into the heat of desire. And they nourish the flames of the fire in themselves, through which they kindle both themselves and others into defilement. And her eyes are white, just as she has been created, because luxury leads the intentions of depraved men to leisurely activity that is not pure, lest they look at something that may be seen as laborious, just so long as what is at hand is according to their wishes. She has white coverings on her feet that are so slippery that she cannot walk or stand on them. This is because, having chosen what she wishes rather than just mortifications of the flesh

while she is alive, she also shows with lascivious gestures that she is not eager to walk through the honor of righteousness nor to endure the mildness of stability in any way while she is alive. Instead, she is anxious to walk in the solitary ways of shameful desire whereby she dances on high but often falls into the depths. And because unclean men are inclined toward the allurements of the flesh and love the filth of human pollutions, making themselves like depraved animals and fleeing heavenly purity, they are subjected by divine judgment to the many passions of their flesh because they desired these things with their own will rather than desired them with a good will, just as it has been written by Paul the Apostle.

43

THE APOSTLE ON THE SAME THINGS

52. *In consequence, God delivered them up in their lusts to unclean practices; they engaged in the mutual degradation of their bodies, these men who exchanged the truth of God for a lie and worshipped and served the creature rather than the Creator—blessed be he forever, amen! (Romans 1:24-25).* This means that because men want to follow their own uncertain desires and do not want to stop doing this, the Creator of all things, in whose power they are and without whose permission they are nothing, according to his just judgment permits them to follow the desires of their own mind and will in order that they many fall into the uncleanness that they want so badly, so that they may turn their flesh upside down in disgrace and contrariness when they commit those things that are not proper. For they start doing whatever they desire and wish, and they forsake God whom they, nevertheless, know with their intellect, paying attention only to what they can do with their own flesh.

53. For by doing this, they imitate the first angel who wanted to change his life by his own very bad will. But he was not able to do this because God surrendered him to death, by which death has been drawn away. For God allows these men to fulfill the desires of their own will even in this manner since they rush to fulfill these desires rather than do heavenly things; they pollute themselves with unclean blood of outrageous moisture and they contaminate themselves so that both in themselves and in others they overturn and dismember human nature with the worst pollution so that they destroy the results of begetting which God established. And so with unclean and inhuman contact, they lay hold of and then desert the teachings of modesty and they transform their bodies

into perversity. For they change the truth, by which God is true God, into a lie by which they blaspheme God when they worship idols who have no truth but only false names. This is because they do not do any good for themselves or others. Creatures subjected to idols serve them as servants when they kneel before them and pour out their prayers to them, forsaking the one who created them and not showing him any reverence. As a result, the devil brings the passions and the unclean burning of their flesh to them, from which they do not want to tear themselves away nor are they able to do so because they desire things from which they are not protected and safe. For being against God, they chose for themselves the creature that Adam knew through his power of reason both by position and by name. They demand salvation from these things and they call God their servant, thereby forsaking the true God who has been called blessed in perpetual honor by every creature since the beginning of time. Thus, however, God is truth; the devil is lying and rushes to incline those serving him to the worst pollutions of body and soul.

54. From her mouth luxury gives forth a certain panting and a certain poisonous froth because she shows and calls forth strife and boasting pride with her words and she brings about whatever she desires with her foul words. At her right breast she is nursing, as it were, a young dog; at her left breast she is nursing a serpent. This is because where she ought to show me nourishing things with righteousness through wisdom, as on the right, she only brings forth foolishness. And where she ought to surround herself with prudence, as on the left, she nourishes bitterness with foolishness, sparing nothing, but bringing scandal to anyone who resists her. She also tears those to pieces who resist her. She plucks some flowers from the trees and some herbs with her hands and smells them with her nose. This is because she prevails upon all things to seek in their works, like the flowers, the greater and unnatural and also the less and natural fires of the flesh which they indiscreetly seek in the odor of familiar taste. When men foully gather together the taste of the odor of unclean filth, they increase their appetite for the worst and most illicit desires. She wears no garments, but is all fiery and because of her burning, she dries out everything lying next to her, just like an open window. This is because she, lacking the beauty of modesty and honesty, shows herself naked in the confusion of all things and she shows herself as a diabolical and infernal fire so that when men rush to her and her filth with the agitated and deceptive seething of their veins and flesh, their holiness dries up, just like the things next to an open window. And she leads them to the fire of fleshly concupiscence, as she showed earlier by

her words. Chastity resists her and warns men to avoid her and to imitate itself faithfully.

44
CONCERNING THE FORM OF ZEAL

55. The fact that, however, to the right side of the man mentioned earlier, you also see standing an image with the form of a human. This means that the zeal of God appears in his righteousness and fortitude. The zeal of God cleans and wipes away the sins of men, because man, made in the image of God and infused with the knowledge of good and evil, ought to be judged by the just judgments of the highest judge who judges all things truly. This image has a fiery face because the zeal of God consumes all unjust things with the fervor of its judgment, just like a fire. It does this not because it cleanses all things with fire, but because it destroys all evil things by burning them up to nothing. And it was clothed with a doubly warm garment since it judges all the things it judges with justice. And the fact that this images cries out against the faults mentioned above means that the zeal of the Lord disproves the illusions of the previously mentioned faults, and it grinds them away completely since these faults, the viscera of the ancient serpent and the outpouring of his wickedness, shoot deadly arrows into men. These faults will be confused by the martyrdom of the Son of God and they will be ground away by the eternal Divinity, being completely destroyed. As a result, death will be destroyed in eternity when God decides to unleash his power, which no one can resist, as Job also bears witness by saying:

45
THE WORDS OF JOB CONCERNING THE SAME THINGS

56. *He is God and he does not relent; the helpers of Rahab bow beneath him (Job 9:13).* This means that God, who created all things and in whose power all things are, has such great strength in his judgments that neither angels nor men have any strength strong enough to resist his examination when he lays bare his vengeance with just judgment against the sinful. For God's anger always fights against the evil of wickedness; his anger is not a friend to evil but casts evil down completely, just as it has cast evil down in an angel and in man. For God established his judgments in such a way that he brings justice to wickedness and correction

to sinners. This is because a sinner is justified through repentance, of course, when he discerns himself with repentance and when he places himself on the cross of repentance and when he wounds himself with tears by confessing his sins to God through a priest. This results from the highest priest, clearly the Son of God, bearing himself on the cross where he wiped away the sins of men by pouring out his blood. No one is able to resist God, since he alone is God and he alone is the just judge, judging all things justly and dispensing all things well. All things are subject to his precepts. These things have strength from him because they are part of a circle, of course, the circle in which the world stands, according to the plan and disposition of God. These things, however, are the sun and the moon and the rest of the planets and the stars with the rest of the constellations, which support the wheel of the circle with their burning strength and which attract water to themselves. They drink those waters, lest this circle catch fire with the burning of those things, but the circle also shines through the water. Further, these things are frequently servants to the judgments of God because they serve men for him, they know their deeds, and they do not do anything other than as they are instructed. All these things have been truly ordered by the highest Creator who orders and disposes all things according to their capacity to be ordered and arranged well. However, let he who desires life grasp these words and store them in the innermost chamber of his heart.

57. Behold, I saw the crowd of the other spirits that I mentioned earlier. They cried aloud and said: "Who is Lord? Lucifer is Lord and there is no other." These spirits show men pride and encourage them to value themselves as more excellent than all others.

46
CONCERNING THE CLEANSING PUNISHMENTS OF THE PROUD ONES

58. I saw a large fire, all of which burned intensely and which contained a multitude of large and horrible worms. In this fire were punished the souls of those who had the exaltation of pride in their deeds and words while they had been alive. Indeed, on account of their pride they were afflicted by the fire, and on account of their boasting they were afflicted by the worms in this fire.

47

CONCERNING THE REPENTANCE OF PRIDE

59. I saw and understood these things. From the living light mentioned earlier I again heard a voice say to me: *These things that you see are true. But let the men who are eager to bind the wicked spirits who bring them pride and who want to flee the punishments of this fault, subdue and chastise their body with a hair shirt, with kneeling, and with scourgings, sighs and tears.*

48

CONCERNING THE SAME THING

60. With such afflictions man's pride is overcome since these afflictions fight against pride. Indeed, the hair shirt prohibits the mind from elevating and raising itself up; the kneeling incites the soul to sighs; the scourgings also constrain pride; the sighs wound it and the tears submerge it. The sighs indeed see God; the tears, however, confess him.

49

PRIDE, THE MOTHER OF FAULTS

61. Pride should be stopped. Since it was the first deception to reject God, it exists as the mother of all the other faults. And just as man guides his whole body with his five senses, so also pride with hate, disobedience and empty glory draws all the other faults to itself and then sends each one of them back into error. For pride wanted to rise above God and tried to do this. It did not, however, want to hate God, but it fought against his justice, resulting in its being wounded many times. Disobedience did not subject itself to God's commands, but declared that God did not have any power. Empty glory also wanted to become what it should not be, clearly because it wanted to be called God. Lying also wanted to put an end to God so it rejected the living God and chose not to listen to him. Just as all humans have come from Eve, so also all the evil of the faults has risen up from pride. The devil even overcame Eve through pride when he persuaded her to eat the apple. Whoever has pride lacks the charity of God and does not sprout anything in the dew of the blessedness of the virtues. Therefore, if man wants to serve God humbly, let him flee pride and let him cast it out completely. These things, however, have been spoken concerning the atonement for the

cleansing and saving of souls, and they are faithful things. A faithful person pays attention to these things and remembers them well.

62. I also saw other spirits in this crowd who cried aloud, saying: "What glory and what kingdom is this that no one can seize it?" These spirits encourage men not to love any gift of God in man, but only what pleases them and what they envy of other's prosperity and good and happy works.

50
CONCERNING THE CLEANSING PUNISHMENTS OF ENVY

63. I saw a large mountain with a cave filled with fire and boiling pitch. There were a lot of vipers crawling around the mountain and the cave had a narrow mouth through which souls entered and left. In addition, near this mountain there was tremendous cold of great horror that had a fiery cloud above it filled with scorpions. The souls of those who had sweat with the hatred of envy while they had been alive were twisted by these torments; they crossed from the punishments of the mountains to the punishments of the cold nearby and then back again. Since they had lifted their hearts above others through envy, they burned in the fire of the mountain; since they had enviously detracted from the prosperity and actions of others, they were stained by the pitch; and since they had tormented others with biting words and actions and with disloyalty, they were twisted by these vipers. But on account of the hatred they had had in their envy, they suffered in the cold near the mountain; on account of the cruelty of their hatred, they were burned by the fire of the cloud; and on account of the biting fierceness of their cruelty, they suffered from the scorpions. Because they had envy with hatred and hatred with envy, they went from one kind of punishment to the other.

51
CONCERNING THE REPENTANCE OF ENVY

64. I saw and understood these things and from the living light I heard a voice say: *These things that you see are true. If men want to avoid the evil spirits who bring envy and hatred and if they want to avoid the punishments for them, let them chastise themselves with a hair shirt and with scourging. And let them bend their knees to God*

since they have stirred up many people with their envy and have robbed many of their prosperity through their envy and hatred.

52
CONCERNING THE SIN OF ENVY

65. The envious do not love the good that they see and find in others. They do not, however, profess their envy openly, but rather proclaim their own deeds as prosperous in plain and righteous ways. God, therefore, allows these people to fall since they do not want to stand with any stability, just as the Jews did not want to stand with stability either, for they rejected what they knew, refused to see what they saw, deserted the righteous ways and walked in unjust ways when they strove by devious means to oppress the one I had sent them for their redemption. For they both rushed to light up the sun of doctrine and then hastened to darken it; they knew the wondrous things of doctrine, but tried to blot them out with the wickedness of their envy. Therefore, I destroyed them and scattered them like the dust since they did not believe the things they saw; whoever refuses to imitate the good and holy things that he sees and knows, falls down in the presence of God and men by righteous judgment.

53
ENVY IS SIMILAR TO THE DEVIL

66. For envy does not do anything good, but whoever is envious fights against good. And so when envy has joined up with hatred, it shakes the very strength of the soul of man, for a man who has the blackness of the hatred of envy does not have the warmth of the Holy Spirit in whom there are rich and infinite days of joy. This joy, however, does not contain any hatred because it does not rejoice in the profit of others. But because envy bites the profit of others with the sharpest of hatred, it is, therefore, like the devil who started hating from his very beginning. As a result, the devil destroyed all the embellishments of heaven because he tried to resist God with envy and hatred. Let people desire to do what those familiar to God do, and let them cast away evil things. These things, however, have been spoken concerning the atonement for the cleansing and saving of souls, and they are faithful things. A faithful person pays attention to these things and remembers them well.

67. I saw some other spirits in this crowd who cried aloud with great clamor: "We will not invoke anyone except Lucifer, because we can have magnificent glory with him." These spirits show empty glory to men and encourage them to trample on God eagerly.

54

CONCERNING THE CLEANSING PUNISHMENTS OF EMPTY GLORY

68. Behold I saw a long and wide marsh filled with filth and vermin of many types and emitting the worst stink. The souls of those who had panted eagerly after empty glory while they had been alive were being punished in it. Because they had been busy trying to receive empty glory, they were stained by the filth of this marsh; because they had been proud of this fault, there were tormented by these vermin; and because they had done all of this indiscreetly, they were offended by the stink.

55

CONCERNING THE REPENTANCE OF EMPTY GLORY

69. I saw and understood these things and from the living light I heard a voice say: *These things that you see are true, and as you see them, so they are. But if men who have sought empty glory are eager to overcome this and want to avoid its punishments, let them afflict themselves with fasting and scourging, let them offer many supplications to God, and let them flee from this fault completely.*

56

CONCERNING THE SIN OF EMPTY GLORY

70. Empty glory looks back to the left, thinking about what it can do irrationally. It wants to have its own will all the time, it decorates itself to show off for others, and it wants to be honored and praised more than others. When it has decorated itself, it does not fear God; when it wants to be honored, it does not choose God; and when it is eager to receive praise, it gives up God's justice. As a result of the delight of its own will, it is not submissive to God, neither fearing him, nor loving him, nor keeping his precepts. Those who follow empty glory think that whatever they learn and give out from themselves is the best since they do not want to worship God or to choose the Son of God, but by their

own will they mock all things that are holy and just. Let those who want to serve God faithfully cast such emptiness down and let them be contrite in their souls with blessed works. These things, however, have been spoken concerning the atonement for the cleansing and saving of souls, and they are faithful things. A faithful person pays attention to these things and remembers them well.

71. I saw some other spirits in this crowd who cried aloud as follows: "God should not be the only God, but there should be another omnipotent one before him." These spirits encourage men to be disobedient and show them how to resist their own anxieties.

57
CONCERNING THE CLEANSING PUNISHMENTS OF DISOBEDIENCE

72. I also saw a very dense darkness that contained the souls of those who had been disobedient while they had been alive. They were walking on a fiery pavement as if they were just wandering around. There were the fiercest of serpents lying on this pavement which were biting these souls with their mouths. Since they had been blind and, therefore, did not want to fulfill the precepts of their forebearers, they wandered about in this darkness; since they had walked so boldly in disobedience according to their own wills, they were burned by the fire of this pavement; and since they had so stubbornly fought against their forebearers, they were attacked by these serpents. I saw and understood these things and from the living light I heard a voice say: *These things that you see are true, and as you see them, so they are.*

58
CONCERNING THE REPENTANCE OF DISOBEDIENCE

73. If the men who had been disobedient want to drive away the spirits leading them to this and if they want to avoid its punishments, let them seek indulgence with the words of humility on bended knee in front of their forebearers. Let them live a solitary life for a time, according to the commands of their forebearers. Let them fast and be scourged and let them wear a hair shirt. Let them, therefore, be drawn back by these means to equal justice among the sons of the Father.

59
CONCERNING THE SIN OF DISOBEDIENCE

74. Disobedience is the worst evil. It does not want to fear God or honor men. Those who are disobedient say to each other: "Vah! What do we see? And what can we do? What is placed before us in this blindness? We do not know what it is. For our justice is greater and more useful than theirs. What will happen to us if we work with envy and hatred? For then we will follow nothing useful since they want to conquer us." Let whoever wants to hope in God lay hold of blessed submission and let him obey the commands of those greater than himself. Let him not follow the one who, not wanting to be submissive to his Creator, fell from the height of heaven down to the depth of hell. These things, however, have been spoken concerning the atonement for the cleansing and saving of souls, and they are faithful things. A faithful person pays attention to these things and remembers them well.

75. I saw some other spirits in this crowd who cried aloud with much clamor, saying: "God will end and another will succeed him." These spirits propose unfaithfulness to men and urge them not to trust in God.

60
CONCERNING THE CLEANSING PUNISHMENTS OF UNFAITHFULNESS

76. I saw a very large fire that was surrounded with great darkness. Under this darkness there was stinking mud of wondrous length, width and depth. And serpents of horrible shapes ran around both in the fire and in the mud. The souls of those who had not trusted in God while they had been alive, but who had valued him as worth nothing, as it were, with scrutiny, were being punished here. Because of the wickedness they had had, they burned in the fire; because of the unfaithfulness by which they did not want to look back to God, they were surrounded with this darkness; because of the unbelief by which they had turned the joys of God's creatures around to deceit and sorrow, they were covered with this mud; and because of the suspicion that caused them to have no hope in God, they were tormented by these serpents.

61
CONCERNING THE REPENTANCE OF UNFAITHFULNESS

77. I saw and understood these things and a voice from the living light said to me: *These things that you see are true. Let those, however, who are consumed with unfaithfulness chastise themselves with supplications on bended knees in order to rise above the spirits making them unfaithful and in order to tear themselves away from these punishments. Let them do this until divine virtue can divert away their unfaithful words and deeds.*

62
CONCERNING THE SIN OF UNFAITHFULNESS

78. Unfaithfulness resists God and fights against men; it does not trust in God or in men, but says to itself: "What am I? What have I been? And what will I be?" Those who say such things are blind because they have no hope of salvation with God and because they do not trust anything since they do not want to know either day or night. For when they do not want to know God, they deny day, and when they do not fear his judgments, they do not fear the night. And when they are unfaithful to men, they despise God's creation; as a result, they are blind since they do not manage themselves righteously. Indeed, these things have been written about.

63
THE WORDS OF DAVID TO THE SAME THING

79. *Punish them, O God; let them fall by their own devices; for their many sins, cast them out because they have rebelled against you (Psalm 5:11).* This means the following. The perverse, being empty because of the malice of their perversity, will fall without any consolation or any salvation of praise and glory when their knowledge is empty. Therefore, you who dispense all things with justice, expel from yourself those who show impiety in many ways. Expel those who anger you by rushing away from you. For there is great impiety in those who refuse to know and do what they are able to know justly and favorably, but instead turn themselves to something else that does not pertain to them and that they neither see nor know. They value this as something more than it is. This impiety is also of the type of unfaithfulness that arranges and distributes

each and every thing, as if it were the creator of such things, and it hates many things since it is always looking back toward something else. As a result, those who associate with such impiety are not worth anything since angering God, they are driven back to nothing; they deny the glory of God and the joy that is in God; they do not worship God, just as a man does not give honor to his enemy. But blessed are those who choose God! They flee from unfaithful works, and holding onto the faithfulness in all good works, they are joined to God since they prefer him more than the devil. These things, however, have been spoken concerning the atonement for the cleansing and saving of souls, and they are faithful things. A faithful person pays attention to these things and remembers them well.

80. I saw some other spirits in this crowd who cried aloud: "Let us hurry up so that Lucifer can do what he wishes." These spirits stir up despair and agitate people so that they do not place any hope in the one who created them.

64

THE CLEANSING PUNISHMENTS OF DESPAIR

81. Behold I saw a very wide ditch that was so deep that I could not comprehend how deep it was. This ditch was filled with a fierce fire that gave forth a tremendous stink. The souls of those who had despaired about having the grace and mercy of God while they had been alive were being punished in this ditch. Because they had given up the hope of salvation, they were in this ditch; because they had committed so many sins of despair, they were burned in its fire; and because they had had no moderation in their despair, they smelled the stink of this fire. And I saw and understood these things.

65

CONCERNING THE REPENTANCE OF DESPAIR

82. Again I heard the voice from the living light saying to me: *These things that you see are true. But for those who despair and do not trust in God, acting as if God did not exist, what else can they have but death? In order to resist these spirits who urge them on to despair and in order to drive despair out of themselves, let them persistently will to offer pure prayers on bended knees. But they should not fast strenuously or do other serious work because this might cause them to fall*

into greater despair, since they already carry a lot of sorrow in their hearts with the bitterest of bitterness because of this fault.

66

CONCERNING THE SIN OF DESPAIR

83. Despair injures the body of man, kills his soul, causes him to despise God, makes his judgment less valid, and causes him to be of little help to others. It says: "What are the things that God has made? And where can I go except into perdition?" Despair is pulled down by good deeds; it is, of course, hurled out by faith; and it is blotted out by the law of the Scriptures because with the Scriptures all good things are studied and found good, just as things are changed and held together with silver. For despair neither trusts in God nor believes in him; neither does it understand nor know what he may be. Because despair is this way, God destroys it in all things and before all things. For if wood did not have greenness in itself, it would not be wood; and if things that bear fruit did not bloom, they would not bring forth fruit. Similarly, man is nothing without the greenness of faith, and without understanding doctrine and the Scriptures, he does not bring forth any fruit. Therefore, the passages in the heart where death bringing despair is found, are destroyed by divine power when God hurls despair down. Nor do any other creatures rejoice with despair. These things, however, have been spoken concerning the atonement for the cleansing and saving of souls, and they are faithful things. A faithful person pays attention to these things and remembers them well.

84. I saw some other spirits in this crowd who cried aloud: "Is anything greater than what Lucifer made? We feel like we are one with him." These spirits drag men down with luxury and encourage them to fulfill the pleasures of their bodies.

67

CONCERNING THE CLEANSING PUNISHMENTS OF LUXURY

85. I saw a very large fire that burned intensely and was steeped with the worst poison and stinking sulphur. As a result of the wicked strength of this fire, the poison and sulphur boiled so fiercely that the infections of these were stirred up and gave out a loud clattering noise. The souls of those who had served luxury and fornication while they had been alive were tormented by these punishments. Because of the burning of

luxury, they suffered in the fire; because of the pleasure of the uncleanness of the things they had done, they were infected with the poison; and because they had not stopped committing this sin, they were punished in the sulphur.

68
CONCERNING THE CLEANSING PUNISHMENTS OF ADULTERY

86. But there was a second fire within this fire in which those wicked spirits who had committed adultery were carried in and out, just as a green twig inside of a snake is bent this way and that. Because they had committed adultery with their bodies while they had been alive, they were put in this fire inside the other fire; and because they had joined themselves to a stranger, they were bent into various shapes by various means.

69
CONCERNING THE CLEANSING PUNISHMENTS OF THOSE WHO HAVE VIOLATED THE VOW OF CHASTITY

87. I also saw that way up high in the air, things were descending that had been mixed with both fire and cold. Way on top were the souls of those who had vowed their chastity to God while they had been alive, but who had violated their vow. They were falling from a great height, but then were blown back as if by the wind, although on the way up they became entangled in the branches of darkness and could not move. The fire and cold then fell upon them heavily. And evil spirits were reproaching them, saying: "Why have you so dishonorably forsaken the vow you made?" Because they broke their vow of chastity, they fell from on high; because they had forgotten their vow when they sinned so freely while they were still bound by their vow, they were hurled into the darkness; and because of the pleasure of the flesh that they held with more esteem than their love of God, they suffered the heavy weight of the fire and cold.

70

CONCERNING THE CLEANSING PUNISHMENTS OF THOSE WHO HAVE TURNED HUMAN NATURE INTO CONTRARY THINGS WITH FORNICATION

88. I also saw a wide and deep swamp filled with mud into which the souls of those burrowed who had turned their human nature, both male and female, into something contrary through fornication while they had been alive. As evil spirits poured fiery water upon them, they tried to hide from their fiery pitch forks by burrowing into the mud. Because they had forsaken their human nature by fornicating, they burrowed into the mud; because they had done this with burning desire, the evil spirits poured the fiery water on them; and because they had cast aside all human shame in their fornication, they were pushed back into the mud by these evil spirits with their fiery pitch forks.

71

CONCERNING THE PUNISHMENTS OF THOSE WHO HAVE MIXED THEMSELVES WITH CATTLE IN FORNICATION

89. I also saw that evil spirits were gathering up the souls of those who had fornicated with cattle. They gathered them to pass them through various fires here and there, shredding them with fiery scourges, just as sharp thorns and thorny plants do. And these fires burned the animals along with these souls. Indeed, because of their inhuman joining together, they were tormented with the sharp points of the flames; because of the contrary lust of their unnatural union, they were afflicted with the fiery scourges; and because they had not thought about what they were doing, they were reproached for their sins. And I saw and understood these things.

72

CONCERNING THE REPENTANCE OF LUXURY

90. From the living light I again heard a voice saying to me: *These things that you see are true, and as you see them, so they are, and there are more things. If men want to overcome the spirits urging them on to the luxury of fornication and if they want to avoid its punishments, let them chastise themselves with fasting and scourging and let*

them wear down their flesh by offering pure prayers as long as neces-
sary to subdue their luxury with the good desires of their spirit.

73

CONCERNING THE FAULT OF FORNICATION

91. For fornication is like the worst snake who deceives with humility. It also contains the wickedness of the devil who attacks and then
leaves justice behind. Therefore, men who choose luxury in fornication
and who neglect the legal institutions attack both their bodies and souls,
just as a beast kills something and then lets its dead body rot.

74

CONCERNING FORNICATION OUT OF MAGICAL DEEDS

92. But those who, doing the worst of deeds, fold themselves together
mutually in unclean copulation, are not worthy to be joined by a legal
institution since they had first joined themselves together in deeds of
idolatrous seduction.

75

CONCERNING THE PUNISHMENTS OF ADULTERY

93. However, if those who have fouled themselves with adulterous
fornication and who have shattered with shameful sin the just copulation
that God joined together want to avoid the punishments for this, let them
wear a hair shirt, fast severely and be scourged according to the recommendation of their superior.

76

CONCERNING THE SIN OF ADULTERY

94. This sin is very wicked since it is incompatible with and intoler-
able to all things. For when God formed the first man, he brought a
woman forth from his rib so that they were made two in one flesh. Infused with this gift from God, they lived in one love. Therefore, when
people who have been joined in a legal union sanctified by a covenant
of ancient authority later violate this covenant and copulate with strang-
ers, they weaken their strength and send virtue away from themselves.

Similarly, Samson was weakened when he deceived his wife; he put himself in great peril and handed himself over to death.

77
CONCERNING THE REPENTANCE OF THE FALLING VIRGINS

95. If those who break their vow of chastity by not observing the vow they made to God as virgins consecrated to God want to lessen the torments for their sin, let them put down the cloak of virginity and with the counsel of their spiritual advisor let them take up the cloak of widowhood. And then let both these and those who made a vow of widowhood to God and then neglected it out of the desire of love, wear a hair shirt, fast and be scourged; let them seek the grace of God by praying on bended knees.

78
THE FACT THAT A VIOLATOR OF A VOW IS SIMILAR TO A PAGAN

96. Whoever made a vow and then broke it by embracing the time that remained to him is like a pagan who worships idols rather than God as a result of placing his own will before God's. Such a person does the same thing Pharaoh did who, having been persecuted, then wanted to seize God's people whom he had sent away; he was submersed in the Red Sea. Likewise the person who must do his own will although he had given it to God is submerged in a crude death, because just as Pharaoh could not have life in the Old Law, so also such a person is no longer able to deserve this life.

79
CONCERNING THE REPENTANCE OF A SIN AGAINST NATURE

97. If those who have abandoned righteous human nature with contrary fornication, both male and female, do not want to be punished for their sins, let them chastise themselves with a hair shirt and with fasting and scourging. And let them appease God with purest prayer on bended knee.

80

CONCERNING THE SAME THING

98. For this sin is shameful and criminal and comes to man through the deceit of the devil, just as death entered man with the fall of Adam when he drew back from God. For God created man for great honor and with a glorious name, but the serpent deceived man and man listened to the devil's advice, thus losing his ability to understand what all the animals say when they make their various sounds. This sin comes from the strength of the very heart of the devil; as a result, he encouraged men to change their natural ways into bestial ways in order to do ugly things. Because of the devil's hatred of the fruit of the first woman, he persecuted her so that she could not bring forth an offspring. And the devil wants men to pollute themselves with unnaturalness. Because God willed that the human race be procreated from a woman, it is a great sin that man uses his semen unnaturally when he fornicates.

81

CONCERNING THE SAME THING

99. But also let those who copulate with cattle so that they join glorious human nature to the worst disgrace and afterwards are aware of their guilt, afflict themselves and punish themselves with severe fasting and scourging. And let them avoid the kind of cattle they sinned with. They will bring scandal to the devil when they repent.

82

CONCERNING THE SAME THING

100. A man who fornicates with cattle is like one who prepares an earthen vessel. Such a person thinks he is his own god and thus dishonors God since he joins rationality to an irrational and contrary nature. He is also like a hard and cold stone because such a man is so hardened that he does not remember the honor he was created for, and he has great coldness since he puts out the fire of the flame of the Holy Spirit in his mind when he commits this very evil sin of blindness. As a result, the soul of such a person, which is inextinguishable in the vessel of his body, suffers when he commits this sin since this sin is more worthless than serpents who do not act according to their nature.

83

CONCERNING THE SIN OF LUXURY

101. When a man walks crookedly in luxury through the taste of the flesh, he makes an offering to the devil. For when he is moved to do evil works through taste, he covers the eyes of his soul from knowing good, as if he were covering his eyes with his hands. As a result, he rushes into the darkness with his evil works, saying: "I am not able to stand up, as if I were not made of flesh. For I live from food and drink, as God made me, and, therefore, I cannot hold myself back from works of this type." And so man rushes into his evil deeds with full knowledge, just like a mill, and he builds a place of ruin for himself through his will to do evil works. Through the kiss and odor of concupiscence, he commits the sins of luxury. For the flame of the fire of luxury is kindled in the navel of a woman, but it is fulfilled in the loins of a man; it is kindled in them by the devil because the devil started his evil counsel with a woman and fulfilled it in a man, just as when fire is blown by something else, it burns harder. But because God created man without emptiness and because he showed him all that is good through his knowledge, he will judge all of man's works according to their merits, just as David, inspired by me to spiritual prophecy, spoke, saying:

84

DAVID TO THE SAME THINGS

102. *He will rule the world with justice and the peoples with equity (Psalm 98:9).* This means the following. God, who discerns all things justly, will judge with just judgment the world he gave man to use and he will renew it since all earthly creatures contain seed. But when the world has been violated with the sins of men, he will cleanse it justly with justice so that it will not be defiled with the blight of iniquity. In addition, with equal righteousness, he will judge men who were created to follow the precepts of God with a quiet mind so that they will be cleansed either in the present or in the future when those who have broken his precepts have been branded. In order to purge themselves when they have neglected the grace of God while they were alive and with knowledge and when they have involved themselves with sins, let them tear themselves away from their sins and punish themselves so that when they look back to the grace of God through repentance, whether slowly or at the end, they will rise up to salvation after they have been cleansed.

These things, however, have been spoken concerning the atonement for the cleansing and saving of souls, and they are faithful things. A faithful person pays attention to these things and remembers them well.

THE THIRD PART ENDS

THE HEADINGS OF THE FOURTH PART BEGIN CONCERNING THE MAN LOOKING TO THE SOUTH AND TO THE WEST

THE HEADINGS OF THE FOURTH PART UNFOLD

THE FOURTH PART BEGINS

CONCERNING THE MAN LOOKING TO THE SOUTH AND TO THE WEST

1. I also saw that the man I mentioned earlier was turned toward the South so that he looked South and West. The earth in which he stood from his knees right up to the calves of his legs had moisture and greenness and was sprouting. As it were, his virtue was flourishing and beautiful since it had been made beautiful through the earth. It is fertile and brings forth offspring, of course, because all things formed in earthly creatures are led forth from the earth. In addition, this material that is the work of God is in man; it is also the material of the humanity of the Son of God. And behold in the cloud I mentioned earlier I now saw eight faults in their various images. The first image had a head like that of a fawn of a deer and a tail like that of a bear; the rest of its body was truly like that of a pig.

1

THE WORDS OF INJUSTICE

2. This image said: "Upon whom should I place my justice? Upon no one. For if I look to this one or that one, I would not be a creature of God but I would be like a little she-ass who walks slowly unless she is threatened with a goad. I am wiser and more prudent than others, I also know the sun and moon and stars and various other creatures, and I establish each and every thing and cause correctly. How can I deny this as if I know nothing? If I were to deny the cause of something, perhaps that thing would do the same with me. If I were to do that, my method would be more useful. Why should I bother with such things, as if I did not know what good is, when all the things that are mine are better and more useful than what belongs to others? For I am just as strong as those who discern and judge all things."

2

THE RESPONSE OF JUSTICE

3. From the storm cloud that reached from the South to the West, the one I mentioned earlier, I heard a voice respond to these words in this way: "O diabolical and shameless craftiness, what have you said? God established everything so that each and every thing looks back to another, for the more one understands from another what it does not know in itself, the more that one knows. Therefore, one has eyes for knowing so that he may see ahead in order to avoid danger and not to venture into peril. If a person were not to look back to another, whose reign would he stand before? What creature would minister to man? Man does what is necessary for himself with the help of other creatures; he digs gardens with a plow, he turns fields with a plow, and he also plows with oxen whom he commands to walk. He takes each and every creature according to its role in life and in the way it is useful to him. Why do you despise man in which heaven and earth is known? Why do you also reject the doctrine and gift of the Holy Spirit which the Holy Spirit poured into men? For man builds a building and an altar for God where he may serve him. The gifts of the Holy Spirit that I know are in man, I know to be the works of God and I am in harmony with them. I also rule over creatures and their deeds like a king with a diadem. I look at their works with honor and I work with their works so that they can have joy in me, since I am their staff helping them along the way of justice. Therefore, let those who despise me fall into a pit. I have come

forth from a leaping fountain and no earthly matters frighten me. I rose up at the break of day and I am a most loving friend of God. I will stay with God and will not leave him, for through him I am solid and complete. I am not burned until I am dried up because I am like the flowers of all the different kinds of trees that have not yet been dried up by winter or knocked down by a storm. I dwell on Mount Sion and I dwell in quietness. I walk in the tameness of the Lamb and I rise up in his victory. I am like the victory of a king. I will not be conquered; no one moves me and no one frightens me because I am not about to fall."

4. The second image had the face of a child and white hair. It was clothed with a pale-colored tunic that hid its arms and hands and feet and its other members so that I could not discern the rest of its form.

3
THE WORDS OF NUMBNESS

5. This image said: "Why should I suffer a narrow and laborious life? Why should I suffer from so many tribulations when I have not committed very many sins? Each and every creature is allowed to be itself. Many, however, weep and howl and make their bodies so thin that they live only with difficulty. They live depraved lives and add sin to sin. What does all this bring them? I, however, live a soft life and avoid hard work; I do not even want any work. If I flee work and other harmful things, God will not destroy me, will he?"

4
THE RESPONSE OF STRENGTH

6. I heard a voice from the storm cloud give an answer to this image: "O ashes of ashes, o glowing ashes of wretched rottenness, you have been poisonous since you first took the shape of your body. Your works are useless. You are not like the serpents that work in their caves and drag in food to feed themselves, nor are you like birds that build their nests and then seek food to restore their bodies again. For what is alive and can give life in this life that can live without care? Nothing, for this life is removed from the anxiously awaited life in paradise where eyes living in blessedness are never darkened. You, however, o wretched one, living without God's wisdom and rejected by God's mercy, desire things that no one can give you since you want to have these things without working for them in your numb sluggishness. But I with the strength of a lion, of course, the humanity of the Savior, serve in the royal bed-

chamber, I sigh for all of God's good things, and I wish everywhere, just like a person who has spread his cloak out widely. Therefore, let people who want to persist in doing good cry aloud to me in all the different languages of all the nations, and let them desire me, but let them value you the same as a dead body."

7. I saw a third image with a head and body like a lizard. It appeared in the presence of those clouds that were black, stormy and misty and that were intermixed with the dense white cloud.

5
THE WORDS OF FORGETFULNESS

8. This image had its forefeet on the cloud I mentioned earlier as it said: "When God does not know me and I do not know him, why can I not do my own will since God does not want me or I him? Whatever I want and find useful to me in any way, I will look for everywhere because I will do whatever I know, understand, and taste. Many, however, cry aloud to me from a life so strange that I do not know it, hear it, or see it. Many also say to me: 'Do this and this.' They show me God, life, and the wages I could receive so that I can know what to do. But many tyrants also run to me and propose wonderful agreements to me that happen to be more false than true, although they do not force these agreements upon me. Whatever I decide to do, however, they allow me to do as if it had been imposed upon me by a precept. I, however, do not want a lot of gods, that is, masters. If God does exist, he certainly does not know me."

6
THE RESPONSE OF HOLINESS

9. I heard a voice from the storm cloud answering this image: "O most rapid destruction, what are you saying? Who created you and who made you alive? God. Why do you not know that you did not do this? I, however, call upon God and ask him for whatever I need; I know all his precepts and follow them by seeing and understanding him. How? I am like a bird with the knowledge of good, by which I also know God and play the lyre of prayer when I adore him and by which I also understand him. If, however, I were to follow the things you do, I would turn away from God. The earth does not give the food, clothing and other things that are necessary for men, but God does. Men see things spring up, but they do not know from what and by what means they spring up,

but they do know that they themselves come from God. For nothing could make man and all the ages of time or even the least thing in the world, except God. And through all this, what God is, is known. Therefore, let men serve God most devotedly in all his works and let him stop doing evil when he acts only according to his own will. For I want to wear the girdle of abstinence and I want to remain like a happy flower of blessedness. Carrying a banner at the ceremonies of God, I am the leader of an ordained line of kings where God can accomplish his work."

10. I also saw a wheel, like the wheel of a wagon, turning in the darkness. This wheel, agitated as if by the winds, turned around like a millstone. There were four spokes thrust into its radius that was large enough for a man to stand up in. Indeed, there was the image of a man standing up among these spokes. He held a spoke with each hand; the other two spokes were behind his back. This image turned with the wheel. This image, however, had curly black hair, hands like those of the forefeet of a monkey, and feet like those of a hawk. Its garment had black and white stripes on it. In addition, this image had spread out a net as if to capture animals, but it did not catch anything.

7

THE WORDS OF CHANGEABLENESS

11. This image said: "Why is it I cannot know what I am? But what I do know, this I do. If I did not do this, I would be foolish. Many do what I admire, of course, because the wise make themselves foolish, the rich poor, and the good vile. What I am, I speak; what I wish, I bring about; what I have, I do not leave behind; and what I am able to do, I do. As long as I can do this, I will not be empty in any way. For a worker who does not do the work he is capable of doing and who forsakes his craft and does not practice it will become a rustic. Fortune also teaches this, for when a man is prosperous, he does whatever he wants to do because when his prosperity has ended, he can no longer do what he wants to do. I speak this honestly."

8

THE RESPONSE OF STEADINESS

12. From the storm cloud I again heard a voice responding to this image, saying: "You are foolish and empty, having been forsaken by the strengths of God's gifts. Think! The devil did what he wanted to do and

fell into hell. What Adam did, he sensed with his taste and he and all his offspring are now mortal. Goliath had confidence in what he did, but a young boy overcame him. Even Nabuchodonosor, your son, received what he could from you, and what happened to him? What happened to your other sons who also received things from you? God gave man the ability to work; he also divided up his knowledge so that he could discern what is honest and what is dishonest. He gave man the sword of good knowledge and the club of evil knowledge. When the flesh sprouts out and the soul agrees with it in doing something good and useful, good knowledge shakes its sword against evil knowledge and evil knowledge stretches its club out against good knowledge. As a result, man should look forward to what is useful, for God put evil knowledge in hell and the ladder of good knowledge in heaven since virtue is from God. O most evil one, you are as good as dead because you have chosen evil knowledge and have despised good knowledge; you have descended into the lake and have rejected the ladder of ascension into heaven."

13. I saw a fifth image that had the form of a man with light colored hair. It stood naked in the darkness, as if in an earthen wine cask.

9
THE WORDS OF CARE OF EARTHLY THINGS

14. This image spoke: "Which care of all the cares of this world is better? Where do the grasses and fruit-bearing things, the grapes and the other things necessary for this life and for sustaining and refreshing men, grow? If I were to shed tears from my eyes and sigh and beat my breast, or if I were to bend my knees, I might then have neither food nor garments, but might rather fall down instead. If I were to cry aloud to heaven and want the things necessary for me to come from the sun, moon and stars, nothing would come to me. Therefore, as long as I live on this earth, I will acquire the things I want by thinking, speaking and working."

10
THE RESPONSE OF HEAVENLY DESIRE

15. From the storm cloud I again heard a voice respond to this image: "O spoiler of souls, what are you saying? Your mind is full of deceit since you do not trust in God who is responsible for all the things you need, for just as the body cannot live without the soul, so also no fruit springs forth from the earth without God's grace. Look, therefore, at the

bones of the dead that lay in tombs and think about what they can do. They do not do anything but lay in rottenness. Similarly, you do not do anything but live in carelessness since you are willing to live without God's grace. Neither do you desire nor seek God with all your cares. I, however, dwell in the highest of places, and I come to each and every creature with grace because I am the life and greenness in all good works. I am the jewel of all the virtues, I am the delight and understanding of the love of God, and I am the foundation of all desire because I do each and every thing God wishes. With wings of good will, I fly above the constellations of heaven so that I accomplish God's will in all his justice. I also ascend above the mountains of Bethel where I look face to face at God's words. As a result, I neither demand, nor desire, nor want anything except what is holy; therefore, I am the Psalter and harp of God's joy. But I am also a representative from heaven in all causes."

11
THE WORDS OF OBSTINACY

16. The sixth image had the form of an ox and said: "I do not by any means have various things and causes in excess and with superfluousness, and when I say such and such, I am not strong enough to bring it forth slowly and gently. If the earth were always soft from fertilizer and rain, it would not be hard enough to bring forth any fruit, or if it were always so soft, water flowing across it would destroy it. How can it be wrong for me then if I am not soft in each and every case when unsuitable and suddenly falling rain harms the earth so much? If, however, I cannot sigh, this may be the case; or if I do not cry, this is of no concern to me because many perish through sorrow and nothing fails because of tears. Every grace that God wants to offer, he still offers. Why should I work for his grace with such determination? Why should I work so hard for something I might not receive? When a person seeks something he cannot get, nothing happens."

12
THE RESPONSE OF SORROW OF THE HEART

17. From the storm cloud I again heard a voice give the following response to this image: "What are you, o stubbornness? Why do you say that you do not have to work during your life when the birds, fish, beasts and cattle and snakes and reptiles all have to work in order to eat? Young animals seek nourishment from their mothers, and the earth gets

its greenness from the atmosphere. Why is God called the Father, unless of course it is because of his sons who call upon him? When God offers good things to his children through grace, they know he is God. Why then do you quarrel against God? I drink from the dew of his blessings, I smile at him from the sorrow of my heart, and I say to him with a rejoicing but woeful voice: 'God, help me.' And the angels respond to me with the sound of an organ, and they praise God since I call upon him. The dawn of grace then shines upon me, and he gives me the food of life because I called upon him so that I would not fail. But since you seek nothing from him, he will give you nothing."

18. The seventh image was similar to a woman down to her shins, but her shins and feet were so covered by the darkness I mentioned earlier that I could not see them. Her head was covered in the manner of a woman, and she wore a white garment.

13
THE WORDS OF DESIRE

19. This image said: "I desire intensely and am intensely eager to attract to myself each and every thing that is rich, that gives honor, and that is beautiful. I am intensely eager to receive each and every small gift that should be given to me and be had by me because the more I have, the more I will know. I am known to be wise and honest because of my beautiful rings, necklaces, earrings and other riches; and I dispense all things righteously with discriminating reasons. If I did not have all these things, I would not have all the goodness and honesty I have. I would be like a rotten branch that is neither hard nor soft. I am, however, able to do good with God and for men; people benefit from my possessions."

14
THE RESPONSE OF CONTEMPT OF THE WORLD

20. From the storm cloud I again heard a voice respond to this image: "You are the worst snare, you who are always measuring with your faculties the various things that are available for your physical pleasure. Certain generations of men have extended their souls to the riches and honors available to them in this life, they have sought signs in the sun and stars, and they have said that they and the things they trusted in were gods. What use is such vanity to them? Where are their riches and honors and lands now? In hell. For they endure the punishments they

have earned since they did not sit with the Holy Spirit and did not desire the things of heaven, but desired only physical and fallen things. I, however, sit with the figure of the Holy Spirit and I make a circle with the chariot of the precepts of God. I walk in his ways everywhere and I call him my father. I cast the fleshly desires for particular pleasures away and I manifest myself everywhere. But if I am tempted with fleshly desires, I quickly awaken my fear of God and the circle of the fire of the Holy Spirit. When people honor me in the name of the Lord and when they want to give me all their possessions, I place no value in this. I seek only enough to sustain me moderately and I say: 'Since these things take me away from the face of God, I blush intensely.' For when sin tempts me, I answer it with this: 'You did not create me and you cannot free me from evil; therefore, I condemn you and your deceit.' When the burning flame of the Holy Spirit kindles me, all the things of the world are consumed in me, and so I travel to heavenly things in a celestial chariot."

21. I saw another image, with its feet lifted up, hanging down in the darkness I mentioned earlier. It had a head like a leopard, but the rest of its body was like a scorpion. It had turned its back to the South and the East and said:

15
THE WORDS OF DISCORD

22. "I deny the East and do not want the South, for the East wants to have all things; the South, however, wants to sustain all things. What do the West and the North have? The dawn, holding the bright sun, shines with a reddish gleam; the West, however, carries the darkness. Can the North do anything? It can. Darkness obscures the sun; the sun, however, does not approach the darkness in order to reduce it. As a result, both hold onto their own strength. The North sustains the things that move about in the darkness. What can the birds of the sky and the beasts and cattle on earth do? What potential do the fish in the water have? Whatever they are able to do, they do. I dwell in all these things and I discern what they are and what they should do, for I turn everything upside down—the noble to the ignoble, the rich to the poor—like a wheel. If I do something for a long time, I become bored, so I stay with things only as long as it pleases me. Each and every thing, of course, rich and poor, noble and ignoble, may do whatever it is able to do. But so can I, for both the East and the South do likewise."

16
THE RESPONSE OF CONCORD

23. From the storm cloud I again heard a voice respond to this image: "You, dreadful and cursing one, what are you saying? You cannot destroy heaven and all its riches, can you? In no way. You cannot so much as make a mouse. You bring about nothing but disgrace with your quarreling. Even if you were to bring forth a thousand words of reproach to destroy your position in life, you would not be able to so much as harm it. You cannot blot out the sun and the stars, can you? No. For the brightness of the sun tramples you under foot like dust. You were thrown into hell the first time you began to fight. You cannot do anything more than other creatures can, for you are their servant, just as an ox is to his master. Furthermore, every male has strength, like the sun, to which the firmament and other luminaries have been subjected, like a female. You do not have any strength, but are useless to all since you have scandalized God's works. Anything that has no good is worth nothing. If a creature were to despise God, as you despise that creature, his power would not fail because he has the power of judgment over you, over Gehenna, over the darkness and over all the things that are in these."

24. Thereupon to the left of the man I mentioned earlier, I saw an image with a human form. On its head there was a fiery circle that gave out fiery tongues, and its face sent out flashes of lightning. I was not, however, able to see the rest of its shape since it was surrounded with a cloth that was as smooth as marble. This image cried out against the fault that had just spoken, saying:

17
THE WORDS OF ZEAL OF GOD

25. "O worst iniquity of the devil's schemes, I will cast you down and blot you out with the fortitude of God, just as the devil was cast down when light first began, and as Goliath and Nabuchodonosor, who wanted to wipe out God's justice since they had been cast down and wiped out by the circle of the fire of the Holy Spirit, were changed back to dust. For I am strength and constancy against all the evil you gather together in your bowels. You will not be able to resist me either."

18

HAVING BEEN RETURNED THROUGH TRUE OBEDIENCE TO GOD

26. I again heard a voice from heaven speak to me: "God, who created the earth and filled it with greenness and the various grasses, holds the earth in his strength so that it cannot be reduced to dust and be dissolved. He does this because man, formed from the earth and then expelled from paradise, remains on the earth and labors on it. Let man be obedient and return to the grace of his Lord so that he can reject the schemes that the devil continually confronts him with and so that he can choose the virtues sent by God and perpetually cling to his Creator."

19

THE FACT THAT MAN MAY ATTEND TO THE LIGHT OF BLESSEDNESS

27. This present vision shows you that the man I mentioned earlier is turned toward the South so that he looks South and West. This is because the omnipotent God moves man with his own piety so that he sees the light of the highest blessedness in the flame and love of true holiness, so that he chooses this flame, and so that he completely rejects the blindness and darkness of the temptations of the devil; he does not volunteer to subject himself to the devil.

20

HOW THE EARTH PRESERVES MAN

28. The earth in which he stands from his knees right up to the calves of his legs has moisture and greenness and is sprouting because the earth contains what God has bound together, with the strength of the earth pressing down and lifting up and sustaining what God made. For the earth contains moisture on high and down low, as well as the subterranean waters, so that it cannot be turned back to dust. It also contains the greenness of all things that are born and grow and that attract the green dye of vegetation. It also contains the seeds for everything that germinates and sends forth flowers of green strength. As it were, this man's virtue flourishes and is beautiful since his virtue has been made beautiful through the earth because the earth, when it produces and nourishes man and when it sustains and supports all the things that man uses, like

the flower of beauty and the embellishment of the honesty of God's virtue, prepares all things with its strength and dispenses them well and justly. Similarly, let God's power be honored through the earth since it preserves man, who should praise and glorify God for all time, with all the things he needs for his body and since it also sustains all the other things that are for man's use when it supports the development of these things. When man praises the excellence of God, man who is from the earth shows his just and holy works to God. Therefore, the earth is fertile and brings forth offspring, of course, because all things formed in earthly creatures are led forth from the earth. All the things that are born from the flesh, as from a mother, or that spring from a seed in the form and life of earthly creation, arise from the earth. Therefore, man, who has the power of reason and the spirit of intelligence, has come from the earth.

21
EARTH, THE MATERIAL OF MAN AND OF THE HUMANITY OF THE SON OF GOD

29. This material that is the work of God is in man; it is also the material of the humanity of the Son of God because God created man from the earth and the earth was also the material from which the Virgin brought forth the Son of God without any blemish in his pure and holy humanity.

22
THE SOUL, THE MATERIAL OF GOOD WORKS

30. Just as the earth brings forth many things that glorify God, so also man's soul that accompanies his blessed works brings forth the seeds of the virtues for the glory of God's name. For the soul in which God is, as in the earth, from the beginning of its strength to the perfection of good and holy works, as it were, from his knees right up to the calves of his legs, contains the sighs, prayers and holy works that lead to God, just as the moisture, greenness and the sprouts of the earth contain the grace of God. All the beauty and embellishment of divine inspiration, as it were, the flowering and embellishment of the virtue of God, as well as divine inspiration itself, are glorified through the soul. For when the soul in which God is, performs good works, God's glory is magnified with heavenly praises since the soul comes from God. The soul is fertile from God's grace and sprouts blessed strengths and virtues. It builds taber-

nacles in heavenly things because things come from the soul just as things formed by earthly creatures come from the earth. But the soul also contains the material for good works and a better life, clearly the contemplative life. The soul exists as something divine in man since it comes from God and it also performs good works, just and well, because of the divine command God gives the soul. It began to do these things, which the incarnate Son of God later finished with his perfect blessed virtues when he showed his true holiness. Being life, he gave life to those believing in him.

23

THE FACT THAT THE SON OF GOD, BEING CONCEALED IN THE HEART OF THE FATHER, WAS MADE MAN

31. Life was hidden in the middle of a great power and this power was silent until a white cloud covered the light so that it could shine forth only with great difficulty. Then the dawn rose up and surrounded the sun, and that sun sent out its rays and built a great city. The sun produced twelve lights, and in the third part of sleeping it aroused those who slept in the middle part. Therefore, all the eagles that dwelt in the white cloud and contemplated offering the sacrifice that had been written on the tablets, grew red when the sun showed its image of holiness in the eye of honesty. And then from the fire of the sun, the new world rose up from the water that covered its hills and mountains. The hills and mountains then sang an angelic song and saw the heavenly light with true faith because the Son of God came into the world and did all these things as he showed the righteous way to those who believed in him, just as David, inspired by the Holy Spirit, also speaks, saying:

24

DAVID TO THE SAME THING

32. *He has pitched a tent there for the sun, which comes forth like the groom from his bridal chamber and, like a giant, joyfully runs its course. At one end of the heavens it comes forth, and its course is to their other end; nothing escapes its heat (Psalm 19:5-7).* This means that the Son of God with the brightness of his divinity took on flesh from the Virgin who existed like a tabernacle for another life for the salvation of the human race. For God is called the burning sun that illuminated everything at the time of creation; from the heat of the sun, the

flesh of the Virgin, like a tabernacle, grew warm so that a man with a brighter faith and with a more burning charity came from it in the same way that God joined Eve to Adam before the fall. God also had created a strong man and a weak woman, from whose weakness the fall came about. Similarly, the divinity of the Son of God is strong, but his flesh is not, although the world was restored to its earlier life through it. This flesh truly came from the womb of the Virgin immaculate and inviolate, for God made it that way. In the same way, the bridegroom receives his bride in the promise of marriage with joy in the marriage bed of his heart when he gives her all his riches and honor with attentiveness. Likewise, the Son of God rejoiced because with the height of his divinity, as a giant he did not have any fear or doubt that some other conqueror would block his way, although he knew that he could run fast in order to show people the way of truth leading to salvation. Coming from the highest God when he came forth from the Father, he came to earth so that having been made man, he was above all else as one Son in power, one Son in work, and one Son in giving freedom. He also returned to his Father with his flesh and all his work when he ascended bodily to heaven with his great miracles. No one can flee from the heat of his divinity because the Word of the Father created all things and being clothed in the flesh, he freed man in the flesh. Therefore, he will judge all things with just judgment. Indeed, he will judge the greatest enemy as well as the newest and oldest enemy since all things exist through him.

25
EIGHT FAULTS FIGHTING AGAINST EIGHT BLESSED THINGS

33. But the fact that in the cloud I mentioned earlier I now see eight faults in their various images. This means that in the concealed unfaithfulness of the various deceits of the devil, these eight faults now reveal themselves through their disgusting signs. They fight against the eight blessed ones whom they cannot conquer because of their divine power. And then they are brought back together so that they can be returned to the same perdition from which they came.

26
CONCERNING INJUSTICE

34. The first image signifies injustice. It does not have any joy in life but clings to the devil, the first evil, because the devil brought this fault

forth first so that he could destroy those things that were and are just. This first image has a head like that of a fawn of a deer because the minds of the unjust are in the forests of perversity, trampling down all the providence and intelligence of those who are good. They fall into the precipice because they want to lead their own conscience rather than ponder what it says to them. This image also has a tail like that of a bear because the unjust do not have any stability on account of their worthlessness and wickedness when they try to resist and fight against everything. As a result, they are cast down, having been conquered by a true and just judgment and having been reduced to nothing. The rest of its body is truly like that of a pig because men who eagerly follow injustice are covered with the dirt of this fault and lie in its filth. Since their works are twisted and shameful on account of their many wrongs, they do not understand the righteousness of wisdom and do not draw just counsel to themselves; they want to do only what they wish. They strive to be superior to others, as this fault showed when it spoke earlier. Justice, however, responds to injustice and warns men not to imitate it.

27

CONCERNING NUMBNESS

35. The second image stands for numbness. It follows injustice because it deserts justice and is not watchful in faith but is blind in its mind so that it does not look back to God with truth. This image has the face of a child and white hair because men who freely choose numbness do not have the discipline of wisdom or the discretion of reason to know what is useful. They are foolish and unstable in their actions and show that they have, as it were, a weak mind so that they do not choose honesty but only uncertain sluggishness. And this image is clothed with a pale-colored tunic that hides its arms and hands and feet and its other members so that I cannot discern the rest of its form. This is because it surrounds itself with the nocturnal and numb darkness of neglect through leisure, that is, they are lazy men. These men conceal their strength when they do not do any good and strong deeds and they hide their footsteps when they should be walking on the path of righteousness. They cover the rest of their works with such neglect and sluggishness that no form of blessed virtue can be found in them. They are bored, they live in boredom, they do not worry about the welfare of their soul, and they do not do any work with their body. But being numb with leisure, they say that they want to live a quiet life, as this fault has shown in the words it spoke earlier. Strength refutes numbness and persuades men not to become dirty with numbness, but to help others as

well as themselves actively in body and soul. Strength also encourages them to use their hands to do some useful work, as it also has been written:

28
WISDOM TO THE SAME THING

36. *When one finds a worthy wife, her value is far beyond pearls. Her husband, entrusting his heart to her, has an unfailing prize. She brings him good, and not evil, all the days of her life. She obtains wool and flax and makes cloth with skillful hands. Like merchant ships, she secures her provisions from afar (Proverbs 31:10-14).* This means the following. Let the man who wants to be faithful throw down feminine fickleness and let him seek manly strength gently and zealously because his glory and fame will rise up from afar since God is glorified through his good works. In addition, let those of greater virtue trust him and show him the honor of their virtues. He will not steal false fame although he could use the praise given him falsely if he chose to. Good rewards rather than evil profits will be given him as long as he continues his good works, doing faithful works with just labor for others. Let him seek both gentleness and harshness so that when he works, he will know when he should be soft and when he should be rough; he should consider carefully what is suitable for others, given their situation.

37. Thus with the help of her highest giver and through the support of her prayers, this woman can carry away the sins of those who have sinned and who are far from the way of truth. She supplies what is necessary for the present moment and for life in general. But she is not spared from the perilous temptations of perverse torments since she carries all those who imitate her to the gate of salvation. The one who chooses wickedness will not find this woman, of course, wisdom, and he will not cast softness down nor take strength up, will he? He will not venture forth either because he is bored or because the journey is long, but will only seek food that does not satisfy him. He is like lightning that lights up things and like a stone that should contain gold. He is very concerned about earthly creatures and works hard for them and does not stop working hard for these things since he thinks they are useful. He values earthly things rather than heavenly ones. This faithful woman, however, prizes spiritual things and collects them in her soul when she contemplates them and in her actions when she does all her work so wisely.

38. She is pleasing to the strongest heart and to the omnipotent God in whom there is no need but only the highest fullness. God lacks nothing and all things can be received from him since he is overflowing with good things. Therefore, God gives her all that is worthy of praise and glory and he does not become less when he does this. She will remain with God since she was always with him and will always remain with him. But with concealed zeal she sought gentleness, like the wool, and piety, like the flax. She did heavenly work according to her own careful counsel when she did this work wisely. She covered the sons of men with her works so that they would not have to walk naked in God's presence, and she does not allow them to be lazy because she shows them many things they should do since she is so accustomed to hard work herself. Therefore, she has intense faith. She is like a ship that faithfully carries all the goods men need; she is like a carpenter since she builds the kingdom of heaven for those who are strong enough to do just labor. From one end of the world to the other, her faithfulness carries the food that can restore all those who want to be restored so that they will not fail along the way in the labor of their souls. Restored by this food, they are so filled with abundance that they cannot eat anything else.

29

CONCERNING FORGETFULNESS

39. You see a third image that stands for forgetfulness. It walks after numbness because numb men are forgetful both in their service of God and in doing other things. They forget God as if they did not know him and they no longer seek to be united with God because of the many questions they ask with diabolical scorn. Since they hold their ideas as more important than God, they, therefore, regard the devil as more important than God. The third image has a head and body like a lizard because the men who choose this fault have stubborn minds and wills, and do all their works stubbornly against God when they do their works hastily and without moderation. Further, envy and disbelief sometimes frighten them so that they do not always even know what they can do. This image appears in the presence of those clouds that are black, stormy and misty and that are intermixed with the dense white cloud because those who forget God remember their own thoughts and are, therefore, now in the impiety of blackness, the disbelief of storminess and the changeableness of mistiness. Nevertheless, all these things please them, the white cloud, when they intermix their work with the pleasure of their will when they do only what they desire. The fact that this same image places its forefeet on the cloud I mentioned earlier

means that those who forget God direct their footsteps in the direction of evil rather than in the direction of salvation. And they divide themselves and their works in two, of course, into the forgetfulness of God and into the hardness of their heart. They pay attention only to what their own mind tells them. Forgetfulness showed this in the words she spoke earlier, but holiness fights against her and warns men to prize forgetfulness less and to love God more truthfully.

30
CONCERNING CHANGEABLENESS

40. The fact that, however, you see a wheel, like the wheel of a wagon, turning in the darkness. This wheel, agitated as if by the winds, turns around like a mill-stone. This means that changeableness, having no stability like the bear mentioned above, has been weighed down with so many excesses and loaded down with so many vanities that it has become sluggish with unfaithfulness. Having been struck down with earthly temptations, it is no longer honest, but runs here and there and overturns all the old institutions with new worries. There are four spokes thrust into its radius that are large enough for a man to stand up in because the slackness that contains changeableness remains steadfast and does not want to forsake its various changes. In the four parts of the world, the various ways of men appear openly as they seek their pleasure when they begin neither with this custom nor with that one and when they transform the old ones into new ones. Indeed, there is the image of a man standing up among these spokes. This stands for the changeableness in the various ways of men in the slackness of their boldness. This image is a man because men are more changeable in their actions than any other type of creature. And this fault protests against honesty because when the unfaithful consider God as worth very little and forget him, they become very changeable. They seize changeableness at the devil's suggestion because the devil is not righteous and does not love moderation. The devil seduces men and drives them to various changes since he chooses instability and is so unstable and, therefore, stirs up those who are stable. This image holds a spoke with each hand; the other two spokes are behind his back. This means that the devil turns the customary actions of men into the pursuit of pleasure while they neglect their other worldly and spiritual actions because the old serpent makes men who serve God and the world very restless so that they now have these customs and then those, and now do these actions and then those. This image turns with the wheel because changeableness does not remain in any particular position but is always unstable. It fans

itself with the winds so that it chooses by measure these things and then neglects them, so that it holds onto by measure the old customs of men and then seizes all the new customs.

41. This image, however, has curly black hair because this fault leads men to thinking they have a lot of knowledge is their mind, which, nevertheless, they do not, since they are not made strong with the fullness of righteousness but instead choose the blackness of perversity with tortuous vanity. Its hands are like those of the forefeet of a monkey because all of man's works are more foolish than they are truly prudent. Whenever man thinks he has the beauty of prudence, he walks in foolishness. It has feet like those of a hawk because man shows bitterness when he wants to do only what is for his own pleasure; what he wants, he does for himself and does not think about whether it is useful to others. Its garment has black and white stripes on it because sometimes man adorns himself with justice while he is actually surrounded with scandals and insults; other times he hides himself on the path of deception when he makes himself appear holy while he is actually wicked. He does not follow the glory and honor of the wise and disciplined but rather follows the despair of those who do not love wisdom and who actually consider it to be a pestilence. People who are consistently honest and upright do not choose or venerate those who are changeable in their words and actions. In addition, this image has spread out a net as if to capture animals, but it did not catch anything because this fault tries to deceive good people and tries to draw them to itself, but it is not strong enough to do this since steady souls remain fixed in their good and honest ways and do not consider changing. This fault, however, values its own motives and thinks those who refuse to follow it are foolish. It thinks it is wiser and more righteous and happier than others are, just as it showed in the words it spoke earlier. Steadiness responds to changeableness and shows that it is foolish and empty and that it will descend with its followers into damnation.

31
CONCERNING CARE OF EARTHLY THINGS

42. The fifth image stands for care of earthly things. It follows changeableness because men who are changeable in their actions and customs as a result of their unstable minds are often concerned with the care of earthly things and resist heavenly things. It does not seek the food and nourishment of life either. As you see, this image has the form of a man, of course, the possession of worldly and earthly cares. It has

pale hair. This is the soul erring with foolishness and with great noise, rushing everywhere, because men who suffer from this fault are very restless in soul and body. But they delight in this just as if they were surrounded with quietness, for what is restlessness to some men is quietness to these and what is quietness to some is restlessness to these who suffer from this fault. This image stands naked in the darkness, as if in an earthen wine cask because the senses and heart of such men are placed in and covered over with the blackness of earthly uneasiness and anxieties. Those naked and without blessedness trample on them with the same pleasure as if they were sitting in pleasant baths. For when they choose the nakedness of ignorance, they do not seek the garment of the salvation from God because they are concerned only with earthly things and with things that are fallen and temporary. This fault demonstrated this in the words it spoke earlier. Heavenly desire responds to the care of earthly things and encourages men to care more for celestial and eternal things than for temporal things.

32
CONCERNING OBSTINACY

43. The sixth image stands for the obstinacy of the mind. It follows care of earthly things because men who care only about earthly things are obstinate in their minds. They have no respect for God in their hearts, as if their hearts had been stained and stuck together with pitch. They speak and act as if God did not exist because they do not know what good is and do not seek the softness of piety. They are, instead, harshly stubborn against God. This image has the form of an ox because this fault makes men's minds rough and hard and makes them ascend to the height of insecure security so that nothing consoles them and so that they have no concern for the power of reason found in others. This fault causes men to oppose each other with the javelin of words and with the bitterness of works. It guides no one, protects no one, but strikes amazement and fear into whomever it can. This was shown in the words it spoke earlier. The sorrow of the heart resists obstinacy and admonishes men to leave harshness behind so that they can sigh for the heavenly things that they can claim from God, seeing that God can mercifully tear them away from the storms of the wicked spirits. The prophet David encourages this when he says:

33

DAVID TO THE SAME THING

44. *Rescue me out of the mire; may I not sink! May I be rescued from my foes, and from the watery depths. Let not the floodwaters overwhelm me, nor the abyss swallow me up, nor the pit close its mouth over me (Psalm 69:15-16).* This means the following. Lord God, through the mildness of your grace, snatch me, a sinner, for the decay that arose in me through my flesh and from the sin that makes me deny you. Snatch me from the concupiscence of my flesh that has become so dirty since the time you created me from the earth. After Adam's fall, I was made unclean mud and perversity shoots up in me everywhere. And cast out the worms from me that are filthy and useless. But from my flesh, by the power of your grace let virtuous things give out the aromas of good works because man's flesh with the knowledge of good and evil can be both useful and useless, although mine has declined into evil. You, however, o God, draw me away from filthy actions so that I will not be found in the decay of uselessness and with the forgetfulness that pierces me like a thorn with the death of destruction. With the sweetest aroma of the virtues, make me rise up from this mud so that I can trample it under my feet with good footsteps. Free me as well from those who hate me and want to steal away all the good knowledge you gave me; these are the ones who taste the sins. And free me from the vanities of the sins that try to suffocate me, clearly the sins of luxury. With the force of your goodness, prevent me from plunging into the perilous storm of wickedness, which is avarice. Do not let me be swallowed by the old serpent because of my depraved works since the devil lives in the infernal pit where he forgets about you. Do not let the abyss, which is the result of all the evil works of pride, close its mouth over me for pride brought death into existence. Do not let death confine me in its closed mouth in case there might be someone who can snatch me out of it. You will be the one to do this, o God, not because of my very few merits, but because of your mercy. That man is blessed whom God listens to and who has a gift from God because that man seeks the things that should be sought after from God.

34

CONCERNING DESIRE

45. The seventh image, however, as you see, signifies desire. It walks behind the obstinacy of the mind because when obstinacy in the per-

verse minds of men does not seek God, desire then succeeds it. Desire has no vision of God, but going around and running around everywhere, like a wolf, it looks for something to devour, disturbing things with its noise and rushing to seize whatever it can. This image is similar to a woman down to her shins, but her shins and feet are so covered by the darkness mentioned earlier that you cannot see them. This is because the softness of vanity touches desire right up to the point where it walks in the footsteps of the complete wickedness of unfaithfulness, resulting in the fact that neither its end nor its footsteps can be discerned in unfaithfulness. For desire makes men speak softly and to say that they do not gather any possession for their present need and that they do not waste anything they might need in the future, but they are completely perverse since no good things are found there when abundance is given to them and to others. The head of this image is covered in the manner of a woman because men who are guilty of this fault hide their intentions with deception, allowing no one to know what is in their hearts since they have no moderation in earthly and heavenly things. This image wears a white garment because it pretends that all of its opinions and its way of life are useful and beautiful and because whatever it is able to seize, it says that it does so only with good intentions and out of necessity. Contempt of the world, however, fights against desire and faithfully persuades men to flee temporal and fallen things and to desire heavenly things eagerly.

35
CONCERNING DISCORD

46. The next image prefigures discord. It follows desire because when wicked men desire many things they are not able to have, they run into discord in the madness of their minds and attack whatever remains, just as a dog growls and attacks a person. With a lot of differences of opinion, with bitterness and with harshness they scatter about and spread around the things God has made; they do not want peace and they rejoice when they can tear others to pieces with their words and actions. With its feet lifted up, this image hangs down in the darkness mentioned earlier because men guilty of this fault are always ready with exaltation and outrage to start on the journey of unfaithfulness. They grant nothing, spare nothing, but agitate all the things they can dislodge into discord. They pay no attention to the goodness of humanity. Those who are prepared to share all their possessions with others have noticed this, as it has been written:

36

CONCERNING THE ACTS OF THE APOSTLES TO THE SAME THING

47. *The community of believers were of one heart and one mind. None of them ever claimed anything as his own; rather, everything was held in common (Acts 4:32).* This means that the multitude that is in the Catholic faith are given many things by the fire of the Holy Spirit who sprinkles their minds so they see God in the unity of the mirror of true faith. This multitude should be of one heart in the unity of the true Trinity in whom they are so on fire that they look at God alone. But they also should have a soul so burning with love that they despise all the kingdoms of the world and by which they consider all the suffering that happens to them as nothing, because when the flesh ascends to the summit of the soul, meritorious flesh is sometimes afflicted. Therefore, let them rejoice in all things. They do not want to be rich, but poor; because their avarice has died and has turned to ashes, they spurn riches. No one has anything according to his own will, but all things he has are a gift from God, so let them possess them with God. Let it not be said that they are lacking anything in their virtue, but let them be with God who gives all good things to the good. What are these good things? Truth and justice, in which all good things are entwined. Those, however, who reject good things and draw evil things to themselves do not want to have a mutual God. But those who choose God and want to have life will hold all things in common. Although the peculiarity of the human will seeks strange gods and drives holiness away, those who choose God do not act this way. God, however, created man and subjected every creature to him, so man has no power over these things except what God allows him to have. Whatever man has today, God with his just judgment will remove tomorrow, whether man wants this to happen or not since all things stand with God and are in God who distributes them righteously.

48. This image has a head like a leopard. It leads the will of wicked men to a double madness when it makes them rant and rave in word and deed. With its fury it also strikes the horror and terror of unquietness into all things so that both quiet and unquiet, in hiding and in the open, it imitates the devil, from whom it came, who makes noise and stirs up everything with is wicked suggestions. But the rest of its body is like a scorpion because everything it does is full of the poison of death since it does not do anything other than cause the perils of unhappiness and

death. This image has turned its back to the South and the East because it opposes the virtues inflamed with heavenly love and because it aids the deceitful deeds of the devil, turning upside down whatever it can. It showed this in the words it spoke earlier. Concord answers discord and points out that it will be hurled into hell.

37
CONCERNING THE FORM OF THE ZEAL OF GOD

49. Thereupon to the left of the man mentioned earlier, you see an image with a human form because those iniquities that are, as it were, to the left since they have forgotten God are being judged with the just judgment of the zeal of God since they have made men sin. The just judgment of God justly judges each and every unjust thing. On its head there is a fiery circle that gives out fiery tongues because the zeal of God, blazing from the beginning of the world and continuing with its judgment of the first fallen angel, burns up every crime kindled by the heat of desire and committed by a rational creature; it does not miss anything or leave anything unexamined either. Its face sends out flashes of lightning because it shows its punishments clearly and brightly when it openly scourges each person according to what he deserves while the others watch on. You are not, however, able to see the rest of its shape since it is surrounded with a cloth that is as smooth as marble. This means that the profound judgments of the zeal of God cannot be completely understood since they are surrounded by such invincible strength that no one has enough strength to soften or to examine them. The judgments of the zeal of God are just because they penetrate everything with righteousness that has not been driven out or punished through repentance. Whatever repentance has cleansed, the zeal of God does not examine because repentance is the fire and scourge of the zeal of God. But whatever repentance does not truly boil away, the zeal of God consumes.

38
HOW A JUST MAN IS A CONCEALER OF HIMSELF

50. A faithful man who has been reproached by God fears these reproaches since he knows he will not be spared from punishment unless he repents. With a sorrowful heart, let him say: "O God, you know all things and accomplish all things. When I sin, I quake in the knowledge of my sins, but when I repent, I do not repent completely and I fear this. When my will takes me on the paths and journeys of wantonness, I

quake; and when I continue sinning until I am old or when I hang onto my sins rather than be sad and have sorrow for them and dismiss them, I fear this. Why is this? Because I also know that there are things of quality. What does this mean? I am like a wheel that sometimes turns to the North, sometimes to the East, sometimes to the South, and sometimes to the West. When I think about being born with original sin, I commit sins either by knowing or by speaking or by working. But when I remember where my soul is from, I sift the barley of my works from the wheat. I, however, do not do this completely since I am flesh and blood. When I rush toward illicit pleasures, which make me dance like a fawn with the temptations of my flesh, I do not hold my flesh and blood in check. When I rush into old age with the weight of sin so that I do not delight quite so fully in them, I want to protect my life and correct my sins, but I do not do this. And so I roll around in all these things with instability, like a wheel. For these reasons, O God, I despise all my sins in whatever way I have committed them since I know in my soul that you do not spare anyone who opposes you boldly with sins. I know this because you cast the first sinning angel into hell, you exiled man after the fall, and you drive each and every wickedness according to its merits back into the stable of its own contrition. I, however, have trust in the fact that you broke heaven open when you put on flesh. Therefore, I abandon my falling and sinning nature to you so that you can wash that part of me with your mercy through repentance; I, a sinner, will then live, having been washed of my sins through you."

39
THE FACT THAT THE ZEAL OF GOD IS INVINCIBLE AGAINST THE DEVIL

51. This image cries out against the various faults because the zeal of God cries out against the temptations of the wicked spirits that make men weary. The zeal of God withholds and wipes out the suggestions in the devil's wickedness through the virtues of the highest judge, just as the ancient attacker and certain of his followers cast out true justice. After they have been cast down prostrate by the fire of divine vengeance, they are no longer considered as worth anything since the zeal of God is strong and invincible against all the deceits of their snares that they hold in their evil. They are not strong enough to resist either because the light will oppress the darkness and good will destroy evil since all things are subject to God.

40

THE FACT THAT THE ZEAL OF GOD STRIKES THE ONE REPENTING LESS

52. When a man, however, punishes himself for his sins and when he stops sinning, the zeal of the Lord strikes him less because this person did not spare himself but did cast away the things he took pleasure in before. This is the other way that can lead man to eternal life.

41

THE FACT THAT THE ACCUSER OF HIMSELF MAKES THE DEVIL BLUSH

53. How? Whenever a man recognizes his sins and forsakes them, he knows God; when he sighs for God in his soul, he sees God; when he has done just and holy works, he cultivates the angelic order; and when the fame of his good works among men flies from him at death, he will write about the secrets of God with the Cherubim. As a result, the devil blushes when he sees man forsake his sins and return to this Creator, which the devil, hardened in the perversity of his wickedness, does not want to do. A faithful person, however, rushes back to God and brings God the glory of his life in order to be saved. He is just and shows his Creator the pious and holy devotion of his heart, just as the Psalm exhorts, saying:

42

DAVID TO THE SAME THING

54. *Give to the Lord, you families of nations, give to the Lord glory and praise; give to the Lord the glory due his name! Bring gifts, and enter his courts (Psalm 96:7-8).* This means the following. You who want to avoid evil and do good, bring the Lord the glory of all things with devotion and the honor of the service of justice with righteous faith when you fill your righteous faith with blessed works. You also bring glory to the Lord when you call him your God; you truly believe that he is your God when you call him your God and when you do good works for him since you are made in his image and likeness. Therefore, adore the Lord of all with bent mind and body in the church's universal institutions that are holy because they reach to the seat of his majesty. Do this by means of abstinence, castigation, and the rest of the virtues that

walk in his temple. Imitating heavenly harmony and angelic order, worship him faithfully. Let your holy and faithful soul do all these things while it is still in your body and let it flee the devil and his temptations. Let your soul cling to its Creator and let it run away from the things that try to suffocate it. However, let he who desires life grasp these words and store them in the innermost chamber of his heart.

55. I saw some other spirits in this crowd who cried aloud, saying: "Lucifer will do whatever pleases him and we will do the same. Neither he nor we will do anything else." These spirits show men injustice and urge people not to give anyone else what is their own.

43
CONCERNING THE CLEANSING PUNISHMENTS OF INJUSTICE

56. I saw a horrible place that was full of fiery thorns and thorny plants and that had the worst worms in it, and with fiery scourges, the evil spirits stirred up the souls of those who had persisted in the ways of injustice while they had been alive. Because these souls had held injustice in their words and deeds, they were punished with these thorns and thorny plants; because they had been harsh in their injustice, they were twisted by these worms; and because they had spared nothing in their injustice, they were afflicted by these fiery scourges of the evil spirits. And I saw and understood these things.

44
CONCERNING DOING REPENTANCE FOR INJUSTICE

57. I again heard a voice from the living light say to me: *These things that you see are true, and as you see them, so they are. Therefore, let the men who want to overcome these evil spirits and who want to avoid the punishments for this fault cast away all injustice from themselves, and let them endure fasting and scourging. Let them also be persistent in the purest prayers in the amount their spiritual director advises.*

45
CONCERNING INJUSTICE

58. Those who choose injustice and hold it in their right and left hands are flattered by other people, but they do not listen to their masters or love the law or wish to serve the institutions of the law; all the things they do, they do only for themselves without any regard for the law and for as long as they wish. Just as there is no injustice in which the moon fails and the stars do not shine, since time cannot be discerned in the night or in the moon or in the darkened stars, so also neither is there any order of equality in injustice. Injustice is like food that is boiled and tasteless since it has been boiled without knowledge and it has been made tasteless without wisdom. It does not have the pleasant sound of reason either since reason has the sound of praise and the pleasure of playing on a lyre in praise of God. Similarly, a faithful man glorifies his Creator with every effort of his mind and body, with a spirit of humility, and with a heart of contrition, for the Creator ought to be praised worthily by his creatures.

46
CONCERNING THE LAMENTATION AND SYMPHONY
OF THE SOUL

59. I who made all things also say: *You who want to partake of the heavenly Jerusalem, praise your Creator with the sound of faith that makes a praiseworthy sound by means of the power of reason in all of God's works, since reason praises God in all good things. Reason is like a trumpet with a living voice; it fulfills its responsibility when it dispenses itself by various methods into creatures and in so far as the various creatures assist it so that they return a good and strong sound. Indeed, through the sound of its living voice, reason makes those things that do not make a living sound resound, for reason, from the time God first breathed in a soul for man, holds the means of gladness. Therefore, praise God with that pure and agreeable knowledge that makes a creature so agreeable, and praise God with the sweet and profound wisdom that dispenses all things wisely and justly, clearly when it discerns heavenly things in man's soul and when it knows earthly things sweetly. But man's soul also has harmony in itself and is like a symphony. As a result, many times when a person hears a symphony, he sends forth a lamentation since he remembers that he was sent out of his fatherland into exile. These things, however, have been spoken*

concerning the atonement for the cleansing and saving of souls, and they are faithful things. A faithful person pays attention to these things and remembers them well.

60. I also saw some other spirits in this crowd who I heard crying aloud: "Who or what God may be, we do not know. But who or what we see, we do know." These spirits lead men to numbness and encourage them to be lukewarm in everything they do.

47
CONCERNING THE CLEANSING PUNISHMENTS OF NUMBNESS

61. I saw darkened air mixed with fire in which spirits were driving here and there with fiery clubs the souls of those who had chosen numbness while they had been alive. Because of the numbness they had had, they were in this darkened air; because of the foolishness by which they had decided that God was not worth anything, they felt the fire; and because of the slothfulness by which they had avoided doing just works, they endured this infestation of evil spirits. And I saw and understood these things.

48
CONCERNING THE REPENTANCE OF NUMBNESS

62. I heard the voice from the living light say to me: *These things that you see are true. But if men are anxious to turn away from the spirits leading them on to numbness and if they want to flee its punishments, let them chastise themselves with fasting and scourging; and after cutting out the disgust of numbness from themselves with the purest prayers, let them serve God with the sharpness of uprightness.*

49
CONCERNING THE FAULT OF NUMBNESS

63. Numbness keeps company with some animals who do not have the quickness of good or the quickness of evil, but who lie down in slothfulness. It does not fear or love God since it does not taste him in fear or harmonize with him in love. It does not reason like man either and it does not call upon God with the breath of its soul. It is as useless as the air of the earth that dries up fruit. Therefore, it says to itself: "If God exists, let God be, because he does not need my work. I desire

nothing more than to live fully." And so numbness postpones doing good. But the man who does not wish to venerate or choose God who created all things and whose kingdom has no end, is foolish; the man, however, who perpetually looks in the mirror of his heart at God from whom he has his body and soul, is wise. These things, however, have been spoken concerning the atonement for the cleansing and saving of souls, and they are faithful things. A faithful person pays attention to these things and remembers them well.

64. I saw some other spirits in this crowd who cried aloud with great clamoring: "Let us go, let us go, and let us hurry to go to that place where we should go." These spirits draw men to forgetting God and persuade them not to remember their Creator or his work.

50
CONCERNING THE CLEANSING PUNISHMENTS OF FORGETFULNESS

65. I saw a great valley that was very long and wide, that was filled with much fire and a most unclean stink, and that had many worms in horrible shapes running around in it. The soul of those who had forgotten about the fear of God when they were alive and who did not want to know and understand what they could do, were punished in this valley. Because they had been unfaithful in their hearts, they were in this valley; because they had chosen impiety, they were burning in this fire; because they had tried to resist God, they smelled this stink; and because they had been full of deceit, they were twisted by these worms. And I saw and understood these things.

51
CONCERNING THE REPENTANCE FOR FORGETFULNESS

66. I again heard the voice from the living light say to me: *These things that you see are true, and as you see them, so they are. Therefore, let men who forget God flee from the evil spirits who entice them to forgetfulness, let them return to their own heart, and let them look back to their Creator and his work. And so that they will not be punished by the things mentioned above, let them remove themselves from other people for a time and let them chastise themselves with harsh*

garments, fasting and scourging, according to the plan of the rector presiding over them.

52

CONCERNING THE FAULT OF FORGETFULNESS

67. Forgetting God gives men the worst of thoughts and it encourages them to say: "How can we know God whom we never see? How can we be strong enough to pay attention to what we never look at?" A person who says such things does not remember his Creator since the darkness of forgetfulness surrounds his heart. When a person fails, every creature is darkened with him. God indeed had created man with complete brightness so that he could see the light of the purest air and could know the songs of the angels. And he clothed him with such brightness that he shone with great splendor, but by breaking God's command so completely, he fell and all the elements fell with him, changing into something worse. Nevertheless, men have some light left in them since they did not continue committing this sin. Therefore, let man understand God and let him take God into the innermost chamber of his heart, knowing that God created him and made all creation come forth. Let man always remember God well, just as it has been written:

53

WORDS FROM THE BOOK OF WISDOM

68. *Remember your Creator in the days of your youth, before the evil days come. And the dust returns to the earth as it once was, and the life breath returns to God who gave it (Ecclesiastes 12:1 and 7).* This means the following. You who desire to have the glorious life and rest of eternity, remember the one who created you by doing good and holy works. You should do this while you are still young, for you should spring forth and proceed in holiness before the time rushes to you when your flesh and blood fail and your bones are made bare. You should do this before the ashes of your body return to the dust of the earth from which you came before you were changed into another form of life. And you should do this before the spirit that quickens your body deserts it and return to the Lord of all who gave this spirit to your body according to the disposition of his grace. God is like a worker who blows on a fire with a pair of bellows and then turns the fire every which way so that he can accomplish his work more fully. When, however, man's spirit is directed by righteous means to do good works so that he can return to the eternity of unfailing joy, he will see the purest light and will hear the an-

gelic song that Adam saw and heard before he broke the command that led to mortality. As a result, let men search carefully for the garment that he tore so that he may again wear it with joy. These things, however, have been spoken concerning the atonement for the cleansing and saving of souls, and they are faithful things. A faithful person pays attention to these things and remembers them well.

69. I saw some other spirits in the crowd who cried aloud: "We will seek all things with our own skills and we will possess all things." These spirits urge men to be changeable and show them changeableness everywhere.

54
CONCERNING THE CLEANSING PUNISHMENTS OF CHANGEABLENESS

70. I saw a very large fire that was full of worms of various shapes. The souls of those who had been very changeable in their words and deeds while they had been alive were punished in this fire. Because of their changeableness with which they had boldly deceived man, they burned in this fire; and because of the many deceits they had had in themselves so vainly, they were twisted by these worms.

55
CONCERNING THE REPENTANCE FOR CHANGEABLENESS

71. And I saw and understood these things. I again heard the voice from the living light say to me: *These things that you see are true. However, if men want to chase away these evil spirits encouraging them to changeableness while they are in this world and if they want to avoid the punishments of this sin, let them lead a spiritual life, or if they are already living a spiritual life, let them be very truthful in their dealings with other people so that they can hurl the wickedness of this fault away from themselves.* This fault speaks to men and says:

56
CONCERNING THE FAULT OF CHANGEABLENESS

72. "How can I walk down just one way when only one way is not shown to me and when the pastures in which I graze are not my own?

Where I seek faith, I do not find it. Those I judge to be my friends are my enemies. Those in whom I find friendship scarcely cling to me. Because of all of this, I cannot have the covenant of stability in any way. I show myself to things the same way they show themselves to me, but if I subject myself to things, they trample me underfoot. I praise whatever I want to praise, I despise whatever seems worth little to me, and I hide myself from whatever I fear; thus I follow my own will. This is just as the Jews did who heard Moses and then did not want to hear him later, but whatever they saw, they heard and believed. Balaam also did the same thing when he praised the Jews and then found other friends for himself. So did the pagans who found in idols the things they wanted to find. Whatever I am able to find, I find; I search many different things eagerly with questions; and in all these things I hold onto some part so that I do not fail. If I did not do this, I would not know what I am, for heaven does not speak to me, earth does not succor me, and no other creature speaks to me so that I can continue with it." Changeableness speaks this way about the areas where it presides because its eyes are blind to faith, its ears are deaf to truth, its tongue is silent to the legal precepts, and its heart is like a stone when it comes to loving God. It does not have any faith in God or men, but it is like an image that neglects God and seduces and deceives men with a lot of hissing. Let those who chose God and venerate men flee changeableness, let them cast deception from themselves, and let them approach what is stable and firm according to God and not according to men. These things, however, have been spoken concerning the atonement for the cleansing and saving of souls, and they are faithful things. A faithful person pays attention to these things and remembers them well.

73. I saw some other spirits in this crowd who cried aloud: "We will dwell in heaven since Lucifer continues on with the same honor he originally had." These spirits lead men to the care of earthly things and encourage men to devote themselves completely to such things.

57
CONCERNING THE CLEANSING PUNISHMENTS FOR CARE OF EARTHLY THINGS

74. I saw a great fire that had a black flame filled with many serpents. The souls of those who did not have any concern for heavenly things but only for earthly things while they had been alive, were being tossed around in this fire from place to place, as if by the wind. Because they had neglected God in the darkness of their unbelief when they de-

sired earthly things, they suffered in this black flame; because they had been greedy for earthly things, they were twisted by these serpents; and because they had not stopped doing these things, they were flung here and there in this fire with great affliction. And I saw and understood these things.

58
CONCERNING THE DRIVING REPENTANCE FOR CARE OF EARTHLY THINGS

75. I again heard the voice from the living light say to me: *These things that you see are true, and as you see them, so they are. Therefore, if men who toil to get earthly things want to overcome the spirits urging them to do this and if they want to avoid the punishments for this, let them chastise themselves with fasting and scourging according to the plan of the rector presiding over them and let them lead their hearts back to heavenly things.*

59
CONCERNING THE FAULT IN THE CARE OF EARTHLY THINGS

76. Those who choose the care of earthly things say foolishly: "We will look for and pay attention to the creation created for our use since that creation feeds and clothes us. Therefore, let God do what pleases us, for if we put our care with God rather than with earthly things, we will fail quickly. What would happen to us then? We are like the birds who look at their faces in the water, for when they do not pay attention, they die quickly. After we have died, we will no longer be with creatures in any way, but we will have only the life God gives to us after death. So if we have shared with creatures and then each and every one is cut off from us, it is not blameworthy since God created these things thus. If they were created for our use and we did not choose them, we would sin greatly. Indeed, we require nothing from these creatures other than what God has given us. Similarly, whoever allows his horse to run unbridled walks not quietly, but dangerously. Further, if we do not have care of earthly things, the earth will sprout thorns and thorny plants. We would then be sinning since the earth is supposed to feed all the animals but could not do so if we did not care for it." Those who put all their effort and care into their present life while they are alive and who do not put any effort into their future life, speak this way, just as the greedy

and unfaithful Jews did when they ignored my Son whom I sent into the world for the salvation of people. Scorning his words, the Jews tried to destroy him completely by putting him to death. Let the faithful man seize a plow with oxen so that he may, nevertheless, look at God who gives greenness and fruit to the earth; and let him walk according to the commands of his master so that, cultivating earthly things, he does not desert heavenly things. These things, however, have been spoken concerning the atonement for the cleansing and saving of souls, and they are faithful things. A faithful person pays attention to these things and remembers them well.

77. I also saw some other spirits in this crowd who cried aloud with a great clamor: "Who is this God who makes us struggle so much?" These spirits stand for obstinacy in men's hearts and they encourage men to be completely obstinate in their minds.

60
CONCERNING THE CLEANSING PUNISHMENTS OF OBSTINACY

78. I saw darkness, burning with pitch and sulphur. The souls of those who had been obstinate in their minds while they had been alive gave forth great lamentation in this darkness. Because they had had harshness against God, they burned in this darkness; because they had not shared in the virtues, they endured this pitch; because they had not shown any benevolence, they were punished by this sulphur; and because they had not breathed forth their hearts to God, they sent forth their great lamentation. And I saw and understood these things.

61
CONCERNING THE REPENTANCE FOR OBSTINACY

79. I again heard the voice from the living light say to me: *These things that you see, are true. But let men who are obstinate in their minds, cast their obstinacy out; let them deny the wicked spirits who make them this way; and in order not to be punished for this, let them chastise themselves with fasting and scourging; and lastly on bended knees, let them make themselves look favorable in the eyes of God.*

62
CONCERNING THE FAULT OF OBSTINACY

80. Those who are obstinate do not see or hear God and are not moved by his breath. For obstinacy is depraved and worthless; it does not want to be softened or changed from the hardness it has. Just like a mole that throws out the earth, it also turns away good things since nothing pleases it except what it chooses itself. It is like glowing ashes that disappear when they are spewed and scattered on high because when obstinacy turns away from virtuous knowledge and looks to immobile wickedness, it leads to nothing.

63
WHY GOD PLACED TRIBULATIONS ON JOY

81. *Obstinacy does not have the fear that Job, my servant, had when he patiently endured all the things that I allowed to be done to him. But because I loved Job so much, I sent him many tribulations since I knew he had great patience and benevolence. Indeed, his patience flourished and his benevolence ascended to me because he gave himself to me and did not gnash his teeth against me. He did not have the obstinacy that is as hard as a stone and as dry as the earth when it does not give forth any fruit.* Let those flee obstinacy who desire to cling to God and to receive the highest reward. These things, however, have been spoken concerning the atonement for the cleansing and saving of souls, and they are faithful things. A faithful person pays attention to these things and remembers them well.

82. I saw some other spirits in this crowd who cried aloud, saying: "Of what use is just one thing? What we seek, we cannot come upon in one God. Therefore, whatever we see and whatever we want, we will draw to ourselves." These spirits encourage men to desire and show them that they should desire all things.

64
CONCERNING THE CLEANSING PUNISHMENTS FOR DESIRE

83. I saw a body of water that was very long, wide and deep. It boiled with the intense burning of fire and contained the worst snakes and very many wicked spirits. The souls of those who had chosen desire while

they had been alive and who had drawn many things to themselves in many different ways were, however, punished here. Because of their unstable desire, they felt the pain of the boiling water; because of the bitterness of their desire, they were tormented by the snakes; and because of the zeal with which they had desired, they were immersed in the fire and smoke of this water. And I saw and understood these things.

65
CONCERNING THE REPENTANCE FOR DESIRE

84. I again heard the voice from the living light say to me: *If men are eager to overcome the spirits who entice them to desire and if they are eager to avoid the punishments for this fault, let them chastise themselves with fasting and scourging, and let them give a lot of alms as repayment for this sin.*

66
CONCERNING THE FAULT OF DESIRE

85. Desire does not love God or trust men, but it tears away whatever it can, it seizes whatever it can, it freely draws to itself whatever it can, and it holds excesses of all things in its mind and body and actions. It is like dogs that run to and from everywhere, but are never satisfied. It is also like an unclean bird caught in a turmoil and storm. Having squalid ways, desire flees the healthy ways of honesty and pours blame out on many; therefore, it does not even know God, but only looks back to things that are foreign. Let those who want to flee death and to choose God and who want to obtain the joys of the eternal promise cast off the overflowing of desire, and let them be moderate in all the things they do, for the sake of God while they live in time. These things, however, have been spoken concerning the atonement for the cleansing and saving of souls, and they are faithful things. A faithful person pays attention to these things and remembers them well.

86. I saw some other spirits in this crowd who I heard crying aloud with a great clamor: "Lucifer is our Lord and no one will attack us when we are with him." These spirits show men discord and urge them to be troublesome and to flee the harmony of the virtues.

67

CONCERNING THE CLEANSING PUNISHMENTS OF MEN NEGLECTING CONCORD

87. I saw a very great fire, near which the densest darkness appeared. It contained snakes with horrible shapes and many wicked spirits that ran back and forth. The souls of those who had neglected the concord of holiness and who had chosen discord while they had been alive, were punished here. They were driven back and forth between the darkness and fire by wicked spirits that struck them. Because they had stirred up every kind of evil with discord, they were burned by the fire; because they had attacked so many with discord, they were twisted around in this darkness; because they had been so cruel, they were afflicted with these snakes; and because they had caused so many others to err through the same fault, they were forced by the wicked spirits to go back and forth between the fire and the darkness.

68

CONCERNING THE REPENTANCE FOR DISCORD

88. And I saw and understood these things. I again heard the voice from the living light say to me: *These things that you see, are true, and as you see them, so they are, and there are more things. If men want to turn away from the spirits dragging them to discord and if they want to flee its punishments, let them wear a hair shirt, let them afflict themselves with the harshest of fasting and scourging, and let them avoid soft things for their body.*

69

CONCERNING THE FAULT OF DISCORD

89. Those who choose and cling to discord have been harassed by a wicked spirit and will, therefore, be ordered to pass from their wickedness to the torments of complete destruction since it is the devil's helper. It murmurs freely, it drags out various deliberations, it scatters good deliberations about, it reproaches others for their deeds, and it gnashes its teeth at the depravity of others. It knows wisdom, but neglects to imitate it. Being full of evil words, it touched heaven with the worst of evils when it sent the serpent into Paradise in order to remove the garment of innocence from man when he told him he could be like God. Discord also laughs at wisdom, scatters good and righteous ways about, and tries

to move the towers of the virtues, thereby stirring up games of anger and ruin, but then freely excusing itself from them. When it has done all these things to others, it then agitates them by saying: "Fate, what did you do?" It says it brings holiness, but this is only an illusion. It is just like a person who mocks holiness by carrying a holy vessel into a place where it might be mocked, thereby committing sacrilege. The devil also deceived man the same way. After discord has gathered a lot of wickedness together, it devours it with blasphemies. It leads things into confusion and disgrace, even if it has not drawn the things to itself. A simple man, however, who is involved with simple sin, does not know about discord; therefore, God will not spurn this one, but will lead him to repentance. The disruptive and unrepentant man, however, falls under God's great anger since by not having fear of the Lord, he walks backwards when he despises the way of justice. Discord also accomplished its work fully when the Jews saw my son having been made man and knew about this wondrous event, but retreated from him because of their wicked hearts. They, therefore, cast themselves down into death, just as it has been written:

70
THE WORDS OF THE GOSPEL

90. *They retreated slightly and fell to the ground (John 18:6).* This should be understood to mean the following. Those who deny the truth and imitate Satan in their works rush to their destruction, walking backward when they shut their eyes of faith and, therefore, falling into the worst temptations that drove them to their destruction. But just as God will raise men up to immortal life on the newest day, so also even now he revives them to life through repentance. However, those who bewail what they have done while they were in their bodies, when their souls have been separated from their bodies, even if they deserve the punishments of purgatory, their souls are, nevertheless, freed more quickly. These things, however, have been spoken concerning the atonement for the cleansing and saving of souls, and they are faithful things. A faithful person pays attention to these things and remembers them well.

THE FOURTH PART ENDS

THE HEADINGS OF THE FIFTH PART BEGIN CONCERNING THE MAN LOOKING OVER THE WHOLE EARTH

82. The Fact That the Voice of the Prophets and Psalmists, Pronounced for the Praise of God, Aid the Necessity of the Suffering, As They Deserved

83. The Fact That God Will Spare These Things for Which Man Offers Alms, according to Which They Are Worthy

84. The Fact That the Good Will of Man Is the Sweetest Odor to God

85. The Fact That God Receives the Labors of Man for the Necessity of the Living and for the Rest of the Dead

86. The Fact That He Who Does Not Serve God, the Striking Angel Will Bear This One Harshly

THE HEADINGS OF THE FIFTH PART UNFOLD

THE FIFTH PART BEGINS

CONCERNING THE MAN LOOKING OVER THE WHOLE EARTH

1. I saw that the man I mentioned earlier looked over all the lands of the earth. From his calves down to the soles of his feet, he was in the waters of the abyss as he stood upon the abyss. The waters of the abyss were, as it were, the strength of his virtues because they restore all things, purify all things, make all things holy, uphold all things, and carry all things. Since they steep all things with their humidity and moisture, they make all things strong, just as the soul makes the body strong. The abyss was also, as it were, the strength of his power since it supports all his institutions and his institutions rest upon it. In addition, the abyss also exists like the building of the highest builder, which contains his tools. And behold from the shins of this man, a certain moist air moved the waters of the abyss around in various ways. Finally, with his feet he pressed down all the elements above the earth, in the earth and under the earth.

1

THE WORDS OF THE MAN LOOKING OVER THE EARTH

2. He said: "You who hear, listen and understand. Practice repentance since God revealed himself to you. If you do not do this, I will punish you with my rod. Therefore, let man be repentant." I then beheld five other images in the storm cloud that contained the various other faults. I saw that the first image had a youthful form from the crown of its head down to its loins. From its loins downwards, however, it had the shape of a crab, as a crab is shaped from its head downwards. It had black hair on its head and was completely naked.

2

THE WORDS OF SCURRILITY

3. It said: "I separate all things and I distribute all things. Wherever you want something to fall, I pay attention and speak about that place. If I did not do this, I would be foolish. Who can blame me for doing this? If I were to praise foolishness and silliness, I would be telling a lie. I will stretch out nets with my words and will catch everything I can, for the more I catch, the more I will have. I can spread out my honor this way so that all things will blush at my words. But I will also stretch out my bow with its arrows of words. What will this hurt? I will not hide anything, I will not be silent about anything, and I will give whatever I have to each and every man according to his measure."

3

THE RESPONSE OF REVERENCE

4. I heard a voice from the cloud I mentioned earlier respond to this image: "If I can renew all the things the Creator made, what am I? I could destroy all the things I did not make or create or give knowledge to; you, o unjust one, agitate all things this way. The mountains sustain me and I walk on the floor of the valleys; these things do not despise me either. I fly both in the highest places and in the lowest places. All the things God created please me. I do not hurt anything, but I do trample you under foot like dirt under my shoes, for you are not worthy since you injure everything you can."

5. I, however, saw a second image that also had a youthful form. But it did not have any hair on its head and it had the face and beard of an old man. Dressed in swaddling clothes, it was in a cradle that was hanging down, as it were, in the darkness I mentioned earlier and that was being moved here and there by the wind. But I could see that this image wore no other garments. Sometimes it lifted itself up out of these swaddling clothes and other times it hid itself in them.

4
THE WORDS OF AIMLESSNESS

6. It said: "It would be foolish of me to remain in one place and with one people. If I show myself everywhere, have my voice heard everywhere, and have my face seen everywhere, I will spread my glory out more. Grass grows and blossoms appear: if this is the case, should man not have glory too? I am like grass with my power of reason and wisdom, and I am like a blossom with my beauty; therefore, I show myself everywhere."

5
THE RESPONSE OF QUIET STABILITY

7. I heard a voice from the storm cloud respond to this image: "You, o diabolical cunning, will fall like the bloom of hay and you will be trampled under foot like the dirt of the road. You are the voice of vanity, you are the look of wickedness; you do not sift through the words of reason but instead walk unsteadily like locusts; therefore you will be scattered about like snow. You do not eat the food of wisdom and you do not drink the drink of discretion, but you imitate the ways of birds who have no stability in their nests. You are like ashes and rotting things. Therefore, I will not give you any rest."

8. The third image had the head of a wolf, the tail of a lion, and the rest of its body was like a dog. This image played with the other images and said: "We are one in all things." The winds roared in its ears, but this image sifted out the noise carefully, hearing what they were and where they had been. This image exalted the winds like they were its gods. It then lifted up its right forefoot and stretched it out to the North wind; it drew the blast of the winds from the elements to itself with its left forefoot.

6

THE WORDS OF WRONG DOING

9. It said: "Concerning Mercury and the other systems of philosophy, I will say that they bound their elements with thorough investigation since they definitely found each and every thing that they wanted. The strongest and wisest men found these things out partially from God and partially from the wicked spirits. What did this hurt? They, therefore, called themselves such names as Mercury and philosophers because they had received a lot of wisdom and information from the sun, moon and stars. I, however, reign and rule with my deeds wherever I want, of course, in the lights of heaven, in the trees and herbs and all the green things of the earth, in the beasts and animals of the earth, and in the serpents both on the earth and in the earth. Who will resist me on my various journeys? God created all things, but I do not injure him in any way with my various actions, for he willed that he be found good in the scriptures and in the fullness of his works. So what would it benefit him if his works are so hidden that no cause might be found in them? It would accomplish nothing."

7

THE RESPONSE OF TRUE CARE OF GOD

10. I again heard a voice from the storm cloud respond to this image: "Which of the two is more pleasing to God—to adore him or his works? Creatures who come from God are not able to give life to anything. What is the life that God gives? Of course, the fact that man is rational and that the rest of the creatures exist in the elements. How? Man is alive with the wings of the power of reason, but every bird and reptile just lives and is moved about by the elements. Man speaks with his power of reason; the rest of the creatures are silent and cannot help themselves or others, but simply do their duty. You, however, o magical deed, have a circle without a hole. For when you ask many questions in the circle of a creature, this creature draws away your honor and riches, and it hurls you into hell, like a stone, since you take away from it the name of its God. Therefore, all the tribes of the earth bewail you since you blaspheme when you lead those who should serve God into error. As a result, you will receive the same rewards that the devil did."

11. The fourth image appeared in the form of a man, except that it did not have any hair on its head and it had the beard of a goat. The pupils of its eyes were small and the whites of them were wide; it drew in

air and blew it out again strongly from its nostrils. Its hands were made of iron, its shins were bloody, and its feet were like the feet of a lion. It wore a tunic woven with black and white mixed together; this tunic was narrower at the top but was wider around its shins. A black vulture stood upon its breast, but it had turned its back and tail toward this image. In addition, in its presence a tree stood that was rooted in Gehenna and whose fruit was pitchy and sulfurous. This image gazed at this tree very carefully, and snatching some fruit from it, it devoured it avidly in its mouth. This image was also surrounded with many horrible looking serpents that made a lot of noise and commotion with their tails in the darkness I mentioned earlier, just as a fish does when it stirs up the water with its tail.

8
THE WORDS OF AVARICE

12. This image said: "I am not foolish, but I am wiser than those who look at the winds and then demand that the air give them everything they need. I snatch all things to myself; I gather all things to my bosom; the more I have collected, the more I have. For it is better for me to have whatever I need than to beg from others. I am not wrong when I carry things away from a person who has more than he needs, for when I have whatever I need, I do not worry about needing something from someone else. When I have all the things I want in my bosom, I fortunately am filled and delighted. At such times I do not fear anybody, but I live in blessedness and do not need anybody's mercy. I am cleverly wise and no one deceives me when I demand all things. How can this hurt me? I am not a thief or a robber, but I take all the things I want and acquire all of them with my own craftiness."

9
THE RESPONSE OF PURE CONTENTMENT

13. I again heard a voice from the storm cloud respond to this image: "O diabolical fraud, you are quick to plunder, like a wolf, and you devour another person's things, like a vulture. But gross pus also boils up in you since you are burdened with illicit desires, like a camel with its burdens. You are like the mouth of a wolf that is open and ready to devour things. You lie in hardness and forget God because you do not trust him, for you are hard and rough without any mercy because you have no wish to be perfect. Just as a serpent hides in a cave, so also you, the vilest rustic, draw yourself up more highly to reach all the prosperity you

can; nothing is sufficient to satisfy you. I, however, sit above the stars where all of God's good things are sufficient for me, and I rejoice in the sweet sound of a tambourine when I trust in him. I kiss the sun when I hold him with joy; I embrace the moon when I hold him in love and when all the things that have come into existence from the sun and moon are sufficient for me. Why should I desire more than I need? Because as a result of my having mercy for all things, my garment is made from white silk; because I am gentle when I use things, my garment has been decorated with precious stones. Therefore, I dwell in the house of a king and have all the things I want. I am in the company of the king because I am the daughter of a king. But you, o worst one, encircle the entire earth and yet are not able to fill your belly. See, therefore, what you are."

14. I saw a fifth image that had the form of a woman. At her back, there was a tree standing whose leaves had dried up completely. This image was entangled in its branches, for one branch had woven itself over the top of her head and one was around her neck and throat. One was around her right arm and another was around her left arm. These branches were not stretched out, but were very tight around her, and they had hands hanging down from them that had fingers like the claws of a raven. In addition, one branch from the right side of the tree and one from the left side were girded around her stomach and legs and surrounded them completely. The feet of this image, however, were made out of the wood of this tree. This image did not wear any garments, except the branches that surrounded it. Finally, wicked spirits had filled this tree with a black cloud and a horrible stench so that the tree bent itself and groaned.

10

THE WORDS OF SORROW OF TIME

15. She said: "Alas that I was ever created! Alas that I am alive! Who will help me? Who will free me? If God knew me, I would not be in such danger. Although I trust in God, he does not give me any good things; although I rejoice in him, he does not take evil away from me. I listen to a lot of things from philosophers who teach that there is much good in God, but God does not do any good for me. If he is my God, why does he hide all his grace from me? If he were to bring something good to me, I might know him. I, however, do not know what I am. I was created for unhappiness, I was born into unhappiness, and I live

without any consolation. Ah! What use is life without joy? Why was I even created when there is no good for me?"

11
THE RESPONSE OF HEAVENLY JOY

16. I again heard a voice from the storm cloud respond to this image: "O blind and deaf one, you do not know what you have said. God created man bright, but through a transgression the serpent seduced man into this lake of misery. Behold the sun, moon, stars and all the embellishments of the earth's greenness, and consider what great prosperity God gives to man in those things while man, nevertheless, sins against God with great temerity. You are a fraud and sorrowful and impious, and you always hold Gehenna in your confidence. You do not realize that salvation is from God. Who gives you these bright and good things unless it is God? When the day rushes up to you, you call it the night; when salvation is present to you, you say that it is a curse; and when good things come to you, you say they are evil. You are, therefore, from Gehenna!"

17. "I, however, have heaven when I behold all the things God has created, which you call harmful. I also gently gather into my lap roses and lilies and all greenness when I praise all of God's works, while you gather sorrow to yourself in all your works. You are like the spirits of Gehenna who always deny God in all their works. I do not do this. I give all my works to God because in some kinds of sorrow, there is gladness, and in some joy, prosperity. This is not like the day and night where one cannot be in the other. For just as God created day and night, so also are the ways of man. For when avarice builds its fortress, God quickly destroys it; when the body desires wantonness, God strikes it down and tramples it under foot; and when the pleasure of the flesh wants to surround heaven with vain glory, God strikes it down and scatters it around. This is just and right. Behold the quality of the birds of heaven and the quality of the worst serpents of the earth, because they are both useful and useless, although they devour each other in turn. Prosperity and adversity are the same way on earth. They should not be destroyed completely, but the useful things should cleanse the useless things, and the useless things should cleanse the useful things, as gold is tried in a furnace. You, however, are like the useless things, while I am not. I evaluate both the useful and useless things just as God created them. The soul bears witness to heaven and the flesh bears witness to the earth; the flesh

afflicts the soul; the soul, however, restrains the flesh. Therefore, o foolish and blind one, think about what you have said."

18. Behold in the presence of the man I mentioned above, a brazen club, like the club of a murderer, appeared fixed in the abyss. It was being moved here and there, as if it were ready to strike. And its movement made a sound that said:

12

THE SOUND OF THE BRAZEN CLUB

19. "O destructive mockers who are opposed to God, you want to ascend to the summit, but you will descend into hell. I will drag you away from honor, I will take away your happiness, and I will cast you down into confusion. I will throw you down like a rotting body that is dead since you live in the throat of the ancient serpent and boil up out of his mouth so that you can deceive men. You pour out your unclean scum upon men from your festering wounds, you strike men with the fiery javelins of your works, and you kill them with the fury of murder. You attack men quickly, hoping that they will forsake God's justice and despise God himself. By doing these things, you hope to lead all of God's works into confusion. Therefore, I will wage war against you and drive you away. I will show you that you do not have God's strength in you when I reduce you to nothing."

13

WATER CREATED FOR THE SALVATION OF MEN

20. I then heard a voice from heaven say to me: *The Creator of all things divided the waters and commanded them to flow into various places, of course, into the higher and lower places, and he gathered the abyss together to hold all those things that are under the earth. He made the waters liquid not only for the bodily needs of those living on earth, but also for the salvation of souls by washing them in baptism. Therefore, let the faithful believing in the Only-Begotten of God cast away the faults suggested to them by the devil by washing away their sins. And let those straining with heavenly desires happily and gloriously stretch to the life of eternal blessedness, as it has been shown to you figuratively in this present vision.*

14

THE FACT THAT ALL MEN ARE UNDER THE PROTECTION OF GOD

21. You see that the man I mentioned earlier looks over all the lands of the earth because the omnipotent God defends the world and all its inhabitants with his protection. This is because all things have received from him what they are, although the ones following his commandments worship, invoke, and venerate him in various ways. Even those who refuse to serve him are, nevertheless, under his protection since they were created by him and, therefore, serve him in many ways although they do not want to. From his calves down to the soles of his feet, he is in the waters of the abyss as he stands upon the abyss. The waters of the abyss are, as it were, the strength of his virtues because God holds the waters of the lower depths in his strength and watches over them with hidden eyes, as under the soles of his feet as he stands upon the abyss, because all things are under his power. These waters of the lower depth show the strength of the Divinity because God rules and protects all things, just as he gathers together all the waters of the earth and protects them. When unfaithful men are led back to life through the water of baptism, they restore all things; when they remove all the uncleanliness of their bodies and souls, they purify all things; when they wipe away the dangers of visible and invisible attacks by sprinkling themselves with water, they make all things holy; when they strengthen all things by pouring water over them so that they do not become dry, they uphold all things; and when they make lands public by unifying them, they carry all things. For they pour the sweat of their humility over all creatures because each and every thing lives its life according to the ways God planned it; clearly, those things that give life, live as men; those things that are fitted with harnesses, live as cattle; those things that have greenness, live as branches; and those things that have a moist red color, live as herbs. The moisture exuding from the earth and air support all these things as part of God's plan so that each and every thing sprouts and produces from this moisture according to the way God established for it.

15

HOW THE WATERS GATHER TOGETHER ALL THE EARTHLY THINGS

22. Since these waters steep all things with their humidity and moisture, they make all things strong so that they grow and do not die and are not scattered about, just as the soul makes the body strong because it nourishes the flesh and strengthens it at the same time as long as the soul remains in the body.

16

THE ABYSS HOLDS ALL EARTHLY THINGS

23. The abyss is also, as it were, the strength of his power since it supports all his institutions and his institutions rest upon it because it upholds all things as God does. As God holds all things in his favor and power, so also the abyss sustains all the things that are above the earth, in the earth and under the earth, seeing that God ordered that all things be placed above the abyss.

17

THE ABYSS IS SUSTAINED THROUGH THE SOLE POWER OF GOD

24. In addition, the abyss also exists like the building of the highest builder, which contains his tools, because the raw material this builder uses is of the type that both burns and does not burn. As a worker pours out and directs his efforts here and there according to his own will, so also the abyss, standing separate from the fabric that the Creator of the world uses, serves the things from which various forms come forth when the abyss sustains both the waters and the earth, the materials of the various creatures. And the support of the abyss is not removed from under creatures unless they are then sustained by God's power.

18

THE ABYSS IS LIKE A CISTERN

25. At its base, the abyss is also like a cistern because as the base of a cistern surrounds the water above it, so also the abyss sustains the things that are higher than it is.

19

THE FACT THAT THE STRENGTH OF GOD MAKES THE WATERS LIQUID

26. And behold from the shins of this man, a certain moist air moves the waters of the abyss around in various ways because from the strength of God, the air, which comes gently and makes most of the water liquid, spreads these waters around here and there throughout all the lands. It also holds these waters back so that they do not go beyond the place established for them at the beginning of time by going forward or by coming back, or by increasing or by decreasing. The spirit of the Lord gives the waters their moisture and a certain course, clearly the fact that they can be vapor or liquid and the fact that they flow just as if they were alive. Otherwise if they remained solid in one place, neither the earth nor the other creatures would be watered.

20

THE FACT THAT GOD HOLDS THE ELEMENTS IN HIS OWN POWER

27. Finally, with his feet God presses down all the elements above the earth, in the earth and under the earth. This is because with his power God maintains the austerity of the elements that flourish in the higher creatures, the lower ones, and the subterranean ones. God's power controls all things so that they are not agitated before the time he planned and so that they do not bring terror and trembling to other creatures.

21

THE FACT THAT GOD EXHORTS THE FAITHFUL TO REPENTANCE WITH FEAR OF HIS BLOWS

28. God also urges the faithful to heed his warning and to repent from their sins since he revealed himself to them in many miracles. Otherwise if they do not repent with their whole hearts, they will feel his blows.

22

HOW THE SOUL PANTS FOR GOD

29. Just as the waters and the abyss show the strength of God's power, so also man's soul, which pants for God, shows its strength and pow-

er in good works. Through the hidden mysteries of his secrets, God is in the strength of the soul, as from the top down to the soles of his feet. God also stands above the soul when it does good works since he breathes holiness into its just and faithful works, as it were, he stands above the abyss. And the strength of the soul has the courage and firmness of holiness to fight against the schemes of the devil through divine help, as it were, the strength of the virtues of this man. This is because men restore all things to justice when they deny the devil and trust in God; they purify all things when they wipe away the dirt and infection of sin through the contrition of confession; they make all things holy when they avoid evil and the danger of death, doing only what is good; they uphold all things when they water their good works with their tears so that their works do not fail; and they carry all things when they do not stop being united with the blessed virtues because if they separated themselves from the virtues, they would then break all their good works open with true and sweet sorrow. By not doing this, they make their desire for heaven solid, just as God made the world solid so that it cannot be dissolved.

23

THE FACT THAT THE DIVINE COMMANDS MAY BE GIVEN TO THE SOUL FOR FULFILLING

30. The soul is also the strength of God's power when it tramples the ancient serpent under foot through divine grace and when it imitates God by doing virtuous works. It then fulfills the divine commands, just as it supports all his institutions, because these commands were given and were made manifest so that they could be fulfilled in a faithful soul, as it were, his institutions rest upon it. And the soul is like the temple of the eternal Creator, just like the building of the highest builder, because it contains just and holy works and all the things that look back to the blessed life that God will give to his faithful ones, as it were, the building contains his tools.

24

HOW THE SOUL ASCENDS FROM VIRTUE INTO VIRTUE

31. When a man's soul follows holiness, God many times works great miracles in it and through it so that others will be so frightened and astonished that they will remove their ignorance. For through the strength

of God's gifts, the Holy Spirit comes softly to a faithful soul and won-
drously brings all its strengths, leading the soul from virtue to virtue,
just as from the shins of this man, a certain moist air moves the waters
of the abyss around in various ways.

25
THE FACT THAT GOD RESTRAINS THE TEMPTATIONS THROUGH THE HUMANITY OF HIS SON

32. Through the humanity of his Son which made the devil grieve,
God restrains the various temptations and their attacks that can entangle
man's soul with spiritual and fleshly and infernal provocations, just as
finally with his feet he presses down all the elements above the earth, in
the earth and under the earth. For the Only-Begotten Son of God came
into the world among men and gave examples to his faithful so that by
casting earthly concupiscence away, they can pant for heavenly things
and can choose eternal holiness.

26
THE FACT THAT GOD URGES THROUGH MIRACLES TO REPENTANCE

33. Therefore, this man who stands for God also warns those who
have hearing ears and understanding hearts to begin repenting for their
sins in the words he spoke earlier. He reveals himself as merciful to
these through many miracles so that they will cast their unjust works out
and will run to him fast. However, God will punish those who neglect
his words of warning with harsh scourgings because they have despised
and rebuked his warning with the stubbornness of their temerity. Therefore, let anyone who wants to be among the faithful in God's house,
chastise his body.

27
THE FACT THAT LUKE URGES TO REPENTANCE

34. Luke urges people to repent when he says: *You brood of vipers!
Who told you to flee from the wrath to come? Give some evidence that
you mean to reform. Do not begin by saying to yourselves, "Abraham is
our father." I tell you, God can raise up children to Abraham from*

these stones (Luke 3:7-8). This means the following. Repentance avoids punishments. Every fault will be examined according to its blame and every soul will receive its dwelling place according to its works, for who else can assign a dwelling place in eternity except God who alone gives rewards? God, however, having been made man, came upon earth because it pleased him tremendously to be able to pardon the sins of those who repent. The Son of God was conceived in the Virgin without sin and was born into a body. He remained innocent when he grew up so just. He then pleased his heavenly Father when he gave man the power to send their sins away and to repent. But those who sin and want to continue to sin are called the offspring of a viper; they were conceived as the result of the deception of a viper since Adam and Eve tore their royal life to pieces. They also destroyed holy innocence and begot their sons into the mortality of sins until they were restored to life by the clean flesh of the Son of God.

35. Who among men, being born in sin this way, has shown you who are also with many sins, how to flee from the overcoming vengeance of the indignation that the Lord has for those who do not repent? Luke shows above that no one can flee from the vengeance of God because neither the first angel nor Adam nor his sons were able to flee from it since from the very beginning, whoever fought against God fell and were conquered. May you, therefore, perform faithful works, and so that you can be freed from sin, believe faithfully in God, approach him with tearful prayer, and leave your depraved works behind. May each and every one of you who has done good works and has repented of your sins, say truly: "Alas, Alas! Lord, I have sinned in your presence!" May you also not speak with false justice because you have a defense in Abraham to whom God showed many miracles and to whom he gave the beginning of the Old Testament; God alone and no one else is able to free you. Therefore, with the certainty of truth, I proclaim to you who hear these things with good will that by the virtue of his grace, the Creator of all things will lead from the harshest harshness the faithful who return to him by cultivating the truth and the true faith and who exist as sons of the highest blessedness. For the Son of God is the corner stone from whom all stones, of course, the holy ones, spring forth and are renewed since he is holy and the holy ones remain in him.

28

THE FACT THAT THE SKILL OF THE JUST DRIVES
BACK FAULTS

36. The fact that you also behold five other images in the storm cloud that contains the various other faults means that in the worst ruin of rash unfaithfulness in which the various abominable faults run about, five other faults show themselves and their significance raging against the five senses of man because they try with every means to entangle and pervert the senses of faithful men into the contrariness of perversity, although the just drive them back with a divine helper who does not allow these faults to dominate them.

29

CONCERNING SCURRILITY

37. The first image stands for scurrility. It comes before the other faults with its lies because it does not like the truth but calls jokingly to this evil and that evil without ever being quiet. It has a youthful form from the crown of its head down to its loins because the ones who choose this fault have incontinence in their words and deeds and wantonness in the vanity of their deeds when through the ignorance that is in their heart they scatter everything about according to their own will. From its loins downwards, however, it has the shape of a crab, as a crab is shaped from its head downwards, because the ones choosing this fault descend from incontinence into changeableness, and while they spoke praise before, they now speak slander; they are headed toward a depraved end. It has black hair on its head and is completely naked because this fault takes the shyness and modesty out of men's minds and makes them foul and unclean. It encourages men to speak and act first with flattery and then with detraction, as this image showed in the words it spoke earlier. Reverence responds to this image and thinks that it is no better than the mud on its shoes.

30

CONCERNING AIMLESSNESS

38. The second image stands for aimlessness. It follows scurrility because running through instability, it leads each and every thing that was disposed correctly into immoderation, and being finite, it thinks God, as it were, can have an end. This image has a youthful form because it does

not reflect upon heaven with joy or earth with care, but it sees only empty vacillation in all the elements. It provides nothing correctly and divides nothing correctly, but does all of its work childishly. But it does not have any hair on its head and it has the face and beard of an old man because, being bored, it turns away from the honor of wisdom. Nevertheless, it wants venerable men to see it as virtuous and religious men to see it as agreeable. Dressed in swaddling clothes, it is in a cradle that is hanging down, as it were, in the darkness mentioned earlier and that is being moved here and there by the wind. This is because men who sweat with this fault and who are foolish in the unfaithful web of their own will, have been bound up, for they scatter themselves around in the diverse vanities of many things and in thoughtless jokes as a result of being tempted by the devil. They begin nothing correctly and end nothing correctly, but are always changing. They rush like restless clouds, always erring everywhere, choosing things they do not know and seeking strange places to dwell in. But you can see that this image wears no other garments since such men do not wear the stability of honesty but instead stagger with instability. Sometimes it lifts itself up out of these swaddling clothes and other times it hides itself in them because such men sometimes want to forsake their own will and to lift themselves up for higher veneration, but they also hide their own will when they refuse to tell anyone else what they plan to do. This fault causes them to be this way since it is never quiet or stable, but always wanders and jokes around everywhere, as it showed in the words it spoke earlier. Quiet stability responds to this fault and urges the faithful to choose honest stability. Quiet stability also speaks with Christ, as it has been written:

31
THE WORDS IN THE SONG OF SONGS

39. *Tell me, you whom my heart loves, where you pasture your flock, where you give them rest at midday, lest I be found wandering after the flocks of your companions (Song of Songs 1.7).* This means the following. Wisdom did indeed say these things through Solomon, for when Solomon knew that he had been steeped in wisdom, he spoke to wisdom with the intimacy of love, like to a woman, and Wisdom said: "I then rose up and shook my mantle off and filled it with a hundred and thousand drops of dew, in which God values man. Thus we in turn spoke. For as I ordered all things when I surrounded the circle of heaven, I also spoke to Solomon about the love of the Creator for the creature and the creature for the Creator. I spoke about how the Creator loved the creature greatly, how the creature wanted to kiss the Creator, and how the

creature obeyed the Creator because it was obedient to him in all things since the creature was kissed by the Creator when God gave it all the things it needed. I imitate the love of the Creator for the creature and the creature for the Creator with the love and faith by which God joins a man and woman together so that they can have children. As every creature proceeded from God, so also every creature looks back to God with his own talents and does not do anything without God's instruction, just as a woman looks to a man so that she can fulfill his commands in a way that is pleasing to him. Similarly, the creature is drawn to the Creator when it is submissive to him in all things and the Creator is present to the creature when he gives it greenness and strength. But the creature is made black when it does not use its talent correctly, but it is beautiful when it does its duty justly. Therefore, good comes to the creature who clings to the Creator for the necessities of life since the Creator brings forth all the things the creature needs."

40. Wisdom also speaks to the Creator with loving love, as if she were speaking to her beloved, asking him where to bring food and where to bring the quietness of her virtue. She does not run around in error with idols who falsely claim the name of the Divinity for themselves. Similarly, man, who is all creature, seeks a kiss from God through the good will of his soul when he obtains grace, and he longs to be with the sweetness of God as he runs strenuously toward him. When he denies the shadow of sin, he restores his beauty through repentance so that he gives out a good and holy aroma with good fame for the daughters of the heavenly Jerusalem, of course, when he rises above his own will. Therefore, man also speaks to Christ, his redeemer, saying: "Through the beauty of your commandments that I follow in my soul since you redeemed me and lifted me up from death, show me the human nature that you received from the virgin and through which you accomplished all your work, just like the smell of good aromas in a garden full of aromas. Your humility as a human moistened all your good works, as a rose from heaven falls upon the earth where it can be watered. Show me where you rest in your burial place of death since in the fullness of faith, the fullest heart of the sun, of course, the Holy Spirit, filled up the faithful when the old law was fulfilled by the Holy Spirit after your resurrection and ascension. Otherwise I might run backwards to the old legal precepts and to the ancient philosophers who were with you when they brought forth those things that you inspired. I will not do this, however, because I do not want to return to squalid ways and idle works that will separate me from happiness."

32

CONCERNING WRONG DOING

41. The third image stands for wrong doing. It follows aimlessness because when men aimlessly wander around in strange places, they also stir up a lot of vanity in other people through the deeds of the devil. They forsake God since they want to do only their own will in each and every thing they do. The devil laughs at them and seduces them into many stumbling blocks. This image has the head of a wolf and the tail of a lion since men who are guilty of this fault search in other creatures through the deeds of the devil for the various things they want to know. As a result, they give their soul to the devil so that he can devour it, just as a wolf devours a lamb. Since they do not direct the end of their work to God through the trust of hope, but only show harshness and roughness in the evil end of their work, as it were, the tail of the lion, they stir up everything they can with hatred and tyranny. The rest of its body is like a dog because directing all their works toward uncleanness, they also use their knowledge for chasing evil things. This image plays with the other images and says that they are one in all things because those who reach out to wrongdoing draw evil to themselves aimlessly and they form a society so that they are not separated from each other since each of them is occupied with its fault just as naturally as the others.

42. The winds roar in its ears, but this image sifts out the noise carefully, hearing what they are and what they have been, because when men direct their efforts aimlessly, they receive many evil suggestions and infernal iniquities in the ears of their hearts, and perceiving them eagerly, they direct their wills to them since they know that these things can be adapted conveniently to their fleshly desires. This image exalts the winds like they were its gods because the unfaithful show a lot of veneration for the devil's suggestions and store and cultivate them in the secrets of their hearts so that they can use them to obtain whatever they want. It then lifts up its right forefoot and stretches it out to the North wind because where these men should put forth righteousness and walk justly with good footsteps, they instead rejoice in depraved footsteps, and through their wrong doing they direct their efforts to the mockeries that are sent from the ancient seducer. It draws the blast of the winds from the elements to itself with its left forefoot because although they should be aware of the danger of these evils, their perverse friends call the provocations of the evil spirits to them. For the demons name their own gods, they cultivate them rather than the true God, they look for the vanities and contradictions of wrong doing from these gods, and they do

this so that they can more promptly and easily fulfill their wish to be unclean, both in themselves and in other creatures. But the true care of God responds to aimlessness and warns men to be on guard against the worthlessness of these mockeries.

33
CONCERNING AVARICE

43. The fourth image manifests avarice. It walks after wrong doing since it is the duty and work of wrong doing. It is also the servant of idols since remaining in the devil's womb, it is not able to accomplish anything according to its own will. This image appears in the form of a man because it desires earthly things and not heavenly things. Except that it does not have any hair on its head; this means it does not cultivate honesty in its will. And it has the beard of a goat since it loves foulness better than its own beauty. The pupils of its eyes are small and the whites of them are wide because it does not rejoice in the prosperity of others, but is terribly envious. It draws in air and blows it out again strongly from its nostrils because with indiscreet desire, it takes worldly concupiscence into itself and then searches for more of it. Its hands are made of iron because it pillages with harshness and bitterness. Its shins are bloody because it uses its strength to kill others for their possessions to please its own desires. And its feet are like the feet of a lion since it walks and plunders ferociously, sparing nothing when it pillages.

44. It wears a tunic woven with black and white mixed together since it takes whatever riches it can, either justly or unjustly, without even asking where they are from or who they belong to. This tunic is narrower at the top but is wider around its shins since it plunders spiritual men with jealous pretense, but when it is in the company of worldly ones who bear earthly cares, it pillages even more. A black vulture stands upon its breast because the enthusiasm with which it plunders encourages its conscience onto the blackness of gluttony. This vulture fixes its feet upon its breast because it directs its conscience to act only according to its own will. But this vulture has turned its back and tail toward this image since it stretches out its strength and the fullness of its iniquities to avarice in all the ways it can.

45. But the fact that in its presence a tree stands that is rooted in Gehenna and whose fruit is pitchy and sulfurous means that in the hearts of the unfaithful, avarice shows care of the world since it does not use all its strength just to destroy, but it also uses it to bring forth foul and stinking fruit through its evil efforts when it does not think about heav-

enly things, but only about earthly things. This image gazes at this tree very carefully, and snatching some fruit from it, it devours it avidly in its mouth because avarice looks at the things of this world cleverly and draws them to its open mouth without any moderation, for men serving this fault are never free from care and do not trust in God, but they immerse themselves violently in difficult things. This image is also surrounded with many horrible looking serpents because avarice is beleaguered by the indescribably and monstrous deeds of the devil. These serpents make a lot of noise and commotion with their tails in the darkness mentioned earlier since they cause a lot of noise and disquiet in the darkness of unfaithfulness with the power of their evil when they do not allow anyone to have any peace and quiet. They do this through wicked men, just as a fish does when it stirs up the water with its tail. When they have been strengthened by the perversity of the depraved works they have done, they then disturb the purity of good knowledge in blessed men so that they take away their things and give them to themselves. This fault showed this in the words it spoke earlier. Pure contentment resists this fault and confidently warns the faithful that God's gifts should be sufficient for them; it tells the faithful that if they follow avarice, they will run into the bitterness of unhappiness. Jeremiah also gives witness to the ones who choose this fault, when he says:

34

THE WORDS OF JEREMIAH THE PROPHET

46. *Where are the rulers of the tribes and those who rule over the beasts on earth, who play with the birds of heaven, who hoard the silver and gold men put their trust in? There is no end to the possessions of those who forge silver and are stirred up, nor is there a trace of their works (Baruch 4:16-18).* This means the following. Where are those who oppress tribes with their tyranny, and what rewards do they receive? Clearly they live in the squalid places they have built for themselves on earth with their own work, and they receive punishments as their rewards since they do not obey the legal precepts, since as despots they have made themselves like gods to rule over the people, and since they have consumed people's possessions with their avarice. They have put their households in charge of the wild animals that live in the wilderness since they know only the bestial on earth. They use their power to control these animals, as if they had made them, not knowing that God created these animals for the service of people. As a result, they abandon the height and width of the highest rewards since they only act according to their own will. They do not lift up their mind to God, but

only serve avarice. Therefore, they receive bestial rewards in the worst darkness. They also fill up their own will with playful things, as if they were birds of the air. Abandoning the harmony of the Holy Spirit that should cause them to rejoice in the precepts of God, they turn their joys to the ways of the birds and play improperly in various ways. Therefore, they will suffer great punishments because they do not serve God. They gather to themselves the silver of mortality and the gold of destruction through their unfair buying and through their profits; they place all their hope in their silver and gold, knowing only earthly things and not heavenly things. They have no meaningful purpose to their lives and have no way of stopping their anxiety since they do not want the silver of good knowing that treasures the holiest of works in heavenly harmony and since they condemn the gold of wisdom that enables faithful men to rule wisely with God's discretion. For the divine precepts have been placed in books, as in private law, so that they will not be forgotten but will rather be fulfilled by just and holy men. They reject the silver of good knowing and the gold of wisdom, and they choose mortal money that causes mortals to die. They also trust in their silver in various ways and are concerned that their earthly and fallen things will be taken away from them. Therefore, their works will not persevere since having been done with vanity, they will disintegrate in vanity. Casting out faith and refusing to be subject to God, they do whatever they want to regarding earthly things, and they say: "God makes all the things he wishes, so we will do whatever we want." As a result, they cast out the sanctity of their holy works that appear as if they had been plated with good virtues, but appearing in the form of the virtues. They anxiously desire an abundance of riches in their hearts, having no concern for the salvation of their souls. Therefore, their depraved works are of no use to them; they do not merit salvation because everything they do in their greedy work dies in death, just as flames are extinguished.

35

CONCERNING THE SORROW OF TIME

47. The fifth image signifies sorrow of time. It follows avarice because when the avaricious cannot have what they desire, they become sorrowful and are not strong enough to free themselves from this. This image has the form of a woman. At her back, there is a tree standing whose leaves have dried up completely. This means that embracing foolishness in feminine fear, man directs all his strength and trust in such a way that he just brings affliction to his soul. This tree is without any greenness since it does not have the protection of holiness. This

image is entangled in its branches since this image is as entangled in contrary things as it is in fertile things. For one branch has woven itself over the top of her head; this is grief that oppresses the beginning and the top of the minds of those who are occupied with evil. And one branch is around her neck and throat; this is the anxiety that constrains the strength that they should use to bear the yoke of the Lord and that constrains the desire that they should have to eat the food of life. One branch is around her right arm and another is around her left arm. These branches are not stretched out, but are very tight around her. This is because the dread of eternal and spiritual works and the fear of fallen and worldly honor enter men so they do not want to work or to extend themselves well and honestly, but instead only want to remain idle because of the heavy oppression in their hearts. They do this with their hands hanging down from them and with fingers like the claws of a raven because their works, done with pride, show harshness in a pit of bold blackness since they trust only in riches and not in sadness, only in prosperity and not in adversity. In addition, one branch from the right side of the tree and one from the left side are girded around her stomach and legs and surround them completely. This is because when men live in the sadness of time, they should be defended by spiritual things, as on the right, but the affliction of their soul only makes them doubt this. When they should cast fleshly things away, as on the left, the affliction of their soul only brings them grief. All of these things squeeze their conscience and the strength of their souls and bodies by taking them here and there through many changes. And all of these things make them live with the worst company so that they do not reach out eagerly to God or to time since they do not have any joy in God or in time. Such men do not correct the ways of their journeys and make them straight with hope and trust, but they put these things in the sadness of time, having no greenness in their strength, but existing like a snake that hides from all the joy and beauty of heaven and earth.

48. This image does not wear any garments, except the branches that surround it, because this image does not give any glory to men who lack honesty and are naked of all happiness. As mentioned earlier, such men are oppressed by the worst calamities since they choose neither these nor the others but only bring heaviness to their lives. Finally, wicked spirits fill this tree with a black cloud and a horrible stench so that the tree bent itself and groaned because the most wicked and diabolical of spirits boast about the blackness of their evil deeds and approach men suffering from this fault with the filth and uncleanness of stinking things. And they drag them away from any consolation or quietness of

mind so that these men, despairing and hating themselves, agree with these spirits and do not trust that any blessedness will come to them, just as this fault said when it spoke earlier. Heavenly joy responds to this fault and faithfully encourages men to cast out the bitterness of sorrow and to cling to God with joy.

36
CONCERNING THE FORM OF THE ZEAL OF GOD

49. Behold in the presence of the man I mentioned above, a brazen club, like the club of a murderer, appears fixed in the abyss. This means that in the sight of God, his zeal stands prepared for the vindication of evil things. And according to God's most profound judgments, the zeal of God does not strike anything or crush anything except what the divine judgments show. This club is being moved here and there, as if it were ready to strike, because it carefully searches for and investigates all the things that should be examined and weighed by the just judgments of God. Its motion, of course, righteous judgments, gives back the sound of the zeal of God, clearly judicial knowledge, which speaks thus, because it cries out that it will take away from all beautiful things and from all the blessed those who seek to fight against God and who strain to stretch to that height that descends into the lowest places. The zeal of God cries out that it will cast those into the outrage of a stinking dead body. This is so because those who follow the gluttony and madness of the first deceiver strive to drag down with themselves whoever they can into the place of worst damnation. But the zeal of the Lord scatters them about and leads them to nothing, because it examines all things justly and judges everything that should be judged justly, as it has been written:

37
FROM THE BOOK OF EXODUS

50. *Thus says the Lord: At midnight I will go forth through Egypt. Every first-born in this land shall die, from the first-born of Pharaoh on the throne to the first-born of the slave girl at the handmill, as well as all the first-born of the animals (Exodus 11:4-5).*

51. This means that when evil became so strong that it thought that no one could overcome it, the Lord ground away every beginning and every head that had raged in the perversity of dark unfaithfulness, clearly from the beginning of pride with the devil when he prepared his seat in the infernal kingdom right up to the beginning of the sin of Adam

when he, having been captured and imprisoned, subjected himself to the devil. For the true God, the just judge, when he confined the devil's pride in the despair of hell and when he pierced Adam's sin with the harshest revenge, crushed all the faults clinging to these. He also crushed every fault of perverse thinking when he examined the thoughts of men because when he cuts these things down in his head, he also wipes them out completely and without any exception. The Lord, as it were, striking down evil through the mediation of his death, led men back to life through the regeneration of the Spirit and water; from the time of the prophets until their servants were imprisoned in their sins, he turned every evil that attacked the old law around into something better. To be sure, he cast down the beginning of faults when he wiped out lust and disobedience in the new law so that most virtues could spring forth where the roots of evil had been pulled up. In the mouth of the old serpent, lust had been formed into a round ball so that the devil could deceive man through food, but from the root of Jesse a girl rose up who divided lust in the womb of the devil when without the taste of lust she bore a child in innocence so childlike that it always rejoices and never has sadness. In addition, the Son of God taught abstinence when he fasted from food for forty days and nights. He also conquered the worst evils of idols when he ground those things down, and he revealed his hidden miracles when he overcame the serpent's sting with his own blood as well as that of his martyrs.

38
THE FACT THAT THE BLOOD OF CHRIST JOINED VIRGINITY TO ITSELF

52. The innocent blood of Christ and his martyrs joined the promise of virginity to itself, which caused the devil to blush since he was all confused by this. As a result, the devil hid in a cave where he could protect himself from these things and where he might arm the various faults in order to deceive Christ and his martyrs. The devil also tried to overturn God's precepts with perverse doctrines, saying to himself: "When, indeed, I have a chance to do what I want, I will put all my efforts into rebelling against God since he oppresses me."

39

HOW GOD OVERCOMES THE ANCIENT SERPENT

53. But I who have been the strongest warrior since the beginning of creation will cast the ancient serpent down completely after he has accomplished the works he planned; I will trample him down completely because of his disobedience. The devil is the father of disobedience and all those who follow his advice about disobedience, persevering in despising God's precepts, are his friends. But they will all be destroyed with the ancient seducer and will be driven back to nothing. The power of the Divinity will then appear as complete since it overcame its enemy; this power also overcomes the devil within man when it converts the publicans and sinners, for God's wide mercy never dries up and it will not change just because something else has changed. God's power always remains stable because God is that life that never began to live, that has nothing similar to it, and that will never end. God indeed raises up repentant sinners who have dried up their sins by forsaking them and who have shipwrecked their sins with tears of repentance. However, let he who desires life grasp these words and store them in the innermost chamber of his heart.

54. I saw some other spirits in this crowd who cried aloud: "Nothing God makes is great, is it? Lucifer is great and we will stay with him always." These spirits urge people on to scurrility and show how they treat everyone with scorn, both in words and deeds.

40

CONCERNING THE CLEANSING PUNISHMENTS OF SCURRILITY

55. I saw some unusual serpents running around in the flames of a fire. The souls of those who had loved scurrility and who had received this sin from other people were punished here. Because they had injured many with the burning zeal of their scurrility, they were dried up in these flames; and because they had forgotten about God in the ignorance of this fault, they were twisted by these serpents.

41

CONCERNING REPENTANCE FOR SCURRILITY

56. And I saw and understood these things. And I heard the voice from the living light say to me: *These things that you see are true, and as you see them, so they are. If men guilty of scurrility have tried to chase away the evil spirits who brought this fault to them and if they have tried to avoid its punishments, let them chastise themselves with fasting and scourging according to the command of their spiritual director and then let them choose silence with the righteousness of agreeable moderation.*

42

CONCERNING THE FAULT OF SCURRILITY

57. Scurrility is filled with the forgetfulness of God and is anxious to tear truth to pieces with false words, because it is like a stinking cloud that makes all the fruit dry up. It does not germinate in honesty and it is not covered by discipline with the mantle of modesty, but it tries to destroy everything that is true with the shadow of its playful works. It makes a hissing sound like a snake, and with its bad habits it entangles itself in blasphemous words against God and man. It attacks the established law, just as a worm destroys a garment; it deceives man by mocking him and thus attacks him through death. Let those who want to choose God with a pure heart and with a disciplined soul cast out the poison of this scorn so that they do not weep later when they really want joy. These things, however, have been spoken concerning the atonement for the cleansing and saving of souls, and they are faithful things. A faithful person pays attention to these things and remembers them well.

58. I saw some other spirits in this crowd who cried aloud: "Our Lord is Lucifer who pierces all things and who knows all things." These spirits show aimlessness to people and persuade them not to chose stability.

43

CONCERNING THE CLEANSING PUNISHMENTS OF AIMLESSNESS

59. I saw a large marsh that was filled with putrid and stinking filth and from which a foul cloud rose up to surround it. The souls of those who had sweat in aimlessness while they had been alive were punished

here so that they walked from place to place and crossed back and forth aimlessly. Because they had sinned with aimlessness, they were in the filth of this marsh; because they had taken delight in their aimlessness, they smelled this stink; and because of the diversity of their aimlessness, they were covered by this cloud. And I saw and understood these things.

44

CONCERNING THE ACTION FOR REPENTING AIMLESSNESS

60. I again heard the voice from the living light say to me: *These things that you see are true, and as you see them, so they are. In order for men to overcome the spirits who urge them on to aimlessness and in order to avoid its punishments, let men chastise themselves with fasting and scourging and let them punish themselves by kneeling and sighing about this sin.*

45

CONCERNING THE FAULT OF AIMLESSNESS

61. Those who are filled with aimlessness do not fear or love God. When they have cast away this fear, they no longer have wisdom; and when they do not surround themselves with the love of God, they no longer have knowing watchfulness. Aimlessness is like the maiden of disobedience and like the servant of luxury. Even if it does not finish its works, it nevertheless still seeks disobedience and luxury as its companions; it wants to see these companions and to subject itself to them. It rages and is lukewarm; it yells at each and every thing. It is not similar in any way to salty meat; it does not have righteous joy or righteous sorrow. Prophecy does not look at it and wisdom does not speak to it because it is neither the root nor the foliage of a fruitful tree. It is not moist with the root of prophecy like the dew in the morning, and it does not rise up in the foliage of the building of wisdom at midday, for it is scum and rottenness. It does not have the taste of wisdom or the food of works, it is not useful, it is not watchful, and it does not lift its mind up to God's authority. It attracts idleness and priggishenss to itself with which it walks blindly through many slippery and outrageous places. Fixing its sight on the diversity of all the things that come to it, it forgets about God when it also neglects its own physical needs. Let whoever desires to be a servant of God in the strenuousness and austerity of his life abhor the vanities of this fault, and restraining his body and spirit, let

him lift himself up to God, for when a man reaches to heaven by seeing the face of God through faith, he kisses him with the most worthy contemplation and he loves him with the strongest love. What has been written is then fulfilled in such a man:

46
THE WORDS OF DAVID

62. *Take delight in the Lord, and he will grant you your heart's requests (Psalm 37:4).* This means the following. You who believe faithfully in God and who perform faithful works gather to yourself all the delight of the virtues and take delight in the one who is Lord of the universe, faithfully following and loving the one who is your Creator. And after you have taken delight in him, he will give you all the things that are good and that give you life, clearly according to what you seek and according to what your heart desires. The faith by which you believe in God allows only what is just to search you out so that contemplation, which teaches faith, seeks only what is pleasing in God's sight and is eternal. For it you sigh for God in proportion to your need and if you cry out to God in proportion to the need of your brother, the aroma of the virtues comes near the love of God with good and holy works, and God does not stop fulfilling whatever petitions are just. These things, however, have been spoken concerning the atonement for the cleansing and saving of souls, and they are faithful things. A faithful person pays attention to these things and remembers them well.

63. I saw some other spirits in this crowd who cried aloud with a great clamor: "Lucifer is Lord because the elements obey his commands." These spirits examine the elements studiously; they entice men to do evil and persuade them to pursue magical schemes and sorcery.

47
CONCERNING THE CLEANSING PUNISHMENTS OF WRONG DOING

64. I saw a great swamp that was boiling like a fire and sending forth the worst stink; it had a multitude of serpents and other vermin in it. The souls of those were punished here who had persevered in doing evil while they had been alive, cultivating many magical and sorceress things with various creatures in their diabolical deeds. These wicked spirits also brought them much disgrace, saying: "These do not have the true Lord." Because they had neglected righteous faith and had fol-

lowed unbelief in their works, they were dried up by this fiery swamp;
because they had not thought about what they were doing, they smelled
the stink of this swamp; because they had placed their trust in the elements and in other creatures and because they had believed these things
to be greater than God, they were afflicted by these vermin; and because
they had chosen such evil deeds, they were infested with the insults of
these evil spirits. And I saw and understood these things.

48
CONCERNING THE REPENTANCE OF WRONG DOING

65. I heard the voice from the living light say to me: *These things
that you see, are true. Let those who have strained to overcome the evil
spirits who led them to this fault and who have strained to flee from its
punishments afflict themselves by wearing a hair shirt, and let them
chastise themselves with very severe fasting and the harshest of
scourgings as demanded by the judgment of justice.*

49
CONCERNING THE BLINDNESS OF WRONG DOING

66. Men who look into creatures the same way that they look into the
scriptures and who strain to see many things in creatures, just as they do
in the scriptures, worship the devil rather than God; they are the servants
of the devil. As a result, the devil cleaves to them, saying: "Whatever
you seek from me, I will give you." And the wretched person who is so
familiar with the devil, says to himself: "I have found salvation in creatures. If I were to look to God and not provide myself with the good
things that please me, God, when he pleases himself, might not bring me
all the things I want. What would I have then? Therefore, what I want, I
will search for in creatures, but I will not place any value in them so that
I do not sin." Such a man mocks himself, thinking this way, but he became this way through his evil and perverse actions. As a result, he is
destroyed both in body and soul since he follows the fall of the first angel and becomes a friend of the devil when he trusts in irrational creatures. Even the devil did not act like this since he trusted only himself.
Let whoever wants to serve God purely and worthily flee these decep-
tions and illusions, and let him turn away from other creatures, for if he
has looked at other creatures with evil beckoning, he blinds the sight of
his own soul. If he has committed depraved and contrary and nefarious

deeds with these other creatures and if he has done things against his nature and his salvation, he sends his soul to destruction. Let him, instead, strive to cling to his Creator. These things, however, have been spoken concerning the atonement for the cleansing and saving of souls, and they are faithful things. A faithful person pays attention to these things and remembers them well.

67. I saw some other spirits in this crowd who cried aloud, shouting: "Lucifer will be enriched with many honors, and we will be made great along with him." They show men avarice and urge them to stretch for more and greater things.

50

CONCERNING THE CLEANSING PUNISHMENTS OF AVARICE

68. I saw fiery air that boiled all over with great flames and that had very small and cutting worms rushing around in it, as if agitated by the wind. The souls of those who had been servants of avarice while they had been alive were punished here; they had grabbed everything they could as they gathered foreign things to themselves in whatever way they could. Because of the incessant panting of the avarice that they had had in themselves, they suffered from the fire of this air; and because of the great losses and torments that they had brought to others with their avarice, they were afflicted by the sharpness of these worms.

51

CONCERNING THE PUNISHMENTS OF ROBBERS

69. I also saw a pit that was so deep that I could not see the bottom of it. A flame came out of this pit, reached up high, and then receded back into it; and it kept doing this. The souls of those who had trained themselves to be robbers because of their avarice were punished here. The flame lifted them up out of the pit and then drew them back down into it again while they bewailed and cried aloud: "Ach! We have sinned!" Because they had been so evil in their avarice, they were burned by this flame; because they had committed so many robberies as a result of their avarice, this same flame lifted them up and drew them back down into this pit; and because they had done this for some time, they were struck by these punishments.

52
CONCERNING THE PUNISHMENTS OF THEFTS

70. I further saw a wide and deep pit that had a lot of wicked spirits running around in it. The souls of those who had secretly stolen things from people while they had been alive were punished here. The wicked spirits tormented them by hitting them all over many times. Because of the thefts that they had committed, they were held in this pit; because of their stealing during the night, they were tormented by the vermin mentioned earlier; and because of their being so blind that they did not see God, they were afflicted by these wicked spirits. And I saw and understood these things.

53
CONCERNING THE REPENTANCE PUT IN MOTION BY AVARICE

71. I again heard the voice from the living light say to me: *These things that you see, are true, and as you see them, so they are. Therefore, let whoever has tried to avoid these wicked spirits that show them avarice and whoever has tried to avoid its punishments, afflict themselves with fasting and scourging, and let them repay with truth and mercy the poor they have defrauded, as much as they can.*

54
CONCERNING THE REPENTANCE OF ROBBERS

72. If whoever attempted robbery without being afraid of taking things from other people wants to be absolved from its punishments, let him chastise his body in which he sinned with a hair shirt and with severe fasting and harsh scourging.

55
CONCERNING THE REPENTANCE OF THIEVES

73. If whoever labored to serve avarice through theft wants to be absolved from its torments, let him punish himself with fasting and scourging and with bended knees.

56

CONCERNING THE PUNISHMENT OF THOSE WHO DRAW ALL THINGS TO THEMSELVES

74. Whoever follows avarice in such a way that he takes from others whatever he can and draws these things to himself, leaving, as it were, no stone upon stone since he scatters their belongings about and makes them poor and needy sinners, will suffer the worst punishments mentioned above unless he cleanses himself with repentance through the grace of God. For I search through all time and I see through all time how each person walks on the way of righteousness, just as David, my servant, inspired by a prophetic spirit shows when he says:

57

THE WORDS OF DAVID

75. *The Lord looks down from heaven upon the children of men, to see if there be one who is wise and seeks God (Psalm 14:2).* This means the following. He who made all things from the secret of secrets looks down upon those who are sons of the flesh, of course, those who walk in the flesh, in order to discern how they have profited from the talent given to them. The Divine sees and considers most acutely how they used their intelligence to look upon him in the mirror of faith and with what kind of search of purity they sought him. For as long as the soul performs good works in the body, it understands God through the taste of holiness, and as long as it brings faith to fulfillment in the virtues, it beholds God by searching in the mirror of most faithful purity. It then sees God with most profound intuition and he rewards each soul according to the person's works.

58

THE FACT THAT AVARICE REMOVES THE BODY OF MAN

76. Avarice is, however, the worst of evils that destroys many, for it not only draws away from someone the things that are outside his body, but it also draws his body away as well.

59

THE FACT THAT A ROBBER IMITATES THE DEVIL

77. A man who practices robbery imitates the devil because just as the devil destroys by winning over the soul of a man, so also a robber takes away the property of another and attacks his body as well. As a result, a robber is separated from God and unless he repents, he is clothed with the abusiveness of abusiveness; he will receive eternal punishment since he accomplished his sins so fully.

60

THE FACT THAT A THIEF IS LIKE THE DEVIL

78. One who steals in the night deceives just like the devil because the devil covers over his will with craftiness since he does not dare to deceive man openly as he carries off the treasure of justice from his heart. The devil hates the happiness salvation brings to man. God, however, carries off all that is unjust and does not allow the devil's will to reach its fullness of wickedness, just as it has been written:

61

THE WORDS OF THE GOSPEL

79. *I was a hard man, withdrawing what I never deposited, reaping what I never sowed (Luke 19:22).* This means the following. I who judge all things am just, sincere and merciful in my judgments since I weigh all sins according to their qualities. Therefore, I mercifully aid repentance, but I judge the unrepentant, removing the injustice that I did not establish and reaping and destroying the evil that I did not spread out. I did not establish what is unjust or sow what is evil, but I reproach these things with my true judgment, just as a fish is caught by a hook against its will. I destroy all that is evil and I bind its throat so that it can no longer stand up. Therefore, I destroy what I do not keep and I reap what I do not sow, just as I carried the devil off to hell and destroyed him according to my wishes. Similarly, I cut the wickedness of the impious away when I turned them back from their impiety. These things, however, have been spoken concerning the atonement for the cleansing and saving of souls, and they are faithful things. A faithful person pays attention to these things and remembers them well.

80. I saw some other spirits in this crowd who I heard crying aloud: "Why is it that that one wanted to be God whom we abhor?" These spirits drag men off to the sorrow of time and persuade them to grow old in sorrow so that they grieve that they even lived.

62

CONCERNING THE CLEANSING PUNISHMENTS OF THE SORROW OF TIME

81. I saw an arid and dry place that was surrounded with darkness and that was full of vermin. The souls of those who had drawn the sorrow of time to themselves while they had been alive were punished here. Wicked spirits chased them here and there in this place with fiery whips while these spirits cried aloud: "Why did you not put your trust in your God?" Because their joy of heavenly things had not been strong, they were in this place; because they had lived with bitterness in their hearts, they endured the torture of these vermin; because they had neglected true and complete blessedness, they suffered the contrariness of this darkness; and because they had been ensnared by these evils and had not trusted in God, they were afflicted by these wicked spirits.

63

CONCERNING THE REPENTANCE OF SORROW OF TIME

82. I saw and understood these things, and I heard the voice from the living light say to me: *These things that you see, are true, and as you see them, so they are, and there are more things. Therefore, if people who have gathered the sorrow of time to themselves are anxious to overcome the wicked spirits who brought this to them and if they want to escape its punishments, let them turn to the spiritual life while they are alive. Or if they are already on a spiritual journey, let them follow the ordinary common strictness, let them submit themselves to humble obedience, and let them contemplate those Scriptures that bring them heavenly joy. However, let them not do all these things boldly, but only under the direction of their spiritual advisor.*

64

CONCERNING FEARFUL SORROW OF TIME

83. Sorrow of time does not have the joy of heavenly things. It is like a wind that does not have the usefulness of greenness or dryness, but that simply scatters everything it touches. Having no righteous stand anywhere, sorrow of time says: "I do not know who or what is said to be God." As a result of not having spiritual breath, sorrow of time dries up all living things. It is also divided into many parts so that it gathers many things to itself with sorrow and finds no joy in them, so that it does not call out to a friend with gladness, and so that it does not try to appease an enemy. After it has done all of this with sorrow, it hides itself in a hole of sorrow, like a snake, because it is afraid of everything that passes by. It is similar to death because it does not pant for heavenly things or trust in the world. Therefore, my zeal will fall upon it, just as it has been written:

65

THE WORDS OF DAVID

84. *Fire is angry with my rage, and it will make things dry right up to the newest things of hell (Deuteronomy 33:26).* This means the following. I who created the sun and moon and all the other creatures made man rational so that he might know me, and by knowing me, he might love me, and so that he might not fight against me with disbelief. Good is more useful to him than evil, but he neglects me as if his salvation did not come from me. As a result, the fire of examination rages in the zeal of my judgments by which I judge all things justly. My fire dries deeply all the evil things that I examine thoroughly. There is no creature beyond reach of my fire or that can extinguish it because it eagerly searches for all the things that resist me. For when I show salvation to man and he neglects it through his disbelief, my zeal will examine him with my just judgment since he did not want to receive the good that was shown to him.

66

THE COMMOTION OF THE DEVIL FIGHTS WITH FAULTS AGAINST MAN

85. And so the devil fights against man with the commotion of this fault, as mentioned earlier, in order to harm man in all places, in all elements, and in all his works.

67

THE FACT THAT BLESSED SPIRITS ARE PRESENT TO MEN

86. But blessed spirits with all their keenness are present to men as well. These spirits hold the powers of all the earth and the power of all the elements through the power of God. And they offer the works of holy people before the throne of God so that they can be judged there.

68

THE BODY MAY BE AFFLICTED BECAUSE OF SINS

87. While man is alive and able to do good and evil, he may bring afflictions to his body because of his sins. Therefore, let him drive his sins away according to the advice of his spiritual director. After he has been cleansed from the filth of his sins, he will not receive the bitterness of punishments but will receive the sweetness of life.

69

THE FACT THAT THE MASTER WILL CONSIDER THE QUALITIES AND SINS OF SERVANTS

88. The master will consider the strength and weakness and quality of the souls of his servants and the quality of their sins, and he will examine the intentions for which they did these things. He will then stand by each one who repents according to the consideration of his nature, according to the manner of his sin, and according to the manner of his repentance.

70

HOW THE MASTER MAY SPEAK

89. Since the master sees how he should hold his correcting rod in his hands for restraining his disciples, he may scourge the hard and rough ones because if he were to allow them to be useful only according to his own will, they might be totally rebellious and kill him. To those, however, who shine with a little light, he will speak softly because if he surrounds them with bitterness, they will be destroyed completely and will become even more evil than they were before.

71

HOW THE MASTER CORRECTS

90. The master may act two ways, of course, with the softness of Jacob or with the harshness of Esau. Jacob indeed failed in his duty, but he was, nevertheless, benevolent; Esau also failed in his duty, but he was harsh. But God chose Jacob on account of his benevolence and reproached Esau on account of his wickedness. The master should do likewise. He should draw to himself the one who failed in benevolence so that he does not revolt, but he should openly rebuke the one who failed in wickedness so that he does not proceed to greater evils. Indeed, the one who has been wounded seriously may ask for help and may lick his wounds if he wants to repent, and the master should consider what kind of cure to apply to him. But if the one remembers that he had been very neglectful in his wickedness, he should repent zealously.

72

WHAT THINGS THE MASTER OUGHT TO PROVIDE

91. But a master who falls upon the good and just who are subject to him with cunning injury is like the Jews who stoned Stephen. And a master who afflicts the innocent and holy and drags them away from their good works is called a wolf. One who keeps company with the vain and delinquent and conceals their depravity is like a thief. Therefore, let him be rebuked by the faithful so that he does not scatter the Lord's flock. A good master, however, should be like a watchful eye during the day and like a careful guard during the night for any disciples of his who sin. Let him praise with a lute those who work well and let him rejoice with his good and best disciples.

73
A GOOD MASTER IS SIMILAR TO PURE AIR

92. Good masters are similar to good air. They rule their disciples with discretion and with immediate correction.

74
GOOD DISCIPLES MAY BE THE CHARIOT FOR THE MASTER

93. Disciples who have been embellished with good service, like gold, and with good works, like gems, should be like a chariot for their master, just as the soil help plants. In such disciples, the advice of the master will be considered as good, and they will be as committed to following it as they are to doing the master's work, which is just like being his chariot or like the soil ministering to plants.

75
CONCERNING GOOD AND DEPRAVED WORK

94. Let man, however, direct the works he does to God, for any work of man that reaches to God will shine with heavenly things; works directed to the devil will be punished. For God created man and subjected the rest of creation to him in so far as man may work with the rest of creation so that God's work is not blotted out. Man's evil works, however, can be blotted out through repentance, for just as when a man willingly sells some of his property and gains a precious pearl that he puts in his pocket, so also one who has repented will shine in God's presence and be a source of confusion to the serpent of deception.

76
THE CONFESSION OF SINS SHOWS THE TRINITY

95. If a man shows his sins to God through a priest's ear, the Holy Spirit will wash away all his uncleanness with his waters, with God washing away his sins with water at the same time. For indeed, a man who accepts the blame for his sins shows the Holy Trinity, of course, the Father in repentance, the incarnate Son in confession, and the Holy Spirit in the moisture of greenness.

77

GOD IS PRAISED BY ANGELS AND MEN

96. As God is praised by the angels and as his works are acknowledged in this praise when the angels sing their music with their voices and their lyres out of duty, so also God should be praised by men with their two parts, of course, one part to praise God and one to do good works. God is known through their praise and God's miracles are seen in their good works, for man is full of God's work and all of God's miracles are accomplished through man's praise and work.

78

THE FACT THAT THE HOLY WORKS OF THE LIVING SUCCOR THE SOULS OF THE DEAD

97. The prayers and alms and other works of holiness that the living do, succor the souls that have not been forgotten but that are still in the memory of the blessed. They bring a saving remedy to these souls that helps cleanse them from their punishments.

79

CONCERNING THE PUNISHMENTS OF THE CLEANSED, CONCERNING THE PARADISE OF THE EARTHLY, AND CONCERNING THE LIGHT OF THE HEAVENLY

98. Through the power of the Divinity, which forgives sins and spoils hell, the punishments that can free souls from purgatory are found in certain elements and come through certain elements. An earthly paradise is given to those souls who have been cleansed and snatched away from these punishments, but the heavenly light, which man cannot look at or discern, is prepared for those glorious souls whose virtues have come from the strength of the Divinity.

80

CONCERNING EARTHLY MATERIALS RENEWED IN THE NEWEST DAY

99. When all the elements of the earth have become full, then even those filthy things that were gathered together when Adam fell, will be torn asunder. After that, they will then shine again, just as they shone when they were first created.

81

PRAYERS ASCEND TO GOD THROUGH THE SPIRIT

100. When a man says prayers in his heart through the gift of the Holy Spirit, those prayers that are brought forth in purity cannot be concealed and will ascend before God.

82

CONCERNING THE SINGING OF PSALMS FOR THE DEAD

101. When the lamenting words of the prophets, which revealed the justice and miracles of God, are sung by people in praise of God in order to free someone from some physical affliction or to bring rest to the souls of the dead, these people help their suffering. When they do this, I help because they speak with sighs and sorrow. God is the foundation and inspiration of all these things because he is touched by them, and God loves man intensely when man has served God with zeal.

83

CONCERNING ALMS

102. In addition, when man offers alms from the possessions God has given him, God recalls Abraham's sacrifice. Just as he spared his son, so also he will spare those for whom alms are offered, in proportion to the worth of the alms. God is delighted in such things because he created man and gave him good things. He does not allow man to lack anything he needs, if it is agreeable to God.

84

CONCERNING GOOD WILL

103. God gives man what he wants because of man's good will. Therefore, good will is the sweetest aroma to God. This is similar to the fact that in the Old Testament, God was not pleased with the blood of goats but rather with the good will of men.

85

CONCERNING LABORS BROUGHT TO GOD

104. When man has worked justly through the gift of the Holy Spirit for some need of the living or for the rest of the dead, God receives this work worthily and justly, just as he had heard Moses and Eli when they worked without ceasing for others who had sinned against God.

86

CONCERNING THE STRIKING ANGEL

105. He, however, who does not serve God in any of these ways will be struck harshly by an angel because of the vanity in his heart. Therefore, every faithful person should never stop working for God, for others as well as for himself, because God will look into the hearts of men and reward their just labor and good will. Every man will be rewarded justly according to his work. These things, however, have been spoken concerning the atonement for the cleansing and saving of souls, and they are faithful things. A faithful person pays attention to these things and remembers them well.

THE FIFTH PART ENDS

THE HEADINGS OF THE SIXTH PART BEGIN CONCERNING THE MAN MOVING HIMSELF WITH THE FOUR ZONES OF THE EARTH

14. The Fact That God Created the Sun and the Moon and the Stars against the Devil

15. The Fact That the Evil of the Devil Is Worse than the Evil of Man, Whence Also He Will Always Be in His Own Punishments

16. The Fact That the Devil Did Not Enter into an Animal That Would Be Swifter for Deceiving Man than the Serpent Was

17. As the Work of God Will Not Be Ended, So the Work of Man Will Not Vanish, the Good of course for Glory, the Evil Truly to His Confusion Unless They May Be Blotted out through Repentance

18. The Fact That the Devil Snares Man with Such a Fault As He Sees Him to Be Delighted with

19. As the Elements Are in Man, So Also the Virtues Are in Faithful Man

20. As Fire Inflames the Body of Man, So Also the Virtues Inflame His Soul

21. As Man Blows Out with Air, So Also the Virtues Make His Soul Draw In for Heavenly Things

22. As Water Moistens the Body of Man, So the Virtues Water His Soul

23. As the Earth Quickens the Flesh of Man, So the Virtues Make Man Bear Good Fruit

24. The Fact That As Nothing Will Be Strong Enough to Manifest Eternal Joys, So Also Nothing Will Be Strong Enough to Manifest Infernal Miseries

25. Concerning the Certain Brightness and Concerning the Joys of the Souls of Certain Men in Time Who Had Renounced Their Sins by Repenting before the Hour of Their Death, and of the Souls of Certain Men in Time Who Had Devoutly Fulfilled the Legal Precepts in Real Life, and Why They May Hold Those Things Thus

26. Likewise concerning the Certain Other Brightness and Concerning the Joys of the Souls of Certain Men in Time Who Had Diligently Observed the Precepts of the Law with an Active Life, and Why They Will Have Received These Things in This Manner

That Nothing Weighted in Mortal Flesh Is Able to Receive in the Knowing of Its Own Understanding

39. The Fact That the Evil of Lying Rose Up without God

40. The Fact That Man Rules over Evil When He Refuses to Do That

41. The Fact That Man on Fallen Earth Is Not Able to See the Immaculate Mansions, unless As God Allows to That One; When, However, Afterwards He Will Gaze upon God, He Will Forget All Earthly Things

42. The Fact That God Shows Diverse Miracles in Every Age of the World

43. The Fact That the Prophets Were Seeing Certain Miracles, Certain Not

44. The Fact That Every Creature and Eternal Life Are from God

45. The Fact That Certain Evil Creatures Are Not Able to Deceive Men unless They May Be through Some Pretense just as if They May Be Heavenly Things

THE HEADINGS OF THE SIXTH PART UNFOLD

THE SIXTH PART BEGINS

CONCERNING THE MAN MOVING HIMSELF WITH THE FOUR ZONES OF THE EARTH

1. I then saw that this man moved, as it were, completely in the four zones of the earth. And behold a unicorn appeared on his left thigh, licking his knee, and said:

1
THE WORDS OF THE UNICORN

2. "What has been done will be pulled down, and what has not been done will be built up. Indeed, man's sin will be examined and his good will be completed with just works. He will then enter into another life." I wondered if some other faults or some other things similar to what I had seen earlier would appear here, but nothing similar was shown to me.

2
CONCERNING THE POWER OF GOD AT THE END OF THE WORLD

3. I again heard a voice from heaven say to me: *God, whose power is stronger than all things, will reveal his power at the end of the world when he will transform the world with a miracle.*

3
GOD WILL SHAKE THE ENDS OF THE EARTH

4. The fact that you see that this man moves, as it were, completely in the four zones of the earth means that God, showing his strength at the end of the world with the powers of the heavenly ones, will shake all the ends of the earth so that every soul will prepare for judgment.

4
CHRIST, THE JUDGE, WEIGHS ALL THINGS

5. And a unicorn appears on his left thigh. This is the one who resisted the devil with his holy humanity and who struck the devil down with the sword of his chastity, clearly the Son of God who came in the form of a man. This unicorn is licking his knee. Receiving the power of judgment from God the Father, the Son of God cries out that the whole world should be cleansed with fire, that it should be renewed, that men's perversity should be judged by him, and that the holiness in the good and righteous works of man should be fulfilled so that the souls of the just can then pass into the greatest glory and joy in the blessedness of eternal life.

5

THE FACT THAT ALL THE STAINED THINGS IN THE WORLD WILL BE CLEANSED

6. After God has perfected the strength of the virtues in man, he will then lift man's strength up into the clouds and will remove the ashes that have covered the elements. He will do this in such a way that all things on earth will be moved with great terror and all the things that had been stained by man's sins will be cleansed. God will then destroy the North and all its strengths and will cast the devil down with his conquering arms as he strips him of his spoils.

6

CONCERNING THE NEW HEAVEN AND THE NEW EARTH

7. Heaven will then appear as glowing with a reddish gleam and the earth as pure since they will have been cleansed along with the other elements. Before this time, the earth and the other elements forgot about heavenly things; after this time, they will shine like new. Man, who is blessed, having also been cleansed along with the other elements, will be like the wheel of the golden circle and will be on fire in spirit and flesh. Every hidden secret will be opened to him. Men who are blessed will cling to God and he will give them the fullness of joy.

7

CONCERNING THE DEVIL AFTER THE END OF THE WORLD

8. The fact that I wonder if some other faults or some other things similar to what I saw earlier will appear here, but nothing similar is shown to me means that at the finite end of the world the devil cannot any longer produce the faults of his deception in men since the world will have ceased to exist in the manner in which it had earlier. Since the faults that had infested men by cunning devices earlier can no longer be committed by men who no longer dwell physically and in time on earth, there is nothing to fight against men since they are not stirred up by wicked spirits and are not judged by any temporal judge; all their memories concerning the earth will have been removed. For at that time, all things pass over into eternity, and the instability and weariness of the

world and all the things in it will have ended. All things will be led through an unfailing change where there will be no fear or danger, as there were earlier when they lived in temporal time. John, my chosen one, shows this in a vision shown to him when he says:

8

THE WORDS OF JOHN

9. *Never again shall they know hunger or thirst, nor shall the sun or its heat beat down on them, for the Lamb on the throne will shepherd them. He will lead them to springs of life-giving water, and God will wipe every tear from their eyes (Revelation 7:16-17).* This means the following. God will remove the shackles of sins, which bring forth tears, from the knowledge of the holy ones, and he will bring them into eternity as if they were the pure linen of living life, as the first man had been created. For at the end of the world death will not come in the usual way, of course, by infancy being finished through youth, youth through old age, and old age through death. The blessed will not dwell any longer in sorrowful exile and they will not expect anything more in life since they will forever have that life that has no weariness. They will not cry out in ignorance since they will no longer seek any hidden testimonies as a result of their seeing God's glory openly forever. Sorrow, the taste of sins, the desire for having things, and the fear of destroying the things they have, will no longer hurt them either; nor will they be troubled by any temporal damnation. For things that disappeared before did so because of all the evil present when they lived in the temporal world and with temporal torments. However, let he who desires life grasp these words and store them in the innermost chamber of his heart.

9

CONCERNING THE LIGHTER PUNISHMENTS OF THOSE WHO ARE WITHOUT BAPTISM

10. I also saw darkness that was diffused into immensity, just like a cloud, and that had some torments in it, but I did not see any punishments of fire, vermin or other serious torments in it. I did, however, see many souls in it who, fettered by the fall of Adam but without any other sins, lacked the sign of baptism. Some of these souls endured a certain smoke in this darkness; others, however, suffered no smoke. These souls did not suffer any grave torments, but they were in the darkness of unfaithfulness because they had not been baptized while they were alive.

Those who had committed some minor sins sustained the smoke while those who had not committed either minor or serious sins but who had not received the sign of the Catholic faith did not suffer any smoke in this darkness; they only endured the darkness of unfaithfulness as mentioned above.

10
CONCERNING GEHENNA

11. I also saw another very black darkness that burned fiercely without the blackness of a flame. It clung to the darkness mentioned above since that darkness had been the strength of this darkness. This darkness contained Gehenna with all its kinds of torments, miseries, stinks and punishments, but I could not see into this darkness inwardly, but only outwardly. I did not want to see Gehenna in it either, but I could hear coming out of it the greatest and most indiscreet wailings from beatings, the greatest and most indiscreet gnashing of teeth from mourning souls, and innumerable and indiscreet clatterings of punishments. These sounded like the crashing of the sea and the rushing of torrents of water. There are all these different types of punishments in Gehenna since it contains the power of the wicked spirits who infused all the faults into the men who know them. These punishments are so numerous that a soul weighed down in the body cannot anticipate and understand them because they are beyond human understanding. And I saw and understood these things through the living spirit.

11
AGAIN CONCERNING THE UNFAITHFUL LACKING BAPTISM

12. I again heard the voice from the living light say to me: *These things that you see, are true, and as you see them, so they are, and there are more things.* For in the darkness mentioned above, there is the weeping and gnashing of teeth, but in the place where you do not see any serious torments there are the souls of those who lived in the ignorance of sin before the flag bearing victory of the Son of God took place. There are also the souls of those who were not weighed down with heavy sin, but who did not have the fiery sign of the sacred fountain because they did not have the vision of the righteous faith. Some of these suffered the punishment of the smoke in proportion to the amount

that they had tasted the temptations of the world; others, however, simply endured the darkness in proportion to their simple ignorance of faith.

12

CONCERNING THE GEHENNA OF THE FALLEN ANGELS

13. But you see Gehenna in the other horrible darkness that burned without a flame because it lacks the bronze of light and the flame of reddish fire by which the other darkness had been touched. Gehenna, rising up at the time of the destruction of the fallen angels, received Satan and contains all the torments for all the miseries, without any hope or consolation. These souls remain here with this ancient inventor of destruction. No mortal creature can understand how many and how much and of what type these torments are and that they will never end. Those who did not seek the grace of God and did not want to look at God or desire to have life will remain here.

13

CONCERNING THE SUPPLICATIONS OF THOSE WHO HAVE BEEN THROWN DOWN IN THE PRESENCE OF GOD

14. What else should human mortals know about these who had forgotten God, but that they have been cast down and are in infinite supplication? The ancient serpent rejoices over them because he does not desire or wish for any good since he is the source of all evil and sin. He looked at God's brightness originally, but then began this evil that ought not to be and that ought not to be done. Every creature was made by God, but this evil that the ancient serpent began was made without him.

14

CONCERNING THE STARS GOD ESTABLISHED AGAINST THE DEVIL

15. Lucifer had been made like a mirror full of embellishments, but he wanted to be the light itself rather than the shadow of the light. God, however, made the sun that makes all creatures brighter than Lucifer's brightness, he made the moon to make the darkness bright against the devil's snares, and he made the stars to shine on all his faults, for God is

the fullness of those things in which there is no emptiness and in which there can be no emptiness. The devil, however, is an empty vessel because from the moment he looked at his own brightness, he destroyed it by being proud. He buried himself in hell where he will remain without any glory or honor of praise because he is the one who spoiled the first man and caused him to be exiled from paradise, who committed the murder of Abel, and who attacked men with evil when he pretended to be God to those.

15
CONCERNING THE EVIL OF THE DEVIL

16. The devil's evil is worse than man's because when man saw God, he did not see him as he is. But the devil shook the very wheel of the nativity of man and deceived him with many evil things. As a result, the devil drew the greatest confusion to himself. And since he also rejoices in the damnation of souls, he will always endure his punishments, just like being in exile without any consolation. His deception, however, also brings him confusion since he blushes tremendously when his followers are snatched away from him by being cleansed through repentance.

16
CONCERNING THE DEVIL AND THE SERPENT

17. The devil, however, had deceived the first man in paradise through a serpent. With all the different kinds of animals, he did not enter one that was swifter than a serpent. Because the devil was afraid to approach man openly, he chose a serpent as the means of his deception, for the serpent is divided into two parts, of course, because it is sometimes in the water and sometimes on the land. In both places, it hisses and is treacherous; from the water it draws out its hisses and from the land it draws out its treachery. In addition, it crawls out into the air from the water and it beckons, as it were, from the land. Its nature is, indeed, such that it deceives man and kills him with deadly poison. But if a man overtakes a serpent, it quickly hides and cunningly moves away from him. Through such craftiness of a serpent, the devil persuaded man that he should not take joy or have trust in God. Therefore, man received the knowledge of evil when he tasted the apple and he knew sin was present through the nourishment of the apple. By these means, the devil sent into man all the evils that have later been suffocated with water.

17

THE FACT THAT THE WORK OF MAN WILL NOT PERISH

18. But just as the work of God, which is man, will endure and not be ended, so also the work of man will not vanish because the work of man, which reaches to God, will shine in heavenly things; the work of man, however, which reaches to the devil, will remain in punishments. For when God created man, he told him to work with the other creatures. Just as man will not end unless he is changed into ashes and as he will rise again, so also his works will be seen, the good, of course, for glory, and the evil in confusion unless the evil has been blotted out through the rite of manifest repentance.

18

CONCERNING THE SNARES OF THE DEVIL

19. Just as the devil, like a watchman, deceives man by joking around, so also he ensnares him with whatever fault he sees man taking the most delight in out of all the elements. For all the faults proceed from the devil and are like his servants since they pillage all the good things that are in man, as much as they can. They also do this with all the elements and with the other creatures with whom man lives and works.

19

CONCERNING THE ELEMENTS AND THE VIRTUES

20. Just as the four elements are in man, so also the virtues of God are in a blessed man whom they turn to good.

20

CONCERNING FIRE AND THE VIRTUES

21. The Holy Spirit is truly an inextinguishable fire. He can never be extinguished; he gives out all good things, kindles all good things, stirs up all good things, teaches all good things, and assigns speech to man with his flames. Through the strong powers of his fire, he also reveals his burning humility that lies under all things and that thinks of itself as the least valuable of all things. His fire also contains coldness, of course, patience, and moisture in the kindness that he shows to all and that is the

work and foundation of humility, for holiness is built up high in the air whereas the evil spirits are driven back down to nothing.

21
CONCERNING THE AIR AND THE VIRTUES

22. The air that has keen powers signifies faith, which is the banner of victory. Just as the flame of fire gives light, so also faith shows the right way. It also shows the dew of hope that moistens the minds of the faithful when they pant for heavenly things and when they hasten to do good in all things everywhere since they have the greenness of perfect charity. Through the breath of repentance, they also bring forth a tearful complaint in a prayer, just as the sweet breath of the air brings forth flowers. Similarly, in the heat of heavenly desire, they bring forth the best fruit, just like the food of life, when they do things that are useful for themselves and for others.

22
CONCERNING WATER AND THE VIRTUES

23. Water with its many powers shows man how to abandon his faults and to pant for the virtues. The Holy Spirit overcomes all unworthy things with water and he perfects his gifts with water. Like the warmth, the Holy Spirit sends prophecy forth to dissolve the coagulation of sins, and like air, he quiets the desire for sin through wisdom so that man can grow fertile in the moisture of justice and can flow toward spiritual things in the flood of truth. He also makes the legal precepts run with speed. Through the paint of chastity, he covers the pretense in the hearts of men; through the taste of abstinence, he grinds away immoderate sins; and through the greenness of the innermost sighs of man, he pours the moisture of remorse on their hardened minds so that being moist with the moisture of the virtues, they will have contempt for the world and will cast all its filth away from themselves. He makes the faithful ascend from virtue into virtue, as if they were flying; he feeds them like fish tarrying in the waters of faith with the food of life through abstinence from sins. He also pours his warmth over them, just like animals, so that they can live another kind of life busily as a result of their love of the heavenly kingdom. But for those crawling in the footsteps of humility, he carries away the foam of pleasure and the habits of the faults and he holds these fast with all the virtues and strengthens them with the endurance of perfection so that they put the love of God before all other things.

23
CONCERNING THE EARTH AND THE VIRTUES

24. The earth with its suitable powers shows that man offers God all his carnal things and leaves all his possessions behind when he dies. For a faithful person, as it were in the summer, shows that he is cold when he is humble and, as it were in the winter, shows that he is warm when he denies the desires of the flesh with the fires of the virtues. He also feeds on the greenness of the heavenly virtues when he dries up the desires of his flesh so that he sprouts the seeds of good works by which he grasps the fruit of holiness. God created man in such a way that he might earn heaven by doing earthly things so that God could overcome the craftiness of the devil in man and so that man might also wave the banner of the Divinity. God made the first angel so bright that this angel could reveal the hidden secrets of the Divinity, but this angel exalted himself in God's presence and stopped praising God, causing his own glory to vanish. God made man in such a way that this one who was lower might overcome that one who is higher, for God perfected all his works in man. He who sustains the animals, as the earth does, suffers many temptations of the flesh; when he turns away from the things of the world, he is just like an animal that flees man; when he turns to the spiritual life, he acts like an animal that runs toward man. Since man conquers all the things of his flesh when he overcomes all the earthly things within himself, he is called the banner of heavenly harmony in celestial victory when he tramples the devil under foot. And so, the works of the Holy Spirit show the powers of the elements in man.

24
THE FACT THAT AS NOTHING WILL BE STRONG ENOUGH TO MANIFEST ETERNAL JOYS, SO NOTHING WILL BE STRONG ENOUGH TO MANIFEST INFERNAL MISERIES

25. Therefore, let whoever is anxious to avoid the infernal torments flee from the devil and let him reject the devil's suggestions. Let him take up the faith of the fiery fountain that was brought by the one who came without any sin and let him guard his faith with just works so that he may come to those joys that have been prepared for those choosing God. But just as no moral language can explain these joys, so also no human knowledge is strong enough to understand the infernal miseries.

These things, however, have been brought forth and spoken from the living voice of the living and unfailing light, and they are faithful things. A faithful person pays attention to these things and remembers them well.

25

CONCERNING THE HEAVENLY JOYS OF MEN IN TIME

26. I saw a great and immense brightness whose splendor was so bright that I could not look at it or at those things that were in it, unless as through a mirror. In this brightness, I knew there was every kind of pleasantness of every flower and the sweetest odor of the various aromas that give delight. In it, I also knew there were the souls of certain blessed ones who had touched God with just sighs and who had worshipped him with just works while they had been alive. These souls had the sweetest joys in all these things.

27. Among these I saw, as if in a mirror, certain ones who were completely clothed in the whitest of garments. Some of them had a halo as bright as the morning on their head, and they wore foot coverings on their feet that were whiter than the snow. Others had a halo as bright as gold on their heads, and they wore foot coverings that shone like emeralds. The rest of the embellishments of all of these were numerous, but they were hidden from me. All of these rested in the brightness mentioned earlier, because they had renounced the devil through faith while they had been alive and because they had consummated their faith with worthy repentance. They were also clothed in the white garment in which Adam had been exiled, because these blessed ones had chosen to follow God's precepts by deserting sin and doing good works.

28. Some of these had a halo as bright as the morning on their heads because through repentance they had fastened in their minds the salvation of redemption by which God redeemed man; they had bewailed their sins by repenting. Because they had returned to life by a righteous journey through the way of salvation, although slowly, they wore foot coverings that were whiter than the snow. For while they had been alive, they had shipwrecked their sins with repentance through divine inspiration before the hour or during the hour of their death, thus gaining salvation. Others truly had a halo as bright as gold on their heads because they had not forsaken God while they had fulfilled their worldly duties, but had fulfilled his precepts in their hearts voluntarily while they lived

in the world. Their foot coverings shone like emeralds because they had followed God's precepts strenuously. While they had been alive, they had not esteemed God less, but they had fulfilled his legal precepts devoutly, although they had been placed in a body in time and in a worldly life. However, the significance of the rest of their embellishments were hidden from me and my understanding.

26
CONCERNING THE HEAVENLY JOYS OF CONFESSORS AND REPENTANTS

29. I also saw another brightness that was much greater and was everlasting, of which I knew no end. It gave forth such a bright light that I was not able to gaze at it; it was beyond human understanding. The brightness that I mentioned earlier clung to it, just as a province is extended to a region, because this earlier brightness had been its beginning and origin. In it, I knew there was every type of delight, every type of music, all the voices of those who sing, all the joys of the happy, and the greatness of all gladness, because I knew it held the souls of the holy ones who had tormented their bodies with great and harsh reproaches while they had been alive. It also held the souls of those who had handed over their bodies to martyrdom for the love of life. But I could not see anything of theirs in this brightness, unless through a mirror, because I was not strong enough to gaze at this brightness.

30. Among these I saw certain ones, as through a mirror, who were clothed as if in the white garment of a cloud. This garment appeared purer than the purest highest upper air and was interwoven with gold. There heads were embellished with halos, as if they were from the elect; their foot coverings were like crystal that shone with purity beyond the purity of the clearest water. They were touched from time to time with a gentle wind that came from the secret place of the Divinity and that had the aroma of all the herbs and flowers. Their voices sounded like a lot of water does. They also had many other embellishments, but I was not able to see them. Because they had come to God through faith with the highest and greatest devotion and because they had worshipped God with their good works, they had infinite joy in the joys of this brightness; because they had observed and fulfilled the legal precepts with the purity of justice while they had been alive, they wore this white garment that was like a cloud; because they had esteemed the legal precepts, their garment appeared purer than the purest highest upper air; and be-

cause they had observed the precepts of the law so carefully, their garment was interwoven with gold.

31. Because they had clearly repented each and every sin in their hearts with pure knowledge, their heads were embellished with halos, as if they were from the elect. Because they had walked righteously and purely on the worldly journey that had been established for them by God's law while they were alive, their foot coverings were like crystal that shone with purity beyond the purity of the clearest water. Because of the generosity of these chosen ones by which they had tearfully shown mercy to each and every wretched one and because they had done this according to the legal precepts that God had established for them when they had clothed the naked, had fed the hungry and given drink to the thirsty, had visited the sick and imprisoned, and had done similar good works, they were touched from time to time with a gentle wind that came from the secret place of the Divinity and that had the aroma of all the herbs and flowers. Because of the devotion by which they had brought forth good fruit with the depth of sighs and the water of tears in their voices and works, they sounded like the sweetest symphony and their voices sounded like a lot of water does. These, however, while they had been in their bodies, dwelling and living in a worldly place while they had been alive, had lived more in body than in spirit but they had fulfilled the law of justice with just works out of fear of their Creator. The rest of their embellishments and their significance were hidden from my sight and understanding.

27
CONCERNING THE HEAVENLY JOYS OF THE OBEYING ONES

32. I also thought about some others who were in the brightness in a similar manner, as if in a mirror. They were clothed, as if with a garment, by the beautiful dawn and by the splendor of the sun, and they were embellished with the noblest of gems. They gave forth the sweetest air of the softness of the sweetest flowers of all different colors, like the aroma of balm. They wore crowns on their heads that were decorated with the noblest hyacinth, and they wore foot coverings decorated with most precious pearls. Their voices were filled with every kind of music, and they sang a new song without any hesitation. They were also illuminated with the clearest and brightest light, coming from the hidden secret of the Divinity, that was so great and so bright that neither man's eye could see it, nor his ear hear it, nor his heart understand it.

33. I could not, however, comprehend the rest of their many embellishments. These also rejoiced with pleasant delights and joys in the presence of the brightness mentioned earlier because of the devotion of their faith and the unfailing strength of their good works. Because they had had good will from the beginning for doing righteous works zealously and had relinquished their own wills, they were clothed, as if with a garment, by the beautiful dawn and by the splendor of the sun, and they were embellished with the noblest of gems. Because they had abstained from their fleshly desires out of obedience, which is the flower of holiness, thereby giving out the aroma of life and giving men examples of the holy virtues, they gave forth the sweetest air of the softness of the sweetest flowers of all different colors, like the aroma of balm. Because they had extended their hearts to God with trusting hope in all their labors, they wore crowns on their heads that were decorated with the noblest hyacinth. And because they had been so steadfast on their righteous journey on spiritual paths, they wore foot coverings decorated with the most precious pearls.

34. Because of the praise by which they had praised God humbly and devoutly with a joyful voice while they had been alive, their voices were filled with every kind of music. Because of the unceasing service of their heart and mouth in saying the divine office where they contemplated each and every virtue, they sang a new song without any hesitation. And because they had offered angelic service in their mind and heart and with their voices and righteous service, they have imitated the praises of the angels by praising God. Obeying the order of their superiors with prayers and silence and with the rest of their good works in the contemplative life, always walking with self control in regard to their fleshly desires, they were also illuminated with the clearest and brightest light, coming from the hidden secret of the Divinity, that was so great and so bright that neither man's eye could see it, nor his ear hear it, nor his heart understand it. While they had lived in their bodies, they had truly dragged themselves away from the material in which they had been conceived and born. They had been truly obedient in their spiritual life and had served their Creator with devotion and very humble subjection by having contempt for the world and its pleasures. The rest of their embellishments and their significance, however, were hidden from my sight and understanding.

28

CONCERNING CERTAIN HEAVENLY JOYS OF THE TEACHERS AND RULERS OF SOULS

35. I also saw some others who were in the brightness in a similar manner, as if in a mirror. They were clothed in a garment of sapphire color, decorated with beryl stone and with ivy. On the breast of their garment there appeared signs of the seven planets that shone brightly in a wondrous manner. On their head they wore crowns embellished with topaz, and they wore foot coverings that were like the purest gold. In their hands they held, as it were, crystalline trumpets that blew forth an aroma that was like myrrh and frankincense. With these trumpets they sang songs and praises like those who are in God's presence.

36. The rest of their many embellishments were hidden from me. Because they had served God faithfully with the perfection of their good works, they rested happily in the brightness and in the joys of the blessedness that I mentioned earlier. Because of the charity they had poured out with mercy on their servants and because of their welcoming sinners and publicans in such a way as to lead them to repentance, they were clothed in a garment of sapphire color, decorated with beryl stone and with ivy. And because of the piety they had in their mind by which they openly saw the gifts of the Holy Spirit when out of love of God they had cared physically for their regular servants in the active life and when they had ruled them spiritually in the contemplative life, on the breast of their garment there appeared signs of the seven planets that shone brightly in a wondrous manner.

37. Because they had restrained the passions of their bodies and had carried true justice in their hearts, when not wanting to resist God with unstable justice they looked upon him with the great constancy of their faithful works, on their head they wore crowns embellished with topaz. Because they had so wisely made their servants walk on righteous paths in God's presence, they wore foot coverings that were like the purest gold. Because they showed true doctrine by word and by example in their works, they were like a mirror for others when they reflected their good works to those who believed, of course, in the esteem of their true steadfastness and in the mortification of their flesh and in their office of holiness, whereby standing day and night in service and praise of their Creator, they have imitated the faith and justice of the patriarchs and prophets and apostles who had made the truth that is in God manifest in their crying aloud, in their hands they held, as it were, crystalline trum-

pets that blew forth an aroma that was like myrrh and frankincense. With these trumpets they sang songs and praises like those who are in God's presence. However, while they had been physically alive on earth, through the inspiration God gives to magistrates and prelates, they were teachers and rulers of God's people, and they presided over their servants with their words and by their examples, snatching their servants from evil and not allowing them to be killed, thereby also bringing themselves to God through their good works. The rest of their embellishments and their significance were truly hidden from my sight and understanding.

29
CONCERNING CERTAIN HEAVENLY JOYS OF MARTYRS

38. I also saw some others who were in the brightness in a similar manner, as if in a mirror. They stood as if above a certain lake that neither remained nor had moisture like water, but that shone greatly. They were clothed in a garment the color of a red hyacinth that was decorated with precious stones above the shoulders and on a border above their feet. They wore crowns on their head that shone with the purest gold and that were distinguished with a circle of very shiny mirrors. They wore foot coverings embellished with emerald and beryl. In their hands they carried palms that shone through, just like clear water, and mirrors that show the many miracles of God.

39. And I heard a voice from heaven cry aloud and speak to me in a way that sounded just like thunder: *The ancient serpent opposed God and was, therefore, cast into hell. But the devil then gathered members who were in the form of man to join him, and through these he persuaded men to harm themselves. In order for men's sins to be absolved, the Lamb, of course, the Son of God, was clothed in flesh and was killed. Because this Lamb was killed, men can now come and pour out the excessive blood of their bodies into the blood of this Lamb.* While this voice spoke, these souls were lifted above the lake and drops of their blood were scattered upon the earth, and so in heavenly harmony they gave testimony to the Lamb who had been killed.

40. As often as this voice called out, all of these souls who sprinkled their blood upon the earth were lifted up to a new song. I was not able to see the rest of their many embellishments. Because they had served God with their faith and works while they had been alive and because they

had scorned their bodies with strong attacks of fortitude on account of their love of God, they received from the brightness the delights and infinite joys of the highest rewards of this mansion. Because they had trampled under foot their anxiety about martyrdom with the strength of their minds, as a result hurling the softness of instability down with constancy, they seized God's most burning love, as if they stood above a certain lake that neither remained nor had moisture like water, but that shone greatly. Because being restrained in their blood, they had worshipped God with great trust, they were clothed in a garment the color of a red hyacinth. Because they had put a lot of effort into divine worship, which they had always done for a good purpose when they sacrificed themselves to God, restraining the members of their bodies and subjecting them to various torments, their garment was decorated with precious stones above the shoulders and on a border above their feet.

41. They also wore the height of hope in wisdom when they showed their brotherly love everywhere with their purity of faith and in their compassion for others, therefore, praising God with their hearts. When they had patience, they did not spare their own members and, therefore, wore crowns on their head that shone with the purest gold and that were distinguished with a circle of very shiny mirrors. Because they ran on the ways of the journeys of God with patience as they poured out their blood, they wore foot coverings embellished with emerald and beryl. Because they won a pure and clean victory without any contamination of pretense with their works when, receiving many examples of constancy and patience, they looked upon God with their total mind, as it were, in their hands they carried palms that shone through, just like clear water, and mirrors that show the many miracles of God.

42. Every voice coming from heaven gave witness to these things and showed that the devil who resisted God and is submerged in hell associates with certain people whom he had encouraged to commit murder. But in order that man might be snatched away from the devil, every voice proclaimed that the Son of God had been made incarnate and had been killed, and it encouraged those who had been near death on account of the Son of God to reflect his martyrdom in their martyrdom. In this voice, those exalting in victory poured out the torments they had suffered at the hands of the unholy and unbelieving for their vindication by the just judgment of God. As a result, every heavenly host, in praise of renewed joy, praises the passion of the Son of God, which is renewed in their passions; as often as the divine majesty touches their passion, they glorify the passion of the Lamb with their own passions. For while they had been alive, they not only gave up their wills, but they also sub-

jected their bodies to many and diverse torments for God's glory. They did not give in to tyrants, but they subjected their members limb by limb to death in martyrdom. The rest of their embellishments and their significance were, however, hidden from my sight and understanding.

30
CONCERNING THE HEAVENLY JOYS OF VIRGINS

43. I also saw air in the brightness in a similar manner, as if in a mirror. This air was purer than the clearest water and shone with a brightness beyond the brightness of the sun. This air was blowing. It contained all the greenness of the herbs and flowers of both paradise and the earth, and its aroma was also full of all the greenness, just as the summer has the sweetest aroma of herbs and flowers. In this air, I saw certain ones, as if through a mirror, who were clothed with the whitest garment interwoven with gold and embellished with the most precious stones from their breast to their feet, in the manner of a hanging sash. Their garment emitted a very strong aroma, like perfume. And they were girdled with a girdle embellished with gold and gems and pearls beyond human understanding.

44. On their head they wore crowns intertwined with gold and roses and lilies and surrounded with pipes of most precious stones. Whenever the Lamb of God used his voice, this sweetest blowing of the wind coming from the secret place of the Divinity touched these pipes so that they resounded with every type of sound that a harp and organ make. No one was playing this song, except these who wore these crowns, but the others who heard this song rejoiced in it, just like a man who could not see previously, now sees the brightness of the sun.

45. They wore foot coverings that shone through, as if they had been taken from the fountain of living water. They sometimes walked as if they were upon golden wheels. They carried lyres in their hands, which they played. And they knew and spoke and understood a foreign language. I was not, however, strong enough to see the rest of their many embellishments.

46. Because they had filled their faith with good works since they had known their Creator while they had been alive, they rested with blessedness and joy in the brightness. Because they had ignored the airy variety of fleshly desires in the purity of their minds and because they had gone beyond the requirements of the legal precepts out of love of the true fiery sun, they have this air that was purer than the clearest wa-

ter and that shone with a brightness beyond the brightness of the sun. Because of their very sweet desire that they had shown to God and to men in the greenness of their virginity and in the flower of their mind and body, as a result rising up in the love of the Holy Spirit when they had sent out the good aroma of many virtues everywhere, they felt that this air was blowing. It contained all the greenness of the herbs and flowers of both paradise and the earth, and its aroma was also full of all the greenness, just as the summer has the sweetest aroma of herbs and flowers.

47. Because with a most chaste heart they had won the trials of the flesh wisely with the holy virtues in the devotion of their hearts right up to the consummation of good perseverance, they were clothed with the whitest garment interwoven with gold and embellished with the most precious stones from their breast to their feet, in the manner of a hanging sash. Because they had done this in the praiseworthy and lovable name of virginity, their garment emitted a very strong aroma, like perfume. They had also restrained their will against perilous rashness by taming their own flesh. Because they had abstained with the sweetness of honesty, changing neither here nor there in many different directions, they were girdled with a girdle embellished with gold and gems and pearls beyond human understanding. Wisely giving glory and honor to God in their hearts and competently denying themselves youthful playfulness with the mortification of their bodies, they had given signs of their vow of chastity to men beyond the precepts of the law, fortifying themselves with the sighs of celestial desires and with the strength and firmness of the virtues, just as if they did not have flesh and blood. Because they had been modest with their bodies and had shown modesty in their faces while they fulfilled their various duties, on their head they wore crowns intertwined with gold and roses and lilies and surrounded with pipes of most precious stones.

48. Because they had inclined themselves to the gentleness of the incarnate Son of God and had lifted their minds to a great height since they had vowed virginity to God and because they had kept their vow worthily and holily, the Lamb of God uses his voice, and this sweetest blowing of the wind coming from the secret place of the Divinity touches the signs of their crowned virginity so that they resound the song of the Lamb that was not in the others who did not have these same signs, although the others can rejoice when they hear this song. Because they had followed in the footsteps God had shown man in his ancient counsel, they wore foot coverings that shone through, as if they had been taken from the fountain of living water.

49. Because they had always walked wisely and humbly and had offered the movements of their bodies with the purest chastity to the sight of the Divinity and because they had piously and mercifully helped those in need with generous alms, they had transcended human nature with the denial of their fleshly desires, giving praise to God with voice and heart and contemplating his divine miracles and professing him in their contemplation, they sometimes walked as if they were upon golden wheels. They carried lyres in their hands, which they played. And they knew and spoke and understood a foreign language. For while they had been alive, they had imitated the angels and had served God in the singularity of their virginity. They had also given themselves completely in good and holy works as an offering to God. The rest of their embellishments and their significance were truly hidden from my sight and understanding.

31
CONCERNING THE BRIGHTNESS OF THE BLESSED

50. In the brightness I mentioned earlier, I also saw another brightness that was much greater and was everlasting, of which I knew no end. By straining, I could understand that the light of this brightness was filled with the most beautiful of all the embellishments, with the greatest delights of all delights, and with the greatest joy of the joys of complete blessedness, which neither the eye saw, nor the ear heard, nor the heart rose to while men were in their fragile and corruptible body. There was also a certain seal opposite me, behind which many more and much greater joys were hidden, which I had seen earlier. And so this sight was shown to me in this way. And I saw and understood these things through the living Spirit.

32
THE WORDS OF THE SON OF MAN

51. I again heard the voice from the living light say to me: *These things that you see, are true, and as you see them, so they are, and there are more.* And behold, I heard the sweetest and softest sound of a voice that was like tasting the dripping of balm say to me:

52. *I am the power of the Divinity, which was before eternity and before time and which did not even have a beginning in time, for I am the power of the Divinity by which God made all things that are to be discerned and probed. I am also the mirror of the providence of all*

things. I thundered with the strongest power as I sounded the word, of course, Fiat, *through which all things proceeded. I also divided the time of times with seeing eyes, considering what things can be or how they can be. I licked my work with my mouth, clearly making a figure from slime, and I embraced this figure with love. And then with flaming breath, I changed this slime into flesh and gave the deeds of all creatures to it.*

53. *After I had rested, I thought about how long and in what way man had been deceived through the counsel of the serpent. I then became like a flame, and approaching the womb of the Virgin, I rested in it. I became incarnate in her flesh that had never given forth any filth, just as the flesh of Adam had originally been. And so I, a great giant, came forth with virtue greater than that of any other man since man did not sow me in the same way; the serpent had mocked the first man through the shattering of blood that is moved through the pleasure of the flesh. Because the devil had stripped man of his glory and had dragged man away from me, I wounded the devil and confused the suggestion of his deception with my legal precepts.*

54. *After being born from the womb of the Virgin, I thought about man while I was being baptized and, therefore, washed the seed of man in the same water. As fire dries up water, I purged all things in this way. I turned my wheel until I renewed those who had been estranged. Because I had kissed the form of man that touched me, I formed a righteous union. Because I placed man over all the other creatures, I planned things in such a way as to hold them all together. Because I was born from the Virgin, I established the rule of virginity for man and woman with these having been separated. I also made a little hole in the middle of my wheel, through which I knew beforehand that spiritual people who did not wear the clothes of the world could be victorious. I also perfected my wheel against the cunningness of the ancient serpent who did not know me since my incarnation had been hidden from him. The ancient serpent had seen Adam but had not known him fully; therefore he tried what he wanted to do and deceived him with his deeds. I, however, bound and destroyed the strong strength of the serpent with my humility, but he did not know me until I sat upon my judicial platform where I confused him completely. And I placed the ones who believe truly and have been truly cleansed and who are truly blessed here in the glory of paradise for the glory of heavenly things.*

33

CONCERNING THE GLORY OF THE SOULS IN PARADISE

55. The glory of paradise, from which the first man was cast out, is surrounded with such brightness, as you see, that man is not able to gaze at it or at those things that are in it, unless as through a mirror. Neither is man able to gaze at the things that have been embellished with the unchanging flourish of pleasantness and the things that have been filled with many delights where the souls of those who have been purged of their sins rejoice. These souls are clothed in the garment of immorality and beauty that Adam had destroyed; these souls have received this garment with great glory. Because they had repented their sins while they had been alive, they touched God; and because they had fulfilled God's precepts by doing good works, they are decorated with these beautiful embellishments, just as the bodies of men are decorated with precious things.

34

CONCERNING THE EMBELLISHMENTS OF THE SOULS IN THE HEAVENLY HEIGHT

56. This great brightness that you are not able to gaze at and that is beyond human understanding comes from the heavenly height from which Lucifer was cast down with his angels. This brightness pours over and illuminates the light of paradise and gives paradise its vigor for greenness and beauty. In this heavenly height there are the rewards and joys ordained by the eternal one for the blessed souls who have put their total effort into their innermost devotion for heavenly things while they were on earth, but these rewards and joys are not fully known to humans who are frail and concealed in a dusty covering, since temporal things cannot understand eternal things unless the Father in his mercy wants to reveal such things to them for his own glory and for the perfection of his faithful ones. More and greater things have been prepared in eternity for the souls of the holy than fallen and human estimation can understand, for the chosen will be embellished with praise and deeds since they had done the brightest of works while they had been with their body and soul together.

35

WHAT KINDS OF SOULS ARE IN THE HEAVENLY KINGDOM

57. There are those in this place who had embraced those things that were celestial in spirit while they served physically in time in the burden of actual life. There are also those who are now dead but who had clung in body and spirit to heavenly things when they subjected themselves to regular discipline and lifted their minds up in contemplation. There are those who had presided over their subjects humbly when they taught them and gave them good examples by helping them both physically and spiritually. There are those who had not wavered in their constancy to truth as their bodies weakened and died as they scorned idols and acknowledged their Creator. And there are those who had honestly preserved the virginity they had vowed to God out of fear and love for him when they denied their flesh and blood.

36

CONCERNING THE INCREASE OF GLORY AT THE RESURRECTION

58. All of these receive the joy of joys and the beauty of unutterable embellishments because they had served their Creator, having been inspired by him to do good works. They are blessed and will be called the blessed of my Father at the time of the judgment of the resurrection when they will receive much greater joy than they have now while they can rejoice merely in the soul. They will then have such unutterable joy in both soul and body that no mortal creature can explain it while it is alive.

37

THE EMBELLISHMENTS ARE OF THE QUALITY OF HEAVENLY JOYS

59. The embellishments of this joy are spiritual, eternal and beyond measure. They are not like gold and stones and gems of earthly dust in eternity, but they are like the chosen who have been embellished spiritually with good and just things, just like a man who has been embellished physically with precious things. For I, the maker of the world, gave work to be done by my work, of course, by man, with the knowledge

that I gave him and by his using the earth and water, air and fire from which he is made. As a result, when man does good things, embellishments are prepared eternally for him as his reward in the brightness of the unfailing light, just as the firmament is embellished with stars and the earth with flowers. When man is sometimes decorated with earthly embellishments, his soul groans, remembering how it is embellished by his works, but when man forges his embellishments with fire and air, water and earth as he makes a garment to fit his body in such a way that it pleases God, God accordingly prepares embellishments for his holy ones whom he raised up from no other material than from himself. He likewise created all creatures from himself, just as a man dictates and does his work through no other creature than himself.

38

CONCERNING THE VARIOUS MANSIONS IN HEAVEN

60. In the heavenly dwelling place, there are many, many mansions and delights beyond measure for man and the works he performed through divine grace. These mansions cannot be shown and understood by humans since they are beyond man's intellect, for in that place there are those mansions that are made manifest to no one weighed down by a body, just as those who dwell there are not known to you or to the temperate in any secret detection. The flesh, pressed down with sin, cannot support the secrets of heavenly things unless it has been strengthened by divine grace. No man weighed down in mortal flesh ever sees perfectly the embellishments and joys of the heavenly miracles unless God wills to show these things to certain holy ones in a vision and to certain prophets who have spoken, as Isaiah spoke concerning the embellishments of the first angel and as John shows in his Apocalypse concerning the embellishments of the heavenly Jerusalem.

39

THE FACT THAT THE EVIL OF LYING ROSE UP WITHOUT GOD

61. God made all things good and just and useful through his Word, but the evil of lying, through which all injustice and all sin rose up, rose up without God. Such things do not touch God in any way and are alien to him; therefore, God judges these things rebelling against him with his ruling judgment.

40
HOW MAN OVERCOMES EVIL

62. Man, however, does not rule over evil except when he refuses to do it. When he has truly done evil, he is its servant.

41
HOW MAN MAY SEE HEAVENLY THINGS

63. But man did desert God and communicated with evil. Therefore, as long as he lives on this red hot ashy and fallen earth, he will not be able to see the pure and immaculate mansions except in so far as God allows him. After, however, he has fallen asleep in such a way that he does not awaken in evil in the life beyond, he will then see these mansions and understand them. When he gazes upon God at this time, he will forget all about earthly things, just as a man does not remember how he was born although he knows that he was born.

42
GOD SHOWS DIVERSE MIRACLES TO HOLY ONES

64. God shows various miracles to his holy ones and prophets in every age of the world so that man's soul does not completely stray from heavenly desires, but so that through faith man might remember eternal life in some of these warnings. Similarly, he gave the stars of the firmament to fallen man so that after he had been separated from light, he would not perish completely in the darkness. The prophets and certain other holy ones, however, saw certain miracles and they prophesied certain things, but they did not prophesy or see the greatest miracles. Moreover, the first angel had not required or expected God's miracles because he wanted to exist as important himself, but he was, therefore, buried in death. Man also wanted to be equal to God as a result of the advice of the serpent that mocked joy in childish ways; therefore, he was cast out into the exile of sorrow. Clearly he will end his existence in time in exile and in sorrow since he had reached out falsely to the eternity of God.

43

WHAT MIRACLES THE PROPHETS WERE SEEING

65. Every creature, however, came forth according to God's will, and each shone bright in eternal life from God, and each is from him. And the embellishments and joys and every voice that is full of the joy of eternal life are from him. Therefore, the works of the chosen, which sprang from the Holy Spirit, give forth light and are embellished with the purest gold and with precious stones and pearls and with other types of embellishments. But these embellishments are not of the kind that come from created material, as it was mentioned above, but they are poured out by the Divinity. You, however, man, you who were made from slime, God embellishes you through your works that enable you to rise above the snares of the first angel who was so proud as a result of his great light. But while the first angel is buried in death where God leaves him, God draws man back to himself, although since the serpent had deceived man and man had sinned, man is covered with such a veil that he cannot see the mysteries of God perfectly as long as he is touched by this veil. But God manifests his miracles to whoever has righteous faith as if through a window and as if through a mirror.

44

CONCERNING THE FALSE MIRACLES OF DEVILS

66. There is, however, a certain type of wicked spirit that cannot deceive man unless through some kind of pretense. Just as this type can appear heavenly and then deceive man when it speaks about the truth, so also this type can show false things to man that man, nevertheless, does not understand are false. But it can deceive man more easily when it shows him true things with the result that those who consent to such things are seduced. Those who truly pay attention to and inquire about what is shown to them are not deceived so easily, but persisting with the strength of truth, they shun those things that they weigh carefully little by little.

45

THE FACT THAT DEVILS DO NOT DECEIVE, UNLESS THROUGH FALSE PRETENSE

67. These things are true and they are shown truthfully in words to this person who is simple, because I who came from the highest Father

and I who received the flesh of greenness from the Virgin mother kept watch over this person so that she might uncover these things without the power of a human magistrate in order to note the simplicity of not knowing by means of the knowledge of experts and so that she might understand the author of these things, who is the unfailing light burning with an inextinguishable flame, in order that the little and great might chastise themselves faithfully in all things.

68. Therefore, that man is blessed who is awakened to heavenly things through a miracle of God. And I heard the voice from heaven say: *The woman who saw these things and who made them known by writing them down, sees and does not see, knows hot ashes and does not know them. And she brought forth the miracles of God not through herself, but through those things touched by God, just as a string that has been touched by the player of the lyre gives forth sound. These things are true and he who is true willed truthfully that these things be made manifest thus. Whoever causes anything to be contrary to these things by letting his mind surpass the scriptures and their distinctiveness should be cast down into the punishments that have been described. Or if he carries anything away from the scriptures in a contrary way, he should be blotted out from the joys shown here.* I then heard the voice of the multitude respond to these highest secrets: "Fiat, Amen, and let it be done thus." I again heard the voice from heaven say to me: *These things have been brought forth and spoken from the living voice of the living and unfailing light, and they are faithful things. A faithful person pays attention to these things and remembers them well.*

THE BOOK OF THE REWARDS OF LIFE HAS BEEN EXPLAINED THROUGH A SIMPLE PERSON FROM THE LIVING LIGHT OF REVELATIONS

GARLAND LIBRARY OF MEDIEVAL LITERATURE

JAMES J. WILHELM
AND LOWRY NELSON, JR.
General Editors

Series A (Texts and Translations)
Series B (Translations Only)

BRUNETTO LATINI
Il Tesoretto (The Little Treasure)
Edited and translated by
Julia Bolton Holloway
Series A

THE POETRY OF WILLIAM VII,
COUNT OF POITIERS, IX DUKE
OF AQUITAINE
Edited and translated by Gerald A. Bond;
music edited by Hendrik van der Werf
Series A

BARTHAR SAGA
Edited and translated by Jon Skaptason
and Phillip Pulsiano
Series A

GUILLAUME DE MACHAUT
Judgment of the King of Bohemia (Le
Jugement dou Roy de Behaingne)
Edited and translated by R. Barton Palmer
Series A

WALTHARIUS AND *RUODLIEB*
Edited and translated by Dennis M. Kratz
Series A

THE RISE OF GAWAIN, NEPHEW OF
ARTHUR (DE ORTU WALUUANII
NEPOTIS ARTURI)
Edited and translated by
Mildred Leake Day
Series A

THE POETRY OF CINO DA PISTOIA
Edited and translated by
Christopher Kleinhenz
Series A

FIVE MIDDLE ENGLISH
ARTHURIAN ROMANCES
Translated by Valerie Krishna
Series B

THE ONE HUNDRED NEW TALES
(LES CENT NOUVELLES NOUVELLES)
Translated by Judith Bruskin Diner
Series B

L'ART D'AMOURS (THE ART
OF LOVE)
Translated by Lawrence Blonquist
Series B

BÉROUL
The Romance of Tristran
Edited and translated by
Norris J. Lacy
Series A

GRAELENT AND *GUINGAMOR*
Two Breton Lays
Edited and translated by
Russell Weingartner
Series A

GIOVANNI BOCCACCIO
Life of Dante (Trattatello in
Laude di Dante)
Translated by Vincenzo Zin Bollettino
Series B

THE LYRICS OF THIBAUT DE
CHAMPAGNE
Edited and translated by
Kathleen J. Brahney
Series A

THE POETRY OF SORDELLO
Edited and translated by James J. Wilhelm
Series A

GIOVANNI BOCCACCIO
Il Filocolo
Translated by Donald S. Cheney with
the collaboration of Thomas G. Bergin
Series B

GUILLAUME DE MACHAUT
The Judgment of the King of Navarre
(Le Jugement dou Roy de Navarre)
Translated and edited by R. Barton Palmer
Series A

THE STORY OF MERIADOC, KING OF
CAMBRIA (HISTORIA MERIADOCI,
REGIS CAMBRIAE)
Edited and translated by
Mildred Leake Day
Series A

THE PLAYS OF HROTSVIT
OF GANDERSHEIM
Translated by Katharina Wilson
Series B